SECOND EDITION

RESOLVING CONFLICT

SECOND EDITION

RESOLVING CONFLICT

A PRACTICAL APPROACH

GREGORY TILLETT

OXFORD

UNIVERSITY PRESS

OXFORD
UNIVERSITY PRESS

253 Normanby Road, South Melbourne, Victoria, Australia 3205

Oxford University Press is a department of the University of Oxford.
It furthers the University's objective of excellence in research, scholarship,
and education by publishing worldwide in

Oxford New York

Auckland Bangkok Buenos Aires Cape Town Chennai Dar es Salaam
Delhi Hong Kong Istanbul Karachi Kolkata Kuala Lumpur Madrid
Melbourne Mexico City Mumbai Nairobi São Paulo Shanghai Singapore
Taipei Tokyo Toronto

with an associated company in Berlin

OXFORD is a registered trade mark of Oxford University Press
in the UK and certain other countries

First edition published 1991
Reprinted 1993, 1996, 1997 (twice), 1999
Second edition published 1999
Reprinted 2000, 2001 (twice)

National Library of Australia
Cataloguing-in-Publication data:

Tillett, Gregory, 1950– .
  Resolving conflict: a practical approach.

  2nd ed.
  Bibliography.
  Includes index.
  ISBN 0 19 551151 4.

  1. Conflict management.
  2. Mediation.
  3. Problem solving.
  I. Title.

302.3

Cover design by Modern Art Production Group
Typeset by Desktop Concepts P/L, Melbourne
Printed through Bookpac Production Services

Contents

Preface

Although the theory and practice of conflict resolution only began to receive serious attention about thirty years ago, the last ten years have seen a dramatic increase in both scholarly and popular books in the field. The literature on conflict resolution ranges from the unhelpfully simplistic to the impractically academic. This book is intended to meet a need that books at those extremes cannot meet: it aims to provide a practical guide to the application of theory and research on resolving real conflicts in the real world.

It offers no magical formulas, instant solutions, guaranteed techniques, or infallible tricks to 'fix' situations of conflict. Although it might be good if such consistently effective methods could be provided, they cannot be, because they do not exist. Suggestions that people involved in serious conflict can, by the application of simple techniques, find easy and relatively painless resolution, guaranteeing a 'win' for all participants, are naïve and unrealistic.

Human conflicts, like human beings, are complex, involving many diverse components. Even when all the components of a conflict are explicitly identified and all possible preparations are made for the process of resolution, there remains an inevitable element of unpredictability. Conflict resolution is not like programming a computer or building a house or repairing a car. Human beings can, and often do, act in ways that are impossible to predict or even, in some cases, to explain, and unpredictable and inexplicable behaviour is more likely in situations of emotionally charged conflict.

The principles of conflict resolution practice outlined in this book have been developed both through academic research and in professional practice. They have been applied, tested, and (on the basis of that testing) reviewed and revised. They have been used in conflicts involving individuals with a strong commitment to find a resolution, and with individuals with powerful enthusiasms for the maintenance, or even the escalation, of the conflict. While it would be encouraging to say that the application of the principles inevitably (and even quickly and easily) brings about the resolution of conflict in every case, that would be simply dishonest. Nor is the failure to achieve resolution always simply explained. Sometimes, of course, it is a consequence of unwillingness to resolve on the part of a third party brought in to facilitate resolution. And sometimes the reason for the failure remains unknown.

Unlike a manual—for example, on a motor vehicle repair—which provides a step-by-step guide to actions that will lead to a certain outcome, this book provides only principles of, and suggestions for, action. The reader will need to reflect on what is offered before applying the principles that are relevant in a particular situation.

The challenge of conflict and, even more, of conflict resolution is to apply analytical problem-solving processes to situations that, traditionally, have been approached through the use of coercive power. All analysis begins in the mind of the individual, and therefore critical and reflective thinking is the first, and most important, skill to be developed.

This book is intended to stimulate thought, analysis, and reflection about conflict and its resolution. As Professor John Burton noted in his foreword to the first edition, it 'invites some rethinking of traditional explanations and remedies, and draws attention to problem-solving alternatives to traditional power and coercive processes'.

The approach taken in this book has been shaped particularly by the work of Burton, and regularly reshaped by the many people who have used it as a teaching textbook (in Australia, the USA, and elsewhere) or have undergone training on the basis of its approach. Teaching and training has been undertaken in universities in Australia and overseas, for organisations ranging from government authorities and commercial organisations through to community associations. The comments, criticisms, and suggestions of students, participants, and clients have contributed to this second edition. The aim of the revised text is the same as that of the first edition, summarised by Burton in these words: 'Those who read this book will understand far better the constant news reports on violence at more remote levels, and hopefully some will be able to voice a resistance to negative and self-defeating policies, punishment and prevention'.

Gregory Tillett
October 1998

1 Conflict and its Resolution

Conflict is an inevitable and pervasive aspect of human life. It arises within individuals and between individuals. It takes place within and between groups, organisations, communities, and nations. Conflict occurs at home and at work and in the neighbourhood. It occurs across neighbours' fences and across national borders.

Conflict is sometimes physically violent, but more often not. Much of it exists within the mind and is expressed in words; some of it, however, is expressed with fists, guns, or bombs. Conflict can occur over a suburban fence or in a family living room, on a battlefield or in a courtroom, in a workplace or a parliament, on a sports field, or in a street. Conflict can erupt suddenly, or it can smoulder for years or even for generations. It can focus on trivia, or concern the future of life on earth.

Conflict is popularly equated with fighting and is generally seen as destructive, unpleasant, and undesirable. It is usually suppressed, avoided, concealed, or fought over. It commonly provokes negative responses, which can have detrimental effects on the individual, on relationships, and on groups. It can break down communication, destroy relationships and lives, increase problems, and erect barriers. Conflict can, however, promote new ideas, encourage better understanding, strengthen personal relationships, stimulate individual growth, and facilitate more effective solutions to problems.

Conflict resolution

Conflict resolution is a multi-disciplinary, analytical, problem-solving approach to conflict that seeks to enable the participants to work collaboratively towards its resolution. John Burton, one of the world's leading scholars in the field of conflict resolution, has commented that:

> the analysis of conflict requires the study of the totality of human relationships, whether conflictual or not, for it is human motivation and values that are involved, conditioned by the totality of the environment—economic, political, social and ecological—in which these relationships are enacted . . . conflict

resolution means terminating conflict by methods that are analytical and that get to the root of the problem. Conflict resolution, as opposed to mere management or 'settlement', points to an outcome that, in the view of the parties involved, is a permanent solution to the problem . . . conflict resolution deals with the total human being, encompassing personal and cultural differences, and deals with this person in the total society, encompassing social differences (Burton 1988, p. 2).

Conflict resolution principles

1   Conflict is inevitable and pervasive. Some conflict can be eliminated; some can be minimised; some needs to be managed.
2   Conflict is essentially based in perceptions (rather than reality) and feelings (rather than facts). It can only be resolved by dealing with perceptions and feelings.
3   There is no simple formula that makes conflict go away, but there are approaches that can minimise the destructive effects of conflict and maximise the possibility of resolution.
4   There are some common negative responses to conflict that maximise its destructive effects.
5   Stress increases the risk of destructive conflict, which, in turn, increases the level of stress; therefore, effective stress management is an integral part of conflict resolution.
6   Most conflict is predictable. The most effective approach to conflict involves predicting and preparing for the conflict.
7   A flexible, adaptive, collaborative approach to conflict is generally more effective, this can be changed to a more directive or even coercive approach where necessary.
8   A collaborative, cooperative approach should usually be attempted initially; by assuming cooperation, one can often promote cooperation. The type of approach can be changed (and quickly) if cooperation fails. Direct confrontation (including threat) usually provokes an aggressive response and should be avoided where possible.
9   The effective resolution of conflict almost inevitably requires talking about it—preferably with the person or people involved.
10 Not all conflicts can be resolved externally, and therefore effective internal (or intrapersonal) techniques of resolution may be necessary. These may include stress management, peer support, counselling, or therapy.

Conflict resolution is a relatively new area of academic and professional study. The study of conflict itself, particularly in the disciplines of anthropology and psychology, is considerably better established than the study of its resolution. Theories of the nature and origin of conflict have a long history and include those of Sigmund Freud and Karl Marx. They range from the biological (such as those

Common negative responses to conflict

- *denial* (for example, suppression, repression, or blocking)
- *withdrawal* (physical, emotional, psychological)
- *submission* (for example, with resentment, anxiety, or depression)
- *immobilisation* (for example, freezing)
- *displacement* (for example, into family)
- *internalisation* (for example, self-blame, guilt, or anxiety)
- *projection* (for example, blame of others, enmification)
- *addictive behaviour* (for example, obsessional thought)
- *drugs and alcohol*
- *violence* (threat or coercion, either physical or psychological)

of Konrad Lorenz) and the psychological (for example, Freud's) to the socio-economic (such as those of Marx), from the inherent to the contingent, and from the individual to the social. Many scholars have studied conflict and its resolution in traditional societies (for example, Max Gluckman's work on Africa).

The generic study of the causes of conflict, how it can be resolved, and the strategies that can be developed to facilitate resolution is a relatively recent development. It is now growing rapidly, largely because of the financial implications of unresolved conflict and the costs to the individual and the community of traditional solutions, such as litigation or violence.

The study of conflict resolution draws material from a wide range of areas, including psychology, anthropology, sociology, history, politics, law, management, philosophy, comparative religion, and social work. Conflict resolution involves both the study and practice of skills in thinking, communicating, and behaving, as well as problem solving, mediation, and negotiation.

This book is not based on an assumption that conflict is in itself undesirable or destructive: conflict can be creative and positive. Most conflict, however, is unnecessarily destructive because it is not effectively resolved. The book outlines a range of practical approaches to conflict and its resolution. Readers are free to accept or reject any or all of these approaches, and are encouraged to develop their own.

The principles and skills of conflict resolution can be applied in both personal and professional life. In management and industrial relations, in social work, psychology and counselling, in law and commerce, and in environmental planning and education—no less than in the life of the individual, in personal relationships, in families, and in neighbourhood—conflicts arise and need to be resolved. Although the context and subject matter vary, the basic principles of resolution remain the same.

Conflict resolution provides a theoretical basis and introduces practical skills for dealing with conflict at all levels—within an individual or between two individuals, between communities or organisations, or at an international level. Although the theoretical base is important, conflict resolution is essentially a practical discipline concerned with resolving actual conflict in real situations.

An outline of the book

The book introduces practical approaches and offers a variety of conflict resolution strategies, suggesting ways in which they might be applied in a wide range of circumstances.

This chapter considers the nature of conflict and conflict resolution, and very briefly outlines the major principles that have been developed. (The reading guide includes suggestions for wider reading in the area of conflict resolution theory.) Chapter 2 introduces conflict analysis and demonstrates the importance of an analytical approach. It emphasises the value of looking at conflict from a human needs perspective, and explores ways in which thinking processes can be improved for more effective analysis and resolution. Chapter 3 examines the important role of effective communication as a tool in conflict resolution. Chapter 4 considers the need for preparation, and identifies the stages through which this preparation ought to go. One aspect of this is the choice of an appropriate process; this chapter outlines the major processes, which are then examined in more detail in later chapters. Chapter 5 discusses collaborative problem solving, the least interventionist of the processes, and suggests ways to improve its effectiveness. Negotiation is one form of collaborative problem solving. Mediation, a process involving an impartial third party to facilitate collaborative problem solving, is examined in chapter 6, and arbitration, the use of an impartial third party to hand down a determination, is covered in chapter 7. Although different processes work in different ways, it is possible to identify a number of basic stages in the conflict resolution process; these are examined in chapter 8, and practical suggestions are offered to increase their effectiveness. Chapter 9 explores a number of ways in which practical psychology can be applied, including the use of a range of interpersonal skills, effective decision-making, and role-play. Conflict resolution will not always flow smoothly: a range of problems and potential obstructions is considered in chapter 10, and basic strategies for dealing with each are suggested. Chapters 11–14 outline some of the particular issues and problems that arise in different areas of conflict, from the interpersonal to the environmental and technical. Chapter 15 provides an overview of the legal and ethical issues of conflict resolution, and chapter 16 offers a summary and conclusion. In chapter 17 a case study is followed by an example of analysis and planning.

What is conflict?

The first question that arises in conflict resolution is deceptively simple: what is conflict? The *Oxford English Dictionary* provides definitions that fit the popular conception: '1. An encounter with arms; a fight; especially a prolonged struggle; 2. Dashing together of physical bodies. The word is derived from the Latin meaning "to strike"'.

In the *Oxford Thesaurus*, the synonyms include 'fight', 'battle', 'combat', 'engagement', 'struggle', 'war', 'fray', 'fracas', 'affray', 'brawl', 'dispute', 'argument', 'controversy', 'wrangle', 'contention', 'disagreement', 'altercation', 'feud', 'quarrel', 'row', 'squabble', 'clash', 'antagonism', and 'discord'. Conflict is most often identified with fighting, whether physically or verbally, with implications of winning or losing. It is useful to prepare a list of as many words as possible that are identified or associated with the word 'conflict', and to consider how they relate to one another. Words that have widely different implications are often lumped together under 'conflict', and it is therefore useful to reflect on how different sorts or dimensions of conflict interrelate.

The range of conflict

Conflict ranges across a broad spectrum. *Intrapersonal* (or intrapsychic) conflict is that which individuals feel within themselves (for example, competing demands, needs, and loyalties; guilt, which is an important form of inner conflict about which much has been written; honesty versus dishonesty; conflicting values). *Interpersonal* conflict is the conflict between two individuals (for example, people living together, including husband and wife; parents and children; neighbours; employer and employee; customer and supplier; professional and client; academic and student). *Intragroup* conflict occurs within a group (for example, between factions within a political party). *Intergroup* conflict occurs *between* groups (for example, racial conflict in towns or suburbs; conflict between developers, community groups, and conservationists in environmental disputes). *Value* conflict is conflict that may occur between or within individuals or groups, and that focuses on values, beliefs, ideologies, ethics, or morals (for example, a moral dilemma within an individual; conflict between political conservatives and liberals; conflict between religious beliefs). *International* conflict occurs between nation states or, arguably, between international corporations, organisations, and/or nation states (for example, Iran and Iraq).

Later in this book, both the common features in all conflict and the special features found in particular areas will be examined.

A typology of conflict

While conflicts generally share a number of characteristics, different types of conflict can also be identified, and the different characteristics of the different types need to be taken into account when attempting resolution. In practice, any given situation of conflict may (and often does) involve types and categories, and may be described by one or more of the participants as being of one type when in reality it is of a different type. The aim of using any typology is not to seek to make definitive and simplistic diagnoses of a particular conflict (for example, 'This is a habituated interpersonal territorial conflict'), but to identify the characteristics of a given conflict, thereby gaining insights that should be helpful in resolution.

To understand conflicts, it is necessary to consider *causes, symptoms,* and *explanations*. The *cause* of a conflict is that factor that, if addressed effectively, would lead to the resolution of the conflict. The identification of causes can be extremely difficult since they may not be disclosed by, may be deliberately concealed by, or may not be (consciously) known to, the participants. The event that was the immediate cause of the conflict can be called the '*trigger*'.

Symptoms signal that conflict exists. In the individual, they indicate 'that something is wrong in the emotional or psychic life of an individual or family. They are behaviours, feelings, or thoughts that both people or that therapists view as pathological, abnormal, or dysfunctional' (Heitler 1990, p. 48). Symptoms are also often:

- attempts at solution, such as a dysfunctional response to the conflict, which alleviates its effects but does not address the underlying cause (For example, an employee suffering a high level of workplace stress may use alcohol in an attempt to alleviate the distress.)
- results of ineffective solutions, such as when an ineffective process of resolution may have led to an apparent resolution, which produces dysfunctional consequences (For example, the apparent resolution of a conflict by coerced collaboration between the parties may not have addressed underlying causes and may lead to displaced hostility on the part of those who have been led to believe that the core conflict has been resolved.)
- 'feelings or behaviours that suggest disturbance of normal functioning' (Heitler 1990, p. 49), including excessive expressions of emotions, decreasing efficiency (whether individual or corporate), increasing problematic behaviour (including workplace accidents), physical symptoms (including increased sick leave), breakdowns in communication (including refusal to communicate or unnecessary formality in communication).

The *explanation* is the event, sequence of events, or issue that one or both of the parties offers as an explanation for the conflict. It is usually the answer to the question 'What happened?' Of course, different parties will often provide different explanations for the same conflict.

In reflecting on different types of conflict, it is important to consider, in each case, the qualities, characteristics, or issues associated with a particular type of conflict that make resolution difficult. It is also important to consider the processes that, on the basis of research and practical experience, are considered to be most effective in approaching each type of conflict.

This typology does not attempt to provide a simple diagnosis–prescription system. However, a recognition of different types of conflict facilitates the analysis of conflict and the identification of appropriate processes for resolution. Each apparent situation of conflict is considered in terms of category, location, and type.

Category

It is important to consider whether the following three concepts are the same, or different: problem, dispute, conflict. If they are different, in what ways do they differ? And does this difference suggest that different approaches should be taken to each?

Although it is important to recognise a distinction between problems, disputes, and conflicts, most of the literature on conflict resolution uses 'conflict' as a generic term to cover the whole area, and uses 'conflict resolution' to include problem solving and dispute settlement. Quite different issues, however, arise in managing a problem, settling a dispute, and resolving a conflict. Throughout this book, the broader common meaning of the terms 'conflict' and 'conflict resolution' will (unless otherwise specified) be used to minimise confusion for readers. However, the distinction between problems, disputes, and conflicts should be kept in mind. It should be recognised that not all situations that are popularly identified as conflicts are of the same nature or dimensions.

Problem

A problem can be resolved by management—by agreement on how something can or should be done. For example, two people who need to meet to discuss a topic may have a problem in finding a mutually convenient time; they seek to resolve this by mutually managing their time. A work group may have a problem in deciding how to undertake a particular task; the group seeks to resolve this by collaboratively managing its time and resources. Problems can become disputes, and can disclose conflicts, but they are not disputes or conflicts as such. Problems are usually managed. There are very good publications on problem solving; some are included in the bibliography. Basic problem-solving skills are an essential part of dealing not only with problems, but also with disputes and conflicts.

Dispute

A dispute arises when two (or more) people (or groups) perceive that their interests, needs, or goals are incompatible and they seek to maximise fulfilment of their own interests or needs, or achievement of their own goals (often at the expense of the others). This may be done through bargaining or negotiating, and the outcome is often reached through compromise: to obtain that which is most important, one party may yield to the other on that which is less important. Disputes are usually *settled*. That is, either a mutually agreed settlement (usually involving compromise) is reached by the parties to the dispute (either with or without the assistance of a third party, such as a mediator or facilitator), or a solution is imposed upon them by an external authority (for example, an arbitrator or a court).

Conflict

A conflict arises when two (or more) people (or groups) perceive that their values or needs are incompatible—whether or not they propose, at present or in the future, to take any action on the basis of those values or needs. Thus, while a problem or a dispute relates to a specific action or situation (for example, a disputed land claim, the purchase of a motor vehicle, the division of joint property), a conflict can exist without such a specific focus. Two parties can be in conflict because of what each believes, regardless of whether any action has been or is being taken on the basis of the belief. For example, religious conflict exists because one person (or group) opposes the religious belief of another person (or group); it may be exacerbated by the belief being put into practice, but it does not depend upon the practice of the belief. Conflict based on racial discrimination centres on the views that one person (or group) holds of a category of people: the people in that category do not have to do anything to provoke the conflict, although their actions may exacerbate it. It is often the case that an underlying conflict (for example, based on racist stereotyping) gives rise to a dispute or series of disputes. For example, if a member of the racial group against whom the conflict is directed moves into the neighbourhood of, or takes up employment in the same company as, the person holding the racist views, it is likely that disputes will arise. But the disputes are essentially the manifestation of the underlying conflict.

Conflicts relate to deep human needs and values. Sometimes they are expressed through problems or disputes, which may be the superficial manifestation of a conflict. Obviously, this is not the case for every problem or dispute. But it may be suspected if:

- the problem or dispute is but one of a sequence characterising the relationship between the parties, and as quickly as one dispute is resolved, another arises (For example, continual minor disputes over meal-times occur in a domestic relationship between two people.)
- the problem or dispute, although objectively minor, provokes an irrational, emotional, or extreme reaction in one or both of the parties (For example, one partner threatens to leave the other because dinner was seventeen minutes late.)
- the problem or dispute, although objectively minor, leads to excessive discussion or argument, or unreasonable expenditure of effort (For example, the couple spends three hours discussing the fact that dinner was seventeen minutes late.)
- the problem or dispute, although objectively minor, seems incapable of resolution despite considerable effort on the part of one or both parties or a neutral third party (For example, all attempts to organise a dinner-time that suits both partners fail.)

In such cases, an underlying conflict may be the cause of the superficial problem or dispute, and unless the conflict is addressed, the dispute or problem will continue, or new disputes or problems will arise.

Location

Intrapersonal

Intrapersonal (or intrapsychic) conflict is conflict that arises within the individual, is usually not obvious to another person (unless disclosed by the individual), and does not depend upon a relationship with someone else (although it is often a result of a relationship). It includes personal decision-making ('Will

I take this new job?'), moral questions ('Will I be honest in my tax return?'), and initiating relationships ('Will I go up and talk to that person?'). Other types of conflict almost inevitably provoke intrapersonal conflict.

Interpersonal

Interpersonal conflict occurs between two or more individuals (excluding intergroup conflict); this includes conflict between individuals in long-term relationships (such as marriage) and in single interactions (for example, a customer and a member of staff in a shop)

Intragroup

Intragroup conflict occurs within a group. It may involve a division of the group into two (or more) opposing factions; divisions may appear to be relatively stable, or they may change according to the different aspects of a conflict. A group is here defined as a number of individuals who want or are obliged to have an ongoing relationship with each other and are, of necessity, required to cooperate. A group may be externally defined (for example, a manager may create a work team) or defined by its members (for example, a social club); it may be relatively permanent (for example, the academic staff of a department) or of limited duration (for example, a task team). Members may face high costs in withdrawing from membership (for example, loss of employment) or very few costs (for example, leaving a social club). Groups can be formal or informal, and can come together either frequently and regularly or infrequently and irregularly. Groups can be of radically varying sizes. The dynamics of a conflict within a group of five people are very different from those in a group of 500; in the latter group, it may be more appropriate to speak of intergroup conflict since the 500 will inevitably be divided into sub-groups.

Intergroup

Intergroup conflict is conflict that occurs between two (or more) groups. In some cases (particularly with large groups), it may be difficult to distinguish intergroup conflict from intragroup conflict because the large group will be divided into sub-groups with a stronger sense of separate identity from each other than of common identity as part of the larger group.

Type

Style

Style conflict arises from negative perceptions of the behaviour of one person by another or others. It results less from what is done than from how it is done and is often described as a 'personality clash'. It is caused by expectations (often unexpressed) and perceptions of appropriate and acceptable behaviour.

Role

Role conflict arises from different expectations and/or perceptions of a role and, therefore, of the effectiveness and appropriateness of the fulfilment of the role. This conflict often arises because the parties assume that there is a common understanding of the nature of a role and its requirements. For example, it might be assumed that a manager and an employee agree on the relative importance of specific components of a position and the relative time and effort that ought to be devoted to each component. If each has different perceptions and expectations of the role, conflict is likely to result as the employee fails to conform to the manager's definition of the role.

Value

Value conflict arises from incompatible values; this includes conflict between individuals, and conflict between an individual and an organisation. Value conflict can arise as a result of mutually incompatible values, the application of particular values, or individuals being expected to act on the basis of values that they do not hold (and that may be in conflict with the values they do hold). Values, which are an integral part of the individual's definition of self, come into conflict where individuals are expected to:
- act contrary to their own values, or
- be seen to support values contrary to their own values, or
- abstain from acting on their own values.

World-view

World-view conflict has its origins in different perceptions of the way in which the world—or a particular component of it (for example, a family, a relationship, a workplace)—is or should be defined, and of how it functions or should function. This can include intercultural and cross-cultural conflict, but is not confined to these areas. People within the same culture can hold radically differing world-views, and people from different cultures can hold very similar world-views. This type of conflict can also include style conflict, although people with very similar world-views can have very different styles. For example, a manager who has a view of the world that centres on order, discipline, structure, and tidiness will tend to evaluate an employee who has a world-view that centres on flexibility, spontaneity, freedom, and relaxation according to the manager's world-view. The employee will be evaluated in terms of what is perceived as an inappropriate approach to life rather than in terms of the quality or quantity of work performance. The manager is likely to see the employee as disorganised, chaotic, uncommitted, indifferent, and non-productive; the employee is likely to see the manager as rigid, authoritarian, obsessive, and inflexible.

Symbolic

Symbolic conflict arises when participants are motivated to engage in conflict not as a result of the matter on which the conflict is purportedly focused, but because of a need to be seen (by themselves or others) as taking a position in relation to the other participants. This can include power conflict, but need not, since some symbolic conflict may weaken the power of either or both participants. Sometimes symbolic conflict will be described using phrases such as 'taking a stand', 'fighting for a principle', or 'not giving in, no matter what'.

Structural

Structural conflict results from systemic or structural problems. For example, a process might have been defined by senior management, who never have to implement it, and so creates unnecessary difficulties for those who do have to implement it, and who have no recourse to consultative processes allowing for revision and change.

Habituated

Habituated conflict arises from a relationship in which conflict is habituated or ritualised (usually as a result of a past conflict or series of conflicts) so that the participants come into conflict because they assume that all interactions in their relationship are conflictual. In some cases, the origin of habituated conflict may lie within one individual, rather than within a relationship between individuals. For example, according to Susan Heitler, 'neurosis from a conflict resolution vantage point is defined as a conflict that persists, repeatedly recurring in varying forms throughout a person's life because it has not been satisfactorily resolved' (Heitler 1990, p. 66). In this sense, it is also displaced conflict, being carried over from one context to another: 'The individual is reacting to new situations as if these were the same as earlier ones in their lives' (Wachtel 1987, as quoted in Heitler 1990, p. 67).

Symbiotic

Symbiotic conflict results from a relationship in which conflict is habituated or ritualised (usually as a result of a past conflict or series of conflicts) so that:
• the participants approach all interactions in a conflictual way because they assume that all interactions in their relationship are necessarily conflictual, and
• each participant in the conflict gains more from the maintenance of the conflictual relationship than would be gained from the resolution of any individual conflict or a change in the relationship.

In some cases, such conflict can also be symbolic conflict or power conflict. But it is usually distinguished by:

1 a frequency of (usually voluntary) conflictual interactions
2 lack of insight by the participants into the consequences of their current style of interaction (that is, regular conflict)
3 frequent complaint by (and sometimes apparent distress on the part of) the participants regarding the conflicts and their consequences, but
4 a failure (and often a refusal) by the participants to change the nature of their interactions.

In some cases, symbiotic conflict is a product of relational definitions (for example, conflict between a union delegate and a management representative) in which each participant believes he or she would lose (for example, in status or support from peers) by taking a non-conflictual approach. It is the classic 'us and them' conflictual relationship, in which any resolution would require a redefinition of who is 'us' and who is 'them'. The participants' expectations that all interaction will be conflictual often lead them to approach every interaction in a way that ensures that conflict will result; this becomes a self-perpetuating cycle.

Power

Power conflict results from a desire to gain or maintain power. Such conflict relates to the need for power rather than to the apparent content of the conflict. Power can be defined as the capacity to ensure that the individual's needs are met and to compel others to comply with directions. There is, arguably, a basic human need to have power, and some individuals need (sometimes to a pathological degree) to exercise, maintain, and gain power frequently, even in situations in which 'winning' is largely meaningless, may provoke further conflict, or even have destructive long-term effects.

Displaced external

Displaced external conflict arises from the acting out within one setting of conflicts external to that setting (for example, an employee whose domestic relationship is in major conflict may act out the frustration and distress caused by that conflict in the workplace). All conflict produces stress, which needs to be released; when it is not released within the arena of the conflict, it will usually be released elsewhere. The widely held view that there is a divide between the home personality and the work personality—or the (more rigidly held) belief that there is (or can be) a separation between the personal and the professional—is little more than a myth. The personal is carried into the professional in the same way that the professional is carried into the personal sphere of life.

Displaced internal

Displaced internal conflict arises from the acting out externally of conflicts internal to the individual. (For example, an employee experiencing intrapersonal conflict may act out the frustration and distress caused by that conflict in the workplace.) The same principle applies here as in displaced external conflict: all conflict produces stress, which needs to be released; when it is not released within the arena of the conflict, it will usually be released elsewhere.

Territorial

Territorial conflict is based in a perception that territory is threatened. Territory should not be understood geographically (although it can be literal territory) but rather symbolically. Thus, territorial conflict may arise when one employee believes that another is taking over part of her or his job, or when one department believes another is seeking to take away some of its resources or clients, or one person in a family believes that another is intruding into her or his area of responsibility.

Individual dysfunction

Individual dysfunction conflict is conflict that has its origins in the psychological dysfunction of one (or more) of the participants. That an individual has, or appears to show symptoms of, some psychological disorder does not define the conflict as based in that individual's dysfunction, although attempts are often made to explain a conflict on this basis. Psychological dysfunction can be as much a consequence of a conflict as the cause of it. The dysfunction may relate to a specific conflict or situation (for example, there may be very high stress at work, but a relatively happy situation at home) or may constitute a personality disorder. The personality disorder may relate directly to the ability to deal with conflict: 'When an individual's conflict-handling repertoire is deficient, rigidified in one counterproductive mode, the person may be diagnosed as having a particular character style or personality disorder' (Heitler 1990, p. 69).

Group dysfunction

It is possible to extend the essentially individualistic definitions of psychopathology to groups; groups tend to operate as though they were more than the sum of their constituent individual members. Groups develop what can be thought of as a 'personality', often described as the group culture but, in fact, going beyond traditional definitions of culture. It is possible, for the purposes of analysing conflict, to talk of a dysfunctional group (or even a corporation), or even a neurotic group (or corporation), in which a number of otherwise potentially functional and healthy individuals are united in a group within which most of them become dysfunctional. In such cases, the conflict within the group is a symptom of group dysfunction.

Stress-related

Stress and conflict are intimately related. A high level of stress in an individual (or a group) increases the risk of conflict. If one or more of participants are under high levels of stress, incidents that might otherwise pass unnoticed, or be effectively dealt with immediately, can provoke conflict or initiate a process that leads to conflict. Stress-related conflict is conflict that has its origins in dysfunctional stress levels, regardless of how it may otherwise be defined by one or more of the participants. Organisations or groups that operate in a situation of abnormal stress inevitably manifest high levels of conflict; the conflict is usually symptomatic of the stress.

Change

Change, even when it is considered to be positive and beneficial, involves the risk of conflict. Where change is perceived as threatening (often because it involves a move from the known to the unknown), the risk of conflict is high. Sometimes this will be stress-related conflict; however, there is also the possibility of change conflict—that is, conflict that results from change as such.

The positive functions of conflict

Although conflict is popularly identified with fighting, with destructiveness, and with discomfort (if not pain), it can also have a positive role. The creative and constructive effects of conflict include prevention of stagnation, stimulation of interest and curiosity, encouragement of the examination of problems, and motivation towards solving them. It can help personal growth and development by challenging the individual, and it can promote group identity and cohesion. Although commonly thought of as destructive of relationships, conflict can stabilise and integrate them, helping to release tensions. It can stimulate and provide the basis for personal and social change by encouraging critical self-reflection. It can encourage interpersonal communication, and promote the exploration and awareness of the feelings, needs, and opinions of other people. Ideally it should encourage creativity and innovation.

The positive role of conflict depends very largely on it being resolved. That is, conflict that has been suppressed, concealed, avoided, or worked around, or in which a fight has produced a winner and a loser, is unlikely to be creative or constructive and is more likely to be destructive. The destructive effects of conflict are not necessarily visible; parties may only appear to establish a harmonious and positive relationship, while, in reality, they continue in a state of tension and unresolved conflict. Appearance need not reflect reality. A workplace described by management as 'harmonious' and 'free of conflict' may, in fact, be seething with unmanifest conflict, with an appearance of harmony only because of an enforced policy or culture that forbids the expression of conflict.

The negative effects of conflict

Most people will probably find it easier to identify the destructive or negative effects of conflict: its ability to provoke anger, anxiety, distress, fear, and aggression. It often breaks down relationships, hinders communication, and obstructs problem solving. Unresolved conflict frequently limits critical self-reflection and hinders self-development. It can destroy group cohesion and identity.

It is not possible to discuss conflict in itself in absolute terms as good or bad, destructive or creative. For example, a relationship conflict—such as an argument about the choice of food—can lead to an enhanced and strengthened relationship, with increased communication and understanding of each party by the other. However, it can also lead to a breakdown of communication, to separation, and to mutual distress—even, in extreme cases, ending in violence.

It is important not to identify conflict with fighting or arguing. The media refer to an 'armed conflict' when they really mean 'violence with weapons'. Fighting (with or without weapons), violence, and physical or verbal aggression are possible *responses* to, or *manifestations* of, conflict. They may be symptoms or expressions of conflict in the same way that domestic violence may be a manifestation of a relationship conflict. The violence, however, is not the conflict, nor is it the only option for expressing or resolving the conflict. There are many ways in which conflict manifests itself. What might be thought of as 'symptoms' often draw attention to the fact that conflict exists. This will be explored in more detail in chapter 2, since the distinction between manifest and unmanifest conflict is critical in conflict analysis.

Options for approaching conflict

This book examines options for manifesting and resolving conflict that may be more productive than fighting, avoiding, or suppressing it. The traditional approaches to conflict have been the classical biological reactions: fight and aggression, or flight and submission. Flight often includes suppression or denial. This is sometimes erroneously called 'conflict management' and is often demonstrated by managers who claim 'there is no conflict' in their workplaces. Conflict is managed when a situation is so structured as to preclude, or at least to minimise, the expression of the symptoms of the conflict. For example, two employees may be warned that if they continue to argue they will both be dismissed. Thus the symptom of the conflict—the argument, in this case—may well disappear. The conflict and the underlying causes of the conflict remain unaddressed and are likely to be displaced into other forms of expression. Conflict management, in this sense, is equivalent to inadequate pain management in health care: it treats the symptom, but does not seek out or treat the cause. In the short term, this can give an appearance of effectiveness; in the long term, however, it is likely that the underlying cause will not only remain unchanged but may also increase in strength and potential for harm. Of course, conflict management as a short-term response and as a preliminary to a more sophisticated approach can be beneficial and, indeed, may be essential. Thus, much of what is called 'peacekeeping' in international conflict is, in fact, conflict management (or, more accurately, 'war management') undertaken in the hope that, while physical hostilities have been minimised, the real conflict may be addressed. Resolution is virtually impossible in the midst of a fight—physical or otherwise—and management (or control) of the fighting behaviour is usually a necessary preliminary to processes for resolution. But conflict management should never be viewed as anything other than a short-term and preliminary process. To continue the medical analogy: symptoms may require treatment to allow time to undertake essential, and more complex, medical procedures.

Most people believe that all conflict represents a fight in which someone will win by using strength to overpower or undermine the other party, and in which someone will lose. They assume that conflict necessarily results in a victory for one side and defeat for the other, or, at best, a compromise in which both sides win a little and lose a little. An effective approach to conflict, however, involves something more than a fight, although some sort of 'fight' (that is, a strong expression of conflicting views) may, in certain situations, be both inevitable and therapeutic.

A definition of conflict

For the purposes of this book, *conflict exists when two or more parties perceive that their values or needs are incompatible*. Values are incompatible if each contradicts or opposes the other (for example, a belief that abortion is always murder and a belief that abortion is not murder). One need would be seen as incompatible with another if meeting that need is thought to prevent, obstruct, interfere with, or in some way make meeting the other need less likely or effective (for example, two job applicants competing for the same, single position). Conflict becomes manifest when one or more of the parties involved seeks to resolve the incompatibility by, for example, discussing, fighting, compelling the other to change, going to the law, or seeking resolution. This working definition, like most definitions, is inadequate and imperfect, but it will serve as a practical basis for this text.

Burton (1988, p. 11), as already discussed, makes an important distinction between problems, disputes, and conflicts. Burton defines conflict as 'a relationship in which each party perceives the other's goals, values, interests or behaviour as antithetical to its own'.

Morton Deutsch, another important scholar in this area, draws attention to the difference between *conflict* and *competition*: although competition produces conflict, not all conflict reflects competition. He defines competition as requiring an opposition of the parties' goals such that the probability of goal attainment for one decreases as the probability of goal attainment for the other (or others) increases. Conflict can exist when there is no competition. Deutsch appropriately distinguishes the *underlying* conflict from the *manifest* conflict, which others have sometimes called the 'presenting problem' (in medical terms, the 'symptom') and the 'hidden agenda' (the 'cause') (Deutsch 1973).

Jay Folberg and Allison Taylor (1988) distinguish between *conflict* (which may, for example, be intrapersonal and unknown, except to the individual) and *dispute*, which they define as an interpersonal conflict that is communicated or manifested.

In considering the definition that will be used in this book, some of the terms are particularly important. Conflict can exist within an individual, but this book will focus on interpersonal, rather than intrapersonal, conflict; conflict can be between two, four, a dozen, a hundred, or a thousand parties. The parties are not necessarily individuals: they can also be families, communities, organisations (for example, a union and an employer body), or nations. Where the parties are not individuals, the conflict will be acted out by individuals, and resolution usually depends on discussions between individual representatives of the groups.

Conflict does not only come about when values or needs are actually, objectively incompatible, or when conflict is manifested in action; it also exists when one of the parties *perceives* it to exist. Much conflict arises from assumptions about what might or will happen if or when one party does something. Much interpersonal hostility in relationships, for example, is a result of unspoken assumptions about the actions of the other or the meaning of these actions. For example, one party might believe: 'I couldn't go out last night because I knew you would have been angry'. The perception need not be reasonable or realistic; bizarre conspiracy theories can provide the basis for beliefs that lead to conflict. Often one role of conflict resolution is to demonstrate that a belief in the incompatibility of values or needs is not based on fact and that the parties do have mutual interests and can (if only minimally) cooperate.

Values and *needs* are often closely related. Values are those beliefs that have significance for an individual; they can include, but are not limited to, religious, political, and moral beliefs, and the holding of particular values probably meets particular needs. Besides physical needs (often the most popularly accepted use of the term), there are needs related to psychological and emotional well-being and self-esteem, and to group identity and acceptance. Conflict is often related to status, power, prestige, self-esteem, 'principle', or religious or political belief, rather than to what would usually be thought of as 'actions'. Essentially the incompatibility can be summarised as: 'You interfere with my doing or being what I want to do or be'.

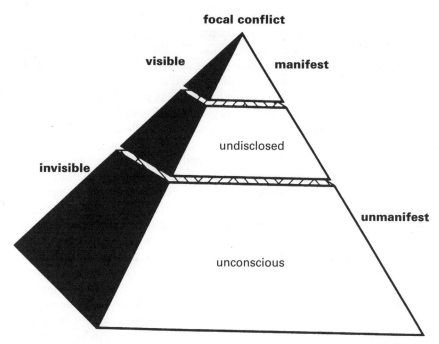

Figure 1.1 Manifest and unmanifest conflict

Manifest and unmanifest conflict

This book deals primarily with manifest conflict, or conflict in which at least one of the parties is trying to do something about the incompatibility believed to exist; an internal, personal sense of competition or mutually incompatible interests is, because of its essentially invisible nature, less easy to deal with. Sometimes it manifests in indirect conflict, or what Deutsch calls '*displaced conflict*'. For example, employee A believes that employee B has the boss's ear and is likely to gain a promotion that A believes he or she should have; A criticises B vigorously about matters related to B's work performance, and a conflict develops. The conflict appears to be related to B's work performance, but clearly it is not.

Among the forms through which parties may seek to resolve what they believe to be incompatible interests are arguments, litigation, physical assault, and war.

Conflict resolution in practice

This book focuses essentially on the practice of conflict resolution. There must be, however, a self-development component, since the practice inevitably relates to personality and personal life, and may challenge and/or assist the individual to become more effective in dealing with conflict. These personal skills

Case study 1

Robert is a fifteen-year-old Aboriginal boy and has been given an apprenticeship in a workshop employing fifteen tradesmen and two other apprentices. The tradesmen and the apprentices spend a lot of time together outside work, and usually go to the local hotel every evening after work. They visit each other's homes and frequently hold social gatherings.

They are not, however, particularly welcoming of Robert. The workshop manager is not sure of the reason for this; he thinks it may be because Robert is Aboriginal, or because he is a quiet young man, not particularly interested in drinking after work, and more concerned about completing his studies at technical college. However, the general lack of interest in Robert develops into unfriendliness and begins to affect his work. The tradesman who is supposed to supervise Robert takes little interest in him, and only mentions him to the manager to complain about his work.

Robert is, in fact, a very good worker, and does exceptionally well at college. This is the subject of ridicule by the other apprentices. The manager is very concerned that Robert will lose his apprenticeship.

Identify the key elements of this conflict, together with the factors that may make it particularly difficult to resolve. Consider whether any particular theories of the origin of conflict may be helpful in understanding what is happening and in attempting resolution.

can be thought of as essentially involving cognition (or thinking), affect (or feeling), and behaviour (including communication).

One of the keys to conflict resolution is *innovative thinking*—that is, breaking out of habits of assuming that things must be done in set ways or that there are only limited options in any situation. In considering possibilities for resolution, it is necessary to be open to change, and to creative and imaginative problem solving.

Just as there are different definitions of conflict, so there are many views of conflict resolution. At its simplest, conflict resolution will be defined as any process that brings about the resolution of a conflict. This can, of course, include fighting (even involving violence), adjudication, negotiation or bargaining, and withdrawal. It is, however, more appropriate to make a distinction between processes that deal with the manifestation of conflict (which can generally be called 'conflict management') and those that deal with the conflict itself (which can be called 'conflict resolution'). For example, if two people in a relationship are in the process of separating, it is possible, and indeed common, to deal with the mechanics of disputes over property without considering any aspects of the underlying conflict.

Just as a distinction has been made between a problem, a dispute, and a conflict, so it is necessary to make a distinction between problem solving, dispute settling, and conflict resolution. Problems can be solved and disputes can be settled even where underlying conflict exists. Burton (1988, p. 2) offers the following definition of conflict resolution: 'conflict resolution means terminating conflict by methods that are analytical and get to the root of the problem. Conflict resolution, as opposed to mere management or "settlement", points to an outcome that, in the view of the parties involved, is a permanent solution to the problem'.

Although much of what is called 'conflict resolution' will involve problem solving, dispute settlement, or conflict management, and although resolution of the underlying conflict may, in many cases, be impossible, Burton's definition should be recalled as the ideal towards which conflict resolution works.

This book provides some basic practical strategies for conflict resolution and, therefore, for problem solving and settlement of disputes.

2 Analysing Conflict

The most effective conflict resolution is one that is *proactive*—that is, a resolution that is planned and prepared for on the basis of an analysis of the conflict. Most attempts at resolution are ineffective because they occur without adequate preliminary analysis, planning, and preparation. Resolution is often attempted at a time of crisis, when emotions are strong and relationships strained, and when the parties are least likely to be able or willing to think clearly about the situation. Most attempts at resolution are *reactive*: they occur spontaneously in reaction to a situation. For example, someone says something that causes immediate anger, and this leads to an argument about a range of past issues.

Trying to remove the emotions from conflict will either be unsuccessful or lead only to a temporary and superficial resolution while the feelings of conflict remain under the surface. Proactive resolution means that at least one party, or preferably all parties, take a positive and active role in seeking to bring about resolution. This may, for example, mean that when something happens to provoke anger and revive a range of past conflicts, the anger is expressed and the need for the issues to be discussed is identified, but the discussion itself is postponed until it can be undertaken more productively.

Arguing and fighting are not necessarily bad; they can have a positive role in releasing emotions. But they need to be distinguished carefully from resolution. A choice to fight is almost always a choice not to resolve.

Principles of effective conflict resolution

It is not possible to prescribe clear and simple rules for the resolution of conflict. One of the first principles to be recognised in effective conflict resolution is that human beings do not behave mechanically and predictably according to pre-determined rules of behaviour. Conflicts, like people, are usually multi-dimensional, multi-faceted, and complex, and are predictable only at some times and within fairly narrow boundaries. The conflict resolver must be adaptable, flexible, sensitive to small and frequent changes, and not dependent on consistency and predictability, but rather be able to deal with the unexpected. However, some general principles for effective conflict resolution can be identified, one of the most important being the need for *conflict analysis*.

Figure 2.1 A model for conflict analysis

A model for conflict analysis

Diagrams and models often provide a useful basis upon which to examine, analyse, and plan. The model presented in Figure 2.1 aims to be simple, easy to remember, adaptable to varying needs, and capable of dealing with the multi-dimensional nature of conflict and its resolution. It is intended to provide a *guide* to analysis, not a *law* of analysis.

This model distinguishes between five elements or dimensions of a conflict: problem, participants, past, pressures, and projections. For each of these, the model distinguishes between *manifest* and *unmanifest*—that is, between visible or known, and invisible or unknown. These dimensions interlink in the problem or conflict. For each dimension there is a *focus*—that is, the aspect that appears to be involved. In some conflicts, of course, the focus *is* the conflict, and there is nothing deeper. Such situations, however, are comparatively rare.

The model locates the multidimensional conflict within a context, structure, environment, and process.

Conflict analysis

The first stage in any effective resolution of conflict is analysis. Premature and unprepared attempts at resolution are often doomed to failure, and may also create extraordinary difficulties for future attempts, however well prepared. For resolution to be effective quickly, it is often a matter of getting the process right the first time.

Analysis can be divided into several stages: investigation, identification, and preparation.

Investigation

Investigation should involve a non-judgmental gathering of as much information as possible about the conflict. It is, in effect, a 'brainstorming' exercise, and in most cases will involve more than simply thinking about what is already known.

The problem, participants, past, pressures, and projections should be actively researched. For example, investigation should seek to identify any aspects of the past—whether of the conflict as such, or of the relationship between the parties—that may be influencing the present conflict.

Identification

Identification involves assessing and analysing the information collected in investigation, and deciding a number of key issues. These include issues relevant both to the conflict and to its resolution.

The conflict
For each participant, identify:
- the problem: what is the conflict (or, more often, what are the conflicts)?
- any other participants: who are the people involved, in varying degrees, in the conflict?
- the relevant past: what history—of the conflict, of the relationship between the parties, and of the parties themselves—may be relevant?
- pressures or needs: what is motivating the parties in the conflict?
- projections or fears: what is obstructing the parties in the conflict from bringing about resolution?

The resolution
Before beginning the process, identify:
- options for resolution
- resources that are necessary or useful for resolution.

At the beginning of the resolution process, seek agreement on:
- the problem (or problems)
- the process.

Identification may be most useful if it involves all the parties to the conflict. Working together on the preliminary aspects of resolution positively promotes a good working relationship between the parties, and can encourage resolution.

The value of preparation

The importance of analysing conflict and preparation for conflict resolution cannot be overemphasised. Although, ideally, conflict should be dealt with spontaneously and openly when and as it arises, the reality is that this is rarely possible, particularly in more complex conflicts. Preliminary work is an investment in effective conflict resolution. Indeed, where the preparatory work is undertaken jointly by the participants to the conflict, the process of preparation not only promotes the resolution of the present conflict, but also establishes a relationship that is likely to promote resolution of future conflicts.

The critical importance of effective communication in conflict resolution makes it a key area for preparation. Chapter 3 looks at the role of communication.

Manifest and unmanifest conflict

The nature of the conflict may seem self-evident—for example, it may appear to be a dispute about a fact, such as the price charged to repair a car, the fact that a tree is growing over a neighbour's fence, the fact that dinner was late, the fact that a mark for an assignment was too low, or the fact that one nation intruded into the territorial waters of another. While care should be taken not to unnecessarily 'psychoanalyse' the conflict, it is also important to consider whether there may be unmanifested issues—what are sometimes called 'hidden agendas'.

It is essential to recognise that almost all conflicts have both visible, manifest aspects and invisible, unmanifest aspects. The visible conflict is usually the one described by the participants. It will probably involve a focus or focal conflict, and there will often be a further level of manifest conflict underlying the focus. The unmanifest conflict includes both undisclosed factors (which are nevertheless known to either or both the participants) and factors that are unconscious. The participants may or may not be prepared to discuss the underlying or unmanifest conflict, and, indeed, may not be consciously aware of some of the unmanifest aspects.

A hidden dimension may be suspected if a relatively minor dispute leads to an extreme emotional reaction, if an objectively minor problem seems incapable of solution, or if a relationship is characterised by repeated minor disputes. For example, if an employer spends forty minutes emotionally denouncing an employee for arriving five minutes late for work, it may be assumed that this minor lateness is not the real issue. Attempting to deal with the manifest conflict when it is but a symptom of something larger is unlikely to be successful, other than in the very short term. Participants in a conflict may, however, be unwilling to deal with, or even to recognise, the deeper dimension, particularly if (consciously or unconsciously) they feel that it is overwhelming and threatening.

A domestic example may be used to demonstrate this: a couple are having a heated argument because one of them did not put the garbage out the previous night and the other is thinking:

> You didn't put the garbage out last night.
> You never put the garbage out when it's your turn.
> You never do your share of work around the house.
> I feel angry because I have to do more than my share of the work.
> I am hiding a backache so I really feel less youthful and vital than I appear.
> You have no commitment to our relationship.
> You don't love me any more and I feel insecure.
> I am fighting with my father/mother.

In some cases, discussion of the conflict will lead to statements indicating hidden layers; the domestic argument that begins with last night's garbage may very well conclude with accusations of lack of commitment and love. Often, however, the focal conflict is limited to the issue of garbage, even though it seems that the real issue is insecurity about the relationship. Either way, the process may involve a series of accusations that are conducive to fighting but not to resolving.

Facts and feelings

Approaches to conflict resolution that focus on 'facts' are unlikely to be effective. It is not facts but feelings that underlie conflicts, just as it is perceptions, not reality, that fuels them. Conflicts exist because facts or reality are perceived in a way that provokes negative feelings. The stronger the feelings, the greater the risk of conflict. Virtually identical situations can be perceived in different ways, provoking different emotions, which may or may not lead to conflict. A simple example: two people make a similar, unflattering comment about someone. In one case, the person making the comment is regarded with indifference, the opinion is perceived to have no value, and the comment is ignored. In the other case, it provokes strongly negative feelings, and a conflict results. The difference between the two situations is not the fact or the reality, but the perception and the feelings.

It is thus very important, as part of the analytical process, to encourage reflection on how the situation that served to provoke (or to trigger) the conflict was seen, and what emotions that perception stimulated. In some cases, the perception may have been based in error, but the feelings that were provoked were real. Thus, for example, if the unflattering comment was over-heard out of context so that the hearer assumed incorrectly that it was directed towards him- or herself, then the hearer, *perceiving* that he or she had been insulted, will respond as though this were the case. The fact that it was not the case is irrelevant. In some situations, careful (and gentle) analysis of the facts and the resulting perceptions can actually lead to a resolution of a conflict based in misunderstanding. However, if this is not approached in an appropriate way, the original position ('You insulted me') may well be maintained, even with greater fervour, in spite of apparent factual correction.

Most people find it difficult to acknowledge mistakes of perception and, even if forced to acknowledge them, may then find themselves in a different conflict relating to a feeling of embarrassment, humiliation, or loss of face. Assisting people in conflict to understand that the other party perceives the situation differently (and that this is not necessarily simply because he or she is dishonest, stupid, or obstinate) is an important part of any conflict resolution process. Skilfully done, it can go even further: it can assist one party to under-stand how the other perceives the situation, and also to understand that (given that perception) their behaviour is understandable (which is not the same as acceptable, good, right, or correct).

The relevance of the past

The conflict and the relationship between the participants both have past as well as present dimensions; the history of each is important in understanding the origins and the nature of the conflict, in identifying the nature of the conflict, and in preparing for resolution.

Conflicts sometimes seem to take on lives of their own so as to exist almost independently of the participants. This is particularly the case, for example, in workplace, intergroup, and international conflicts of long duration: people may come and go, taking up positions in the conflict that seem to continue irrespec-tive of their involvement. There are many cases in which those involved in a continuing conflict cannot recall its origins: 'We haven't spoken to them for five years. I don't know why, but I'm not going to start now'.

The history of a conflict and of the relationship between the participants provides vital information for resolution. The roles played, the issues raised, and the attempts at resolution by various participants during its history can give valuable insights into the present situation.

Conflicts often follow a process of incidents and increasing tension over time. A chain of relatively minor incidents, each provoking tension in a rela-tionship, can build to a point of crisis (which, itself, may focus on a minor inci-dent). The outcomes of this process can include *war*, an escalating series of incidents resulting from one or both parties deciding to resolve the conflict by attack. *Stalemate* is the maintenance of the level of tension, without future inci-

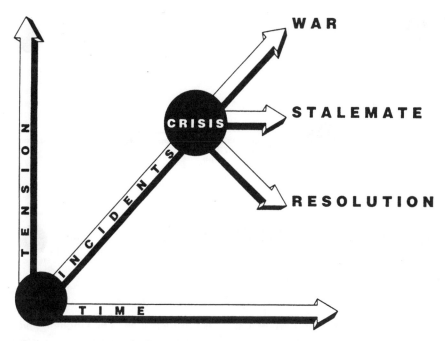

Figure 2.2   History of a conflict

dents, by the parties deciding to resolve the matter by withdrawing (whether physically or psychologically). Resolution will lead to an eventual decline in the level of tension as a result of the parties' decision to resolve the conflict, but is likely to involve a dramatic short-term increase in the level of tension during the resolution process, a sort of therapeutic catharsis.

Participants

The identity of the participants may be deceptively obvious. The visible participants, the actors, may not necessarily be the real protagonists, or the only participants. This is not to suggest that all conflicts have hidden motivators, but that the possibility needs to be considered.

Conflict resolution is not effective if it is worked only with apparent protagonists who regularly appear to agree to resolution, and who may go away, only to return to engage in conflict all over again. Therefore, it is vital to identify and consider the roles and importance of real, as contrasted with apparent, protagonists—that is, the focal, manifest, and unmanifest participants.

Focal participants are those at the focus of the conflict: the two neighbours arguing over the fence, for example. *Manifest participants* are those whose involvement in the conflict is known and recognised: the neighbour's husband or wife who is standing by during the conflict, for example. *Unmanifest*

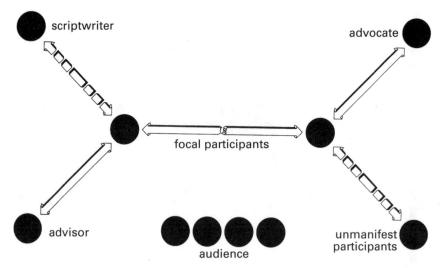

Figure 2.3 The participants in the conflict

participants are those whose involvement is not identified. They include *undisclosed participants* (whose participation is known to one participant but is not revealed) and *unconscious participants* (whose involvement is not consciously recognised). Undisclosed participants can play a range of roles, including 'script-writers', 'advisers', and 'cheerleaders'.

Manifest participants may be *advocates* and *representatives* (including, for example, lawyers and trade union representatives), who usually want to speak and to argue a case on behalf of a real participant, who may be more or less, or indeed totally, silent. Conflict resolution is rarely successful if worked through advocates or representatives alone.

Advisers often claim simply to be 'supporters' but are frequently playing a kind of vicarious protagonist role: they are often important in taking a negative approach to proposals for resolution because the resolution may not suit them (regardless of how suitable it is for the actual protagonist): 'Well, you must make the decision for yourself, but I know if it were me I'd . . .'. If the adviser is powerful and important, he or she must be involved in the conflict resolution process.

Script-writers often provide suggestions for verbal responses: 'Why don't you say . . . and if she says . . . you could say . . .'. Once again, if the script-writer is important, he or she should be involved in the conflict resolution process.

Cheerleaders mobilise support for one of the protagonists, and have a vested interest in the conflict as entertainment or as a game rather than in its resolution. The classic cheerleader is the person in the hotel or schoolyard who stands behind one of the people in an argument saying encouraging words like: 'Bill sure told him . . . Bill won't take that from anyone . . . Good on Bill . . . ' while looking encouragingly at the part of the audience who appear to be Bill's supporters. Cheerleaders are best removed from the conflict resolution process, but can then become 'prophets of doom', seeking to convince the protagonist and any audience that the participant was 'done' in the process, and that a proposed resolution cannot work.

Supporters are less active and influential than cheerleaders; however, the importance of those who are perceived to be supporters cannot be underestimated. Most people want to appear successful in the eyes of friends, acquaintances, and colleagues. This is difficult if, as part of conflict resolution, there seems to be a 'backing down', or 'giving in', or 'letting the other party get away with something'.

It is important to recognise that 'loss of face' (so often, and erroneously, assumed to be a concern primarily of Asian cultures) is a universal human concept. In some situations, individuals (or groups) will 'fight to the death' (even when obviously losing all that they claim to be seeking) to avoid being seen to 'back down' or 'lose face'. Where the status and reputation attributed by the group is of primary importance, the dominant concern will be for group approval; the group may attribute (or may be assumed to be going to attribute) greater status to a martyr who achieved nothing but did not give in than to someone who recognised the limits of a situation and pursued a realistic goal through sensible compromise. The supporters (or what may be called the 'cheer squad' in some situations) may be more concerned with group image than with individual needs.

A *general audience* is also an important factor, and parts of the audience can move in and out of other roles. The presence of an audience generally makes it more likely that the protagonists will want to be seen to win, and that they will be less prepared to resolve than to fight. Performance, rather than actual achievement, can become the most pressing concern in the presence of an audience.

Pressures or needs

Pressures or constraints, real or perceived, are important factors in conflict and resolution. Pressures include needs (for self-esteem, recognition, and being seen to be successful) and values. They also include (both real and perceived) limitations on time, resources, and options. Pressures are what drive individuals in conflict.

Projections

Projections are the expectations and fears of the participants: what they believe may be the outcome of the conflict and of any resolution process, both in terms of what they hope to achieve, what they think they may achieve, and (often more importantly) what they fear they may lose. This involves, whether explicitly or implicitly, a cost–benefit analysis: what are the advantages and disadvantages, costs, and pay-offs? This leads to a consideration of the advantages and disadvantages of seeking resolution rather than leaving the conflict in existence or seeking to 'win'. Negative projections are what restrain individuals in conflict from working towards a resolution.

The context of conflict

Conflicts do not occur in vacuums: they have personal, interpersonal, social, industrial, commercial, legal, political, and doubtless many other contexts. The context is an important consideration in preparing for resolution. If one conflict is a part of the context of another larger conflict (involving other participants and different issues), the smaller conflict may be little more than a theatre in which the larger conflict is to be played out. The smaller conflict may appear simple and easily resolved, and one of the participants and any mediator may be confused by their inability to resolve it. The significance of the smaller conflict will be lost unless the context is understood and taken into account. It may, in some circumstances, be a waste of time to try to resolve the smaller conflict before the larger one is dealt with.

Context also refers to the pre-existing relationships between the parties. If the parties have very positive personal relationships, they are likely to find conflict resolution relatively easy in, for example, an industrial setting. If, however, they have recently gone through a destructive marital breakdown, for instance, they are unlikely to be able to keep the personal context away from any professional work.

Context involves the social and cultural rules, norms, and values of the relevant society, and also of any sub-group or sub-culture involved.

Issues

A conflict will include both matters in dispute—for example, a tree is growing over a neighbour's fence—and issues. The issues are often more important, and need to be dealt with in the conflict resolution process. To take the simple (but very common and often heated) tree dispute as an example. The matter in dispute is whether or not the tree should grow over the fence and, presumably, is easily dealt with: the offending branch could be chopped off. The issues involved, however, may relate to a sense of territory and to feelings of intrusion. It may be that the neighbour does not care at all about the tree, and would be happy to allow it to continue growing over the fence if permission had been sought. Listing possible issues is a positive way of identifying the kind of key factors involved in a particular conflict.

Interests and positions

Most people begin to deal with a conflict by taking a position—'You told me it would cost $50 and that's all I'm going to pay'—and then fighting for it. They frequently become locked into defending a position, and attacking that of the other person (whom they see as their opponent). This presupposes that there can only be three possible outcomes: I win and you lose; you win and I lose; we compromise and both lose. As will be seen in discussion of the resolution process in chapter 8, fighting for positions is generally ineffective conflict resolution and ineffective negotiation technique.

It is important to identify the positions of the participants: these are the demands they make, and are usually the starting point for the dispute. They may have 'up-front', 'negotiating', and 'fall back' positions. It is even more important to identify the known or probable needs or interests of the participants; these may not be identified by them or, in some cases, even consciously known to them.

Innovative methods of conflict analysis

A range of imaginative, innovative techniques can be used to facilitate the analysis of conflict. Often techniques that externalise the conflict are particularly helpful—that is, methods that enable the conflict to be put into a format from which the participants can stand back. This includes the use of diagrams, flow charts, and other drawings. The use of a whiteboard in mediation, for example, can be very helpful in assisting the parties to a conflict to focus on an externalised representation of the conflict.

Other techniques (largely drawn from various forms of psychotherapy) can also be helpful. These include:
- life space mapping
- life line
- drawing and other graphic representations
- sand play
- clay modelling
- picture creation using fixed components
- picture creation and story telling.

Although some of these techniques sound, initially at least, as if they could not be used with adults, they can be and have been. It is often a matter of finding a technique with which the participants (or, in some cases, an individual) feel most comfortable. Individuals often derive considerable benefit—both in terms of coming to understand a conflict and of emotional release—from using a practical technique to represent the conflict.

Case study 2

David and Martin both work for the same company and have long been friends. Their respective wives, Sarah and Julie, are less friendly, and have sometimes argued, often about matters related to their husbands' work. Although David and Martin essentially do the same sales work, they report to different managers and work in competing divisions of the same company. Each division sees itself as a team in competition with the other, and the friendship between David and Martin is sometimes seen as verging on disloyalty to their teams.

David and Martin jointly own a holiday home in the country. David has announced his intention of taking the other members of his sales team and their wives up to the holiday home over the next long weekend, even though he had originally planned to go there with Martin and his wife. Martin says this is unacceptable; David says it is unavoidable since he has already issued the invitations, and it was his turn to use the house.

Analyse this conflict. It may be useful to try to draw a 'map' of it, identifying the major components. Pay particular attention to the needs of the participants, and consider how understanding their needs may assist in resolution.

3 Communication and Conflict Resolution

Language can provoke conflict, and language can encourage its resolution. Both conflict and conflict resolution inevitably involve the use of language, verbal and non-verbal. Most conflict has its origins in communication or, probably more often, the lack of effective or adequate communication—for example, an individual's inability to communicate needs or feelings. Given that conflict resolution is essentially a communication process that works with and through language, it is important to consider the role of communication, language, and interpersonal behaviour in conflict and conflict resolution. Appropriate preparatory work on communication, even if only thinking about the right language to use, will help to maximise the effectiveness of conflict resolution.

Virtually all conflict and conflict resolution are based on communication and language. Even physical violence usually begins with an exchange of words prior to the exchange of blows or bullets.

Culture, communication, and conflict

Every culture and society has largely unwritten rules about communication and conflict, and the relationship between the two, about arguments and fights, public and private, and about the appropriate ways of expressing anger, disagreement, dissent, hostility, and other negative feelings. When and how it is appropriate to say what to whom is socially defined. It is useful to consider the rules that apply in the society in which a conflict occurs. For example, in the case of a neighbour causing excessive noise by the use of power tools late at night, there is a range of ways in which this problem could be communicated to the neighbour, from polite request through to physical violence. These can be ranked in terms of social acceptability and appropriateness.

Societies also have subsets of rules for sub-groups. Different communities, different families, and different individuals will have different approaches to communicating about conflict. Some may be happy to have a public verbal (or physical) brawl; others will never engage in any public manifestation of hostility at all. Most people do not like conflict, and do not like communicating about issues that may provoke or relate to conflict; they tend to avoid the subject, or to attack the person, and neither approach is conducive to communication.

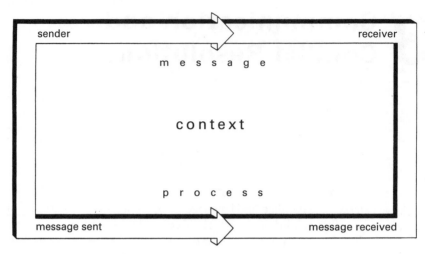

Figure 3.1   The communication process

The communication process

The communication process, very simply described, involves a *sender*, a *receiver*, a *message*, a *process* by which the message is sent, and a *context* and an *environment* within which the message is sent. This is the case whether this is done by face-to-face verbal communication, by telephone, or in writing.

Communication begins with the intention of one party to send a message to another. The message that is sent may not be the message that was intended. Either consciously or, more often, unconsciously, the sender may distort the message. If the sender, for example, does not really want to send a message, but feels obliged to do so, the message may not be clear. Similarly, if the sender is fearful of the consequences of the message, it may be vague or unclear and therefore distorted. The message can also be distorted by the process through which it is sent, or by the context within which it is sent. The context includes the past relationship between the sender and the receiver: close friends, for example, can often exchange 'shorthand' messages, which they understand but which would be confusing to others. Similarly, a relationship of hostility often causes distortion.

The context also includes the physical environment (for example, background noise), the presence of other people, interruptions, and physical discomfort. Pressures and constraints may also apply to either party: limits of time, for example, can cause problems by forcing the sender to try to communicate quickly what may be a complex message.

The receiver may clearly receive the message sent, but not the message that was intended. Resulting conflict may appear, to the sender, to have been provoked by the receiver. The receiver, however, will have received the message sent. The problem lies with the sender's failing to send the message intended.

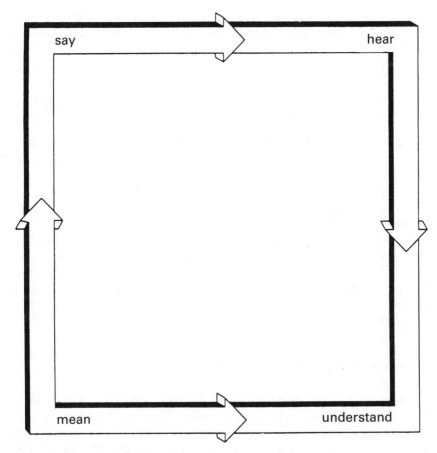

Figure 3.2 Effective communication

Communication presupposes that the message will be received, but the message that is received is not necessarily the message that was sent. The receiver's assumptions, perceptions, expectations, and projections may distort the message: this is often referred to as 'interpretation', and may be unconscious rather than conscious. The receiver may not want to hear what is being said, or may want to hear a specific message that is not being said; interpretation can change the message sent into a different message received.

Effective communication

Effective communication means that what is meant is said, and that what is said is meant; it means that what is said is heard, and that what is meant is understood.

Saying and meaning, and hearing and understanding, are affected and distorted by a number of factors, both internal and external to the participants. Noise, interruptions, and the presence of others are obvious examples of external factors. Internal factors may include fear of conflict, or eagerness to engage in conflict, which can distort communication: if one party is anxious to avoid conflict, a message may be phrased (often unconsciously) so as to minimise the risk of the receiver actually understanding what is being said. Similarly, if the receiving party is eager to avoid conflict, the message may (usually unconsciously) be interpreted so that the meaning that could provoke conflict is softened or removed. This often leads to future conflict, when one party claims to have sent a message that the other claims not to have received.

The aim of effective communication for the sender, therefore, must be to ensure that the message sent is the message intended, that the message sent is the message received, and that the message received is understood. For the receiver it means ensuring that the message sent is the message received, that the message heard is the message understood, and that what is meant is understood. This requires active participation and attention by both sender and receiver. Sender and receiver fulfil these aims by their own actions and responses, through the relationship of each with the other, and by their control over external factors.

Non-verbal communication

Communication does not only consist of verbal language; it also involves a range of non-verbal means of communication. There are, however, dangers in taking a too literal approach to the interpretation of non-verbal messages, or in accepting unquestioningly some of the popular works written on this subject. These often suggest simplistic interpretations of body language, usually in isolation from the accompanying context and verbal language. Although, for example, folding the arms may, in one context, suggest defensiveness, it may equally indicate that the person is cold, has aching arms, or simply feels comfortable holding them that way. Drawing conclusions from body language alone is risky and liable to inaccuracy. It is also important to recognise that non-verbal communication varies from one individual to another, from one group and context to another, and cross-culturally.

Non-verbal communication includes a number of elements. *Body contact* is something about which all societies have rules regarding not only whether or not body contact is permissible, but also under what circumstances and in what forms it is or is not acceptable. Touching has all manner of psychological implications and effects, and is generally very 'powerful'. In Western society there remain very strong taboos on physical contact (with some notable exceptions— for example, in sport). Rules on body contact include prescriptions about who may touch whom (including contact between members of the same or the opposite sex, within relationships of kinship and common membership), in what context, and on what part of the body. Body contact can provoke both conflict and resolution—for example, pushing someone away as a sign of rejection, or shaking hands as a sign of reconciliation.

'*Physical proximity*' refers to what is sometimes called 'body space', or 'personal territory', meaning how close people are prepared to be, or the limits of comfort in being close. All societies have rules about physical proximity: how close, when, and with whom. People moving into or out of physical proximity convey important messages, and can both provoke conflict and promote resolution. The degree of physical proximity will vary during a process of conflict and resolution. It is sometimes suggested that forcing people into close proximity also forces them towards resolution; it can, equally, provoke such discomfort as to increase conflict.

Orientation is the way in which people are placed in relation to others—for example, sitting or standing, beside, opposite, above, or below. There are many theories about the effects of juxtaposition in conflict resolution: the effects of placing participants opposite one another, or beside one another, or of having one participant behind a desk and the other in front of it. Orientation includes the act of facing towards, or turning away from, the other party. All societies have rules about appropriate and inappropriate orientation, and this often relates to status and position. Orientation can also be used to demonstrate power, to throw out challenges, or to make gestures of reconciliation—for example, the employer who stays seated behind a desk and leaves the employee standing, or the employer who leaves the desk and joins the employee in sitting on a couch.

Body posture and gestures play important roles in communication in all societies—and not only in those that are popularly represented as 'speaking with their hands'. Body posture conveys messages about one's emotional state, including anger, depression, or tension. There are social rules about appropriate and inappropriate body posture, and different postures indicate different conditions in different societies. Body posture is often an important indicator of whether the person is tense or relaxed; there is some evidence that the posture can have an effect on tension as well as reflecting it. It is difficult to be tense for long if your body is relaxed. Gestures involve movements of parts of the body, especially the hands. They often convey emotions, and show involvement and interest in the conversation. They may convey unspoken messages—for example, thumping a table. There are social rules about appropriate and inappropriate gestures, and about the contexts in which certain gestures may be appropriate. Some gestures that communicate aggression and hostility can provoke or heighten conflict, while others may suggest cooperation or forgiveness.

Head movements can be particularly important indicators in listening. Nodding can suggest attention; nodding and shaking can convey understanding or sympathy. Similar head movements differently carried out can convey very different feelings: turning slowly to one side and looking away for a while may suggest thoughtfulness; abruptly turning away may indicate anger and rejection.

Facial expressions, including looks of displeasure, pleasure, boredom, and lack of understanding, add to verbal meaning. Facial expression is very important in monitoring communication since it is often an unconscious 'mirror' of communication effectiveness: a person may be showing confusion, boredom, disinterest, or increasing tension. A change of facial expression can ask a question without words or can indicate that a statement was not understood. Eyebrow movements can indicate understanding or lack of it. The facial expression will either support or contradict the verbal message.

All societies have rules about the appropriateness of different ways of looking at other people, of the significance of not looking at a person, and of *eye movements* generally. In contemporary Western culture, looking at a person while communicating is generally regarded as positive; looking away, gazing out of a window, and checking the time suggest lack of interest, attention, respect, and honesty. It is important, however, to appreciate that not all cultures regard looking someone directly in the eyes as being polite. In some cultures, looking down is interpreted as respectful, loyal, honest, and sincere; in many modern Western cultures it would probably suggest shiftiness, guilt, wilfulness, and other negative attributes. Staring directly and continuously into the eyes of the other person, however, is also likely to suggest something odd. Direct gaze may be very appropriate when making important statements of personal feeling or belief: 'I really want to work through this problem . . . ', or 'I really did believe you said . . . '.

Clothing and accessories, and other aspects of *physical appearance* can give non-verbal messages, again with cross-cultural variations. The degree of formality of appearance will often indicate the seriousness with which the individual views the situation: does a person wear jeans and a T-shirt to a criminal trial in the Supreme Court, and if not, why not?

All the non-verbal aspects of communication need to be considered together in the flow of communication; trying to interpret any individual action (for example, a gesture) in isolation from other non-verbal elements, from the verbal communication, or from the context, is unlikely to be helpful or accurate. Non-verbal messages, no less than verbal messages, require clarification before they are taken as the basis for serious action. A person who appears to be uncomfortable and moves around a lot in a chair, with occasional frowns, may be finding the topic discomfiting, or be showing signs of rejection or distress; but they may also have a lower back problem or want to go to the toilet. If in doubt, clarify: 'I feel you're not really comfortable . . . ' may lead to a simple explanation. Even if the response indicates that the person is otherwise fine, care needs to be taken before assuming some deep hostility.

Similarly, if a person's body language is causing distress, it is important to deal with it openly and assertively: 'I don't really feel comfortable when you stand over me like that . . . ' or 'I don't understand why you keep poking me in the chest . . . '.

Non-verbal elements of speech

Speech also includes what can be described as non-verbal elements: those aspects that add to the meaning of the words. They can give non-verbal indications of meaning, mood, tension, emotion, and interest. *Volume* can convey important messages, regardless of content. Speech can move from the barely audible whisper to the threatening shout; different volumes can reflect mood. Low volume may indicate nervousness, despair, depression, lack of interest, or hostility (if it seems that the intention is to make the other party unable to hear). High volume may indicate anger, frustration, or loss of control. However, account must be taken of usual individual speech patterns.

Inflection—that is, the way in which the tone rises or falls—usually differentiates a question from a statement: a question rises at the end; a statement falls. However, added meaning can be given to a sentence by changing the usual inflection. For example, uncertainty or tentativeness is suggested by something that appears to be a statement but that has rising inflection. 'I could reconsider your assessment' can be a statement or a question depending on inflection. Definitive statements with clear falling inflection do not promote negotiation or discussion. 'It is not my intention to reconsider your assessment' with a falling inflection suggests a final, non-negotiable position; a rising inflection suggests a tentativeness, an openness to ongoing negotiation. The word 'but' is implied, and the message may be understood as: 'It is not my intention to reconsider your assessment, but it might be possible if you could . . . '. Inflection is very important in conflict resolution and negotiation because of its power to imply either finality or tentativeness.

Tone is an aspect of speech that often conveys significant messages but that is difficult to define: statements such as 'I don't like your tone' or 'It wasn't what he said but the way he said it' reflect the importance of tone. It often denotes emotion and involvement. 'I don't care' can be said in such a way as to suggest that it is completely and depressingly true—or that it is the opposite of the truth.

Speech can be slow or fast. Increasing *pace* suggests increasing emotional activity and involvement, or impatience. Decreasing pace suggests despair, depression, indifference, or seriousness and thoughtfulness.

Pauses are mini-silences. They can add to and change meaning—for example: 'It is not my intention to reconsider your assessment, but [pause] . . . '. Pauses may suggest thought and reflection: 'I see [pause]. Perhaps we ought to . . . '. Unusual pausing often suggests tension or nervousness as the individual strives to maintain control in a highly emotional situation. Pauses are very useful in implying tentativeness, or openness to suggestion or offer (particularly at the end of unfinished statements).

Silence often conveys more meaning than words. Long silences can create extraordinary tension. Who breaks a silence and how it is done can be very important. Silence can be an intimidating tactic, particularly when it follows a provocative statement: 'Tell me why you wrote such an illiterate and hopeless report . . . [silence]'. Silence is often interpreted as an inability to respond adequately: 'Well, if you can't give me an explanation . . . [silence]'. It can indicate a sense of hopelessness, powerlessness, and despair, or a refusal to participate and a high degree of hostility.

Active listening

Communication is generally assumed to involve only the sending of messages, usually by speaking or writing. The communication process depends, however, as much on receiving or listening as it does on sending or speaking. Unlike speaking, listening is often assumed to be a passive process, like sunbathing. This assumption is fundamentally wrong: listening, to be effective, must be an active skill consciously cultivated and developed, and requiring active attention and concentration during the communication process, particularly when that process is stressful, difficult, or important. As previously stated, effective listening implies ensuring that the message being received is the message intended to be sent—that what is said is what is meant, and that what is in fact meant is what is understood.

One aspect of effective listening that is often overlooked is setting the environment: ensuring a sense of safety and comfort. Being explicit on these matters is preferable to ignoring them: setting a time and place for a discussion, when freedom from interruption and distraction can be assured, is better than trying to cope with interference. Openly discussing distractions (such as telephones, background noise, people coming in and out, or the presence of others) is important in ensuring good communication.

The environment can be said to include the emotional environment—effective communication may not be possible, for instance, immediately following a heated argument. It is preferable to openly recognise this, to allow a period for the atmosphere to calm, and to set a time for further discussion. Expressing anger when one is angry may be important, but attempting to resolve conflict or to solve problems at a time of high emotions is unlikely to succeed. It may be better deliberately to defer the matter.

Effective listening must include the skills of attending, following, and reflecting. *Attending skills* involve indicating attention and interest, and include adopting a posture of involvement, appropriate body movement (for example, nodding the head), eye contact, occasional verbal cues ('Ah ah', 'I see', or 'Mm'), and the ability to ignore distractions. *Following skills* involve indicating that the communication is being followed and listened to, and include encouragement, occasional questions (to draw further information), attentive silence (but too much silence can suggest either hostility or lack of interest), and occasional clarifying questions or indicators of attention. *Reflecting skills* are used to ensure that communication is effective by checking that meaning is understood, and include paraphrasing, reflecting feelings, reflecting meaning, clarifying questions, and summarising.

Reflecting skills are particularly important in conflict resolution to ensure that both parties understand precisely what is being said and what is being meant: ambiguity, uncertainty, imprecision, and misunderstanding must all be resolved in a non-threatening, non-accusatory way. Paraphrasing is helpful: statements such as 'It seems that you feel . . . ', 'So you think that . . . ', or 'You believe he said . . . ', said with rising inflection to indicate a question, allow the speaker to respond either 'Yes, that's right' or 'No, what I said/felt was . . . '. Paraphrasing can include statements such as 'I want to make sure I understand. It seems to me that . . . '.

Clarifying questions are important in reflecting, particularly questions relating to key issues, such as 'Let me make sure I've understood you: do you want . . . ', and direct questions, such as 'And what did you say then?' Feelings are very important in conflict, and it is essential that they are expressed and understood. An active listener will often reflect feelings with statements such as 'It seems you were very upset when . . .', 'How did you feel when that happened?', or 'It sounds to me that you were . . . '. Encouraging and promoting the expression of feelings not only helps the communication process, but also suggests interest, concern, and empathy. On key questions of fact and disputed interpretation in particular, meaning must be clarified, and it is important to reflect meaning: 'It seems that you meant . . . ' or 'Did you mean that . . . ?'

At the end of a period of receiving messages, it is useful to engage in *summarising*, and in some cases to ask the sender to summarise as well. This can be done reflectively—'Let me see if I've understood . . . You're saying . . . '—or more directly: 'I want to summarise what I think you're saying to make sure I've got it right . . . '. It should be noted that the focus is on the listener (with the suggestion that he or she may not have understood), not on the speaker (with the implication that he or she may not have been clear in their expression).

All these approaches should be tentative, questioning, and open-ended, allowing for correction, addition, and explanation. They should not be presented as conclusions, accusations, or 'evidence'. They should seek clarification, rather than imposing interpretation.

Note-taking

Effective listening can be assisted by note-taking, not usually by taking a verbatim transcript, but by noting key points. Such note-taking is an indication of attentiveness. If the other person finds (or may find) note-taking threatening or discomforting, it may be valuable to talk about it at the beginning: 'I'd like to take some notes to make sure I know exactly what we're saying . . . '. A note summary to which both parties agree can be very valuable, and can be copied so that both parties have access to it. Here the use of electronic whiteboards is particularly valuable in group conflict resolution. Such a summary need only include key points, for example:

A wanted: 1, 2
B wanted: 1, 3
A agreed to: 1, 2
B agreed to:1, 2, 3
A and B agreed to: 1, 2
B to complete more detailed proposal for 3 by Friday
A to plan 2 and report back on Monday
A and B to meet again 2.00 p.m. Monday

Such note summaries are not formal minutes (let alone legal agreements), although in some cases such minutes may be useful or even necessary. Mutually agreed summaries, particularly where they outline what different parties have agreed to do, are helpful in minimising subsequent arguments, and facilitate evaluation at further discussions. This will be considered further in an outline of the conflict resolution process in chapter 8.

Goals of communication

To be effective, communication should involve motivation to communicate, effective disclosure, clear, precise messages, assertiveness, clarity of thought and language, empathy, effective listening, and an appropriate environment. Effective communication begins not when words are first used, but in the thought processes that precede speaking or writing. Preliminary analysis and reflection is essential, especially when preparing to communicate on complex, sensitive, difficult, or potentially contentious subjects. Identifying the goal of the communication is an essential prerequisite, and should be followed by identification of the key message(s). Unrealistic goals—for example, to change totally the behaviour of the other person—should be avoided. The focus should be on practical, attainable goals—for example, an explanation of one person's feelings about the other's behaviour.

Single complex messages should be avoided. Where it is necessary to communicate a complex and difficult message, it can usually be divided (or fractionated) into a number of simpler, less complex segments to be given in sequence. Each 'sub-message' is likely to be easier to communicate, and is more likely to be understood. It can be useful when planning to communicate a complex or difficult message to write it out, and to consider appropriate language. The meaning should be carefully considered, and what is going to be said should be planned. Any difference between what is meant and what is going to be said should be identified and corrected. For example, if the meaning is 'Unless you improve your work within a week, you will be dismissed', saying 'Your work could do with a bit of improvement' is inappropriate and will be ineffective.

Reflecting on how the receiver of the message may feel—that is, being empathic—will help in deciding how to make the communication more effective, and in considering possible difficulties in advance.

Barriers to communication

Communication is often ineffective because barriers get in the way. There are different ways of looking at those factors that prevent, hinder, disrupt, or interfere with communication. They can be divided into two categories: *barriers to message* and *barriers to meaning*. Barriers to message include factors that are external to the participants (noise, distractions, other people listening or

observing, interruptions, physical discomfort) and factors internal to the participants (including non-verbal communication). Barriers to meaning are forms or
styles of communication that are likely to prevent the listener from understanding what is meant; they include criticising, name-calling, ordering, threatening, moralising, avoiding, and diverting.

Further divisions can be made, between *barriers in sending* and *barriers in
receiving*. In both cases, these divide into *personal barriers* (for example, body
language, manner), *contextual barriers* (for example, hidden agendas, personal
context), and *environmental barriers* (for example, noise, other listeners). Actual
or potential barriers to effective communication in a given situation can usually
be identified in advance, or during the process, and should be dealt with.

Verbal skills are essential to conflict resolution: both the ability to communicate clearly and to understand communication clearly. Conflict often arises
through breakdowns in communication, particularly where meaning and understanding are obscured. Conflict resolution depends on effective communication, and the development of a high level of interpersonal communication skills
is of critical importance. It is also important, however, to recognise and take
account of differences between individuals and cultures in approaches to
communication and communication style.

The preliminary work of analysis and consideration of communication and
language lead into the practical preparation for conflict resolution; this is
outlined in the next chapter.

Case study 3

Ruth is a senior manager in a government department. Her deputy, John,
was one of the applicants for the position she holds, and he was very angry
when he was not appointed. John treats Ruth in a formal, unfriendly but
polite manner. He carries out her instructions precisely, but never does
more than she explicitly tells him.

Ruth decides that the tension between them is destructive, both for
her and for the workplace, and decides to meet with John in an attempt to
'clear the air'. Although he agrees to the meeting, he insists that there is no
problem, that his treatment of her is entirely appropriate, and that he has
no wish to have any sort of informal or personal relationship with her.

Consider what communication problems exist in this situation, and
what skills Ruth might need, or what strategies she might use, in attempting resolution. It will be useful to consider how a person who does not wish
to communicate might be motivated to do so.

4 Planning and Preparation for Resolution

Because the most effective approach to conflict resolution is one that is *proactive*, and that is based on preparation and planning, it should not be left to chance: 'If they raise the issue, then I will talk about it' or 'If I meet her, we can discuss it'. To plan and think about conflict resolution is not to remove spontaneity; it is to set an appropriate context and environment within which spontaneity (an essential part of conflict resolution) can occur. Part of the planning and preparation includes understanding the full range of resolution processes.

The range of conflict resolution responses

There is a wide range of processes for the resolution of conflict; there is no universally right, correct, and proper way of approaching all conflicts at all times and under all circumstances. A process must be selected to facilitate resolution. This might be simply two participants discussing the matter together—that is, a process involving no external intervention. Even that apparently simple process can, however, involve numerous variations with, for example, different degrees of formality. Sometimes it will be decided that external intervention is necessary or desirable. Conflict resolution can include processes ranging across a spectrum from minimum to maximum external intervention, from minimum to maximum formality in the process, and from minimum to maximum enforceability of outcome.

A participant or the participants may respond in various ways to a conflict, either taking positive action, no action, or negative action. Positive action is intended to bring about a resolution, and includes initiating discussions with the other party, seeking the assistance of a third party (for example, a mediator), trying to negotiate a solution, or taking some form of unilateral action to encourage, or force, the other party to move towards resolution. Negative action is essentially related to fighting. It includes attacking, defending, and diverting, together with a range of other forms of attack and defence mechanisms, many of which will be considered in chapter 10.

Figure 4.1   Range of conflict resolution processes

Processes can be divided approximately into:
- those involving only one party (monadic)
- those involving only the two parties (dyadic)
- those involving a third party (triadic).

One-party actions

Sometimes one party to a conflict will take action intended to resolve—or, more often, to avoid—the conflict. One possible approach is an attempt at *coercion*—that is, endeavouring to force the other party or parties to take particular action. Coercion involves the arbitrary use of power (including emotional, psychological, physical, and financial power) and is intended to force compliance regardless of the needs, interests, or desires of the party or parties being coerced. At its lowest level, this may be described as influence or persuasion; at its highest level, it may involve threatened or actual violence. Although coercion can be highly effective and efficient in bringing about an apparent resolution of a conflict, it rarely produces a long-term and permanent resolution and may create further conflict relating to the means used.

Some people will endeavour to deal with a conflictual situation by *withdrawal*—that is, by endeavouring to escape from the conflict. Of course, this can be effective, but its effectiveness depends upon being able to withdraw without serious consequences. Sometimes a physical withdrawal (for example, leaving a relationship or resigning from employment) deals only with the external conflict and leaves the individual with considerable internal conflict, some of which may derive from self-blame (for example, 'Why did I let that person drive me away? Why was I so weak that I couldn't stay and fight?').

One type of withdrawal can be *submission*—that is, simply giving in or yielding to the demands of the other. Submission can be an entirely appropriate approach in some situations; for example, if confronted by someone using a gun to demand the surrender of a wallet, submission to the demand is almost certainly the most sensible response. But submission—where the individual does not regard it as the best possible option under the circumstances—can lead to internal conflict and self-blame.

Sometimes conflict will be re-defined by the individual so that it is dealt with by *internal suppression*: the individual explains the conflict away to him- or herself as a rationalisation for taking no action. It is most often a form of denial. This is, of course, different from a decision—based upon a realistic evaluation of options—that a matter is not worth pursuing.

In some cases, individuals will endeavour to bring about *internal resolution*—that is, to resolve the conflict personally without the involvement of any other party or parties. Individual counselling and psychotherapy are processes often used to bring about internal resolution, particularly in relation to conflicts that were not resolved in the past and that continue to cause distress. Internal resolution is sometimes the only realistic option—for example, if the other parties refuse to participate in any process for resolution, or are not accessible (having gone away or died), or if the real risks in attempting to involve them are too high. Internal resolution rarely works where an attempt at external resolution is possible.

Collaborative processes

Collaborative processes are those in which the parties, without external assistance, seek to reach a resolution. The most common means whereby parties seek to resolve conflict is by *communication*—that is, by talking together about the conflict. In some cases this, in itself, will lead to a resolution as the conflict is discovered to have been based on miscommunication or misunderstanding. In other cases, the communication will establish a basis for collaboration or negotiation.

Collaboration is commonly used to resolve conflicts: it involves the parties discussing the conflict (formally or informally) and reaching a mutually acceptable decision about its resolution. It often, although not invariably, involves negotiation. The least interventionist, formal, and enforceable process is collaborative problem solving by the parties to the conflict (which may or may not involve negotiation). This is the form of conflict resolution that most people use most of the time: they communicate (sometimes effectively, but often not) in the hope of reaching resolution. The resolution sought is often a victory rather than a resolution, although at its best, collaborative problem solving ought to be exactly what the term implies. This approach to conflict, including negotiation, is considered in chapter 5.

Negotiation is a process whereby two or more parties confer to reach agreement, each making and responding to offers, demands, or proposals from the other. Negotiation implies that the subject of the conflict is negotiable (for example, money, land, contractual obligations) and that each party is willing and able to make at least minimal compromises. In matters that are essentially not negotiable (for example, absolutely held moral values), negotiation is not only impossible, but attempts at it may also make the conflict worse. There are usually no formal rules governing negotiation, although there are cultural norms, and within particular contexts (for example, industrial negotiations) there are many externally imposed constraints (for example, legislation). The process of negotiation leaves most control with the people involved, but there may be no safeguards for a less powerful party. The process is consensual, and may be formal or informal.

Third-party intervention

Processes involving the intervention of third parties (sometimes described as 'third-party neutrals') are many and varied, and the terms used to describe these processes (for example, 'mediation' or 'arbitration') have been defined in different ways by different writers and practitioners. Unfortunately, there is no definitive or universal set of definitions. Thus, two agencies or individuals describing what they do as 'mediation' may, in fact, apply distinctly different processes.

The National Alternative Dispute Resolution Advisory Council (NADRAC), established by the Australian government, sought to facilitate a common understanding of, and discussion regarding, third-party processes by developing a set of working definitions (NADRAC 1997a). NADRAC distinguished between processes that are facilitative, processes that are advisory, and processes that are determinative:

> Facilitative processes involve a third party providing assistance in the management of the process of dispute resolution. Generally the third party has no advisory or determinative role on the content of the dispute or the outcome of its resolution, but may advise on or determine the process whereby resolution is attempted. These processes fall into three categories: mediation, conciliation and facilitation.
>
> Advisory processes involve a third party who investigates the dispute and provides advice as to the facts of the dispute, and, in some cases, advice regarding possible, probable and desirable outcomes and the means whereby these may be achieved.
>
> Determinative processes involve a third party investigating the dispute (which may include the hearing of formal evidence from the parties) and making a determination, which is potentially enforceable, as to its resolution (NADRAC 1997a, p. 5).

Determinative processes can be further divided between those in which the determination is *enforceable*—whether by external authority (as with the court system) or by internal agreement of the parties (as with arbitration based on a preliminary agreement to accept the decision of the arbitrator)—and those in which the determination is *not enforceable*.

Facilitative processes

Facilitative processes can be divided between those that focus on a specific conflict or dispute (and which are dealt with in the NADRAC definition) and those that focus on the relationship between the parties.

Dispute resolution

Processes that focus on the resolution of the dispute include mediation, conciliation, and facilitation. There are many different approaches to, styles of, and processes described as *mediation*, and therefore there are many different definitions. NADRAC (1997a) defines mediation as:

> a process in which the parties to a dispute, with the assistance of a neutral third party (the mediator), identify the disputed issues, develop options, consider alternatives and endeavour to reach an agreement. The mediator has no advisory or determinative role in regard to the content of the dispute or the outcome of its resolution, but may advise on or determine the process of mediation whereby resolution is attempted.
>
> Although the components of mediation—identifying the disputed issues, developing options, considering alternatives and endeavouring to reach agreement—usually occur, they do not necessarily occur in every mediation and are not necessarily sequential.
>
> The general term mediation may be further defined by the addition of one or more of the following descriptors: therapeutic, community, shuttle, victim–offender or expert, or by the addition of descriptors referring to the agency within which mediation is undertaken (for example, Community Justice Centre, Family Court). Each agency should be able to define mediation more specifically insofar as its practice differs from the general definition given above (NADRAC 1997a, p. 5).

Mediation is characterised by the involvement of an impartial third party who:
- is concerned only with the process of resolution and not with the content of the conflict or the outcome of the process
- has no authority to make decisions on content
- does not provide advice or make recommendations on outcomes
- must be perceived by the participants to be impartial.

The mediator, whatever conclusions he or she may reach or have reached regarding the conflict or the participants, must avoid manifesting partiality.

Different mediation programs will provide services to meet the particular needs of different participants (for example, cultural requirements), and in some cases (for example, where highly technical or specialist matters are involved), there may be a need for the mediator to have a good knowledge of the subject area to enable him or her to understand the language of the content so that the process can be managed effectively.

Co-mediation is mediation using two mediators who work collaboratively. *Shuttle mediation* is mediation in which the parties are not brought together (or not kept together all the time) and the mediator moves between them; this movement need not be physical but may involve, for example, telephone or even written communication. *Expert mediation* involves the use of a mediator with a specialist knowledge of the subject matter of the mediation. *Community mediation* involves the use of a mediator who is chosen from the community within which the conflict to be mediated is occurring.

Mediation is a process in which a third party intervenes in a conflict, usually with the consent of the parties, to facilitate a mutually acceptable resolution that requires the agreement of the participants for implementation. In a sense, it is facilitated collaborative problem solving or facilitated negotiation. Mediation will be explored further in chapter 6.

In some facilitative processes, the third party who assists the parties to a conflict to reach a resolution does so within constraints that are externally imposed (for example, by legislation). Such third-party assistance, which might otherwise be described as mediation, is often termed *conciliation*. NADRAC defines conciliation as:

> a process in which the parties to a dispute, with the assistance of a neutral third party (the conciliator), identify the disputed issues, develop options, consider alternatives and endeavour to reach an agreement. The conciliator may have an advisory role on the content of the dispute or the outcome of its resolution, but not a determinative role. The conciliator may advise on or determine the process of conciliation whereby resolution is attempted, and may make suggestions for terms of settlement, give expert advice on likely settlement terms, and may actively encourage the participants to reach an agreement.
>
> Statutory conciliation is a process in which the parties to a dispute which has resulted in a complaint under a statute, in which the parties to the dispute with the assistance of a neutral third party (the conciliator), identify the disputed issues, develop options, consider alternatives and endeavour to reach an agreement. The conciliator has no determinative role on the content of the dispute or the outcome of its resolution, but may advise on or determine the process of conciliation whereby resolution is attempted, and may make suggestions for terms of settlement, give expert advice on likely settlement terms, and may actively encourage the participants to reach an agreement which accords with the requirements of that statute.
>
> The general term conciliation may be further defined by the addition of one or more of the descriptors given above for mediation: therapeutic, community, shuttle, victim–offender or expert, or by the addition of descriptors referring to the agency within which conciliation is undertaken (for example, Human Rights and Equal Opportunity Commission, Industrial Relations Court), or by agency-specific descriptors (for example, conciliation counselling in the Family Court). Each agency should be able to define conciliation more specifically insofar as its practice differs from the general definition given above (NADRAC 1997a, p. 7).

Conciliation (as distinct from mediation) essentially refers to a process of mediation that is undertaken by or on behalf of an agency empowered to intervene in a conflict at the request of one party (who has often lodged a complaint or notification of a conflict with the agency). Conciliation occurs with or without the agreement of the other party, and the conciliator, although acting generally as a mediator, is required to ensure adherence (in the conciliation process and in any agreement that may result) to the principles upon which the agency is based. It is usually, but not necessarily, a process established by statute. In Australia, conciliation is frequently referred to in legislation, but is almost never defined. In some cases, the conciliator (or the agency) is required to undertake an initial investigation into the conflict, and there is often (but not necessarily) a process whereby matters not resolved in conciliation can be referred for arbitration or adjudication.

Facilitation is usually used to refer to third-party assistance provided to groups. NADRAC defines facilitation as:

> a process in which the parties (usually a group), with the assistance of a neutral third party (the facilitator), identify problems to be solved, tasks to be accomplished or disputed issues to be resolved. Facilitation may conclude there, or it may continue to assist the parties to develop options, consider alternatives and endeavour to reach an agreement. The facilitator has no advisory or determinative role on the content of the matters discussed or the outcome of the process, but may advise on or determine the process of facilitation (NADRAC 1997a, p. 8).

NADRAC also identifies two other processes that relate to facilitation:

> *Facilitated negotiation* is a process in which the parties to a dispute, who have identified the issues to be negotiated, utilise the assistance of a neutral third party (the facilitator), to negotiate the outcome. The facilitator has no advisory or determinative role on the content of the matters discussed or the outcome of the process, but may advise on or determine the process of facilitation.

> *Indirect negotiation* is a process in which the parties to a dispute use representatives (for example, lawyers or agents) to identify issues to be negotiated, develop options, consider alternatives and endeavour to negotiate an agreement. The representatives act on behalf of the participants, and may have authority to reach agreements on their own behalf. In some cases the process may involve the assistance of a neutral third party (the facilitator) but the facilitator has no advisory or determinative role on the content of the matters discussed or the outcome of the process, but may advise on or determine the process of facilitation (NADRAC 1997a, p. 8).

Group facilitation refers to the use of an impartial facilitator to manage the process whereby a group seeks to resolve a conflict. It can range from formal facilitation (in which the facilitator takes the role of the chairperson of a meeting) to informal facilitation (in which the facilitator takes a role as discussion leader). The facilitator is concerned to ensure that the agenda determined by the group is worked through in the most effective and efficient manner, that time constraints are kept to, and that the participation by members of the group is maximised.

Facilitated decision-making refers to the use of an impartial facilitator to manage the process whereby two or more people seek to make a decision or decisions (which may or may not relate to a conflict or conflict resolution). It can range from formal facilitation (in which the facilitator takes the role of the chair of a meeting) to informal facilitation (in which the facilitator takes the role of discussion leader). As with group facilitation, the facilitator is concerned to ensure that the agenda determined by the participants is worked through in the most effective and efficient manner, that time constraints are kept to, and that the participation of the parties is maximised.

Conferencing can be broadly defined as the facilitating of a meeting between the parties to a conflict (and sometimes their legal or other advisers). The facilitator usually takes the formal role of the chairperson of the meeting.

Relationship resolution

There are third-party processes in which a third party assists the parties to resolve problems in the relationship between them (without a primary focus on a specific conflict or specific conflicts); these processes include counselling and therapy.

Counselling, as understood in the context of conflict resolution or conflict settlement, generally refers to a process in which a trained counsellor assists a client to explore thoughts, feelings, the past, the present, and the future, to enable the client to reflect upon her or his present situation and to consider options for the future. There are many, diverse (and indeed, conflicting) schools of counselling. All would, however, begin by addressing the client's discomfort, distress, or conflict (which may be related to a specific conflict or conflicts). They would also seek to enable the client to bring about personal, psychological change to minimise or eliminate the cause or causes of the discomfort, distress, or unhappiness, or to take actions (including seeking advice from others) that may assist the client. Counsellors, like mediators, vary greatly in the degree to which they actively intervene in the process, and in the extent to which they deal with immediate problems while exploring underlying causes.

Therapy, as understood in the context of conflict resolution or conflict settlement, generally refers to a process in which a trained therapist assists a client to explore thoughts, feelings, the past, the present, and the future, to enable the client to reflect upon her or his present situation and to consider options for the future. There are many, diverse (and indeed, conflicting) schools of therapy (for example, Freudian psychoanalysis, Jungian psychotherapy, rational emotive therapy). However, all would, like counselling, begin by addressing the client's discomfort, distress, or conflict (which may be related to a specific conflict or conflict). They would also seek to enable the client to bring about personal, psychological change to minimise or eliminate the cause or causes of the discomfort, distress, or unhappiness. Therapists, like counsellors and mediators, vary greatly in the degree to which they actively intervene in the process, and in the extent to which they deal with immediate problems while exploring underlying causes. For example, classical Freudian psychoanalysis would emphasise the past (specifically childhood psycho-sexual development) rather than immediate problems, and short-term problem-solving therapy would focus on assisting the client to discover practical options for dealing with immediate concerns.

The difference between therapy and counselling is now difficult to define with precision; in the past, counsellors tended to work on short-term problem solving and therapists on longer-term personal change, but this is no longer true. There are now therapists who use short-term problem-solving therapies, and counsellors who see clients over long periods.

Therapy and counselling have traditionally been individual client-centred processes. But in modern times it has been recognised that individuals in relationships with one another, especially in long-term relationships (such as marriage), may have problems that cannot be effectively dealt with on an individual basis. Many counsellors and therapists now work with both parties in a relationship (although they may also work with the individuals separately) in what is known as *relationship therapy* or *relationship counselling*. Some counsellors and therapists now work with groups in what is known as *group therapy* or *group counselling*.

Group work refers to any process (including group therapy) that involves a group of people in an attempt to resolve a conflict or to improve relationships within the group. Group work can include the use of problem-solving exercises, facilitated decision-making processes, role-plays, simulations, and games.

Reconciliation can be used to describe processes that may include facilitation, group work, counselling or therapy, or other conflict resolution methods, in which the aim is to effect the establishment or restoration of a functional and relatively harmonious relationship between the parties. Parties in processes of reconciliation are usually large groups, often groups with different values or cultures, and often groups who have a history of disharmony. In Australia, it is particularly used to refer to processes designed to develop better relationships between Aboriginal and non-Aboriginal Australians.

Advisory processes

Advisory processes are those in which a third party investigates and/or hears evidence and/or arguments regarding a conflict and provides advice on the conflict (or on one or more aspects of a conflict). These processes include a range of different approaches.

Case presentation is generally a formal process in which the parties to a conflict (or their advocates) present their respective cases in the conflict before an impartial third party. The process of presenting evidence and arguments may in itself lead to a partial or complete resolution of the conflict as each party (or its advocate) comes to understand the other side's position. The third party provides advice as to the probable outcome should the matter go to litigation or adjudication. In this sense, case presentation is similar to mini-trial, but it is more often used in conflicts in which the matter that is the subject of the case presentation will not proceed to litigation. The third party in case presentation may not be legally qualified, but may be an expert in the subject area of the conflict (for example, an engineer or a medical practitioner). It is thus related to independent expert appraisal.

Independent expert appraisal and *expert appraisal* are third-party interventions that will assess the arguments (or some of the arguments) that will be put forward by both parties, and may advise on the probable outcome. Its use may be principally to create doubt in the minds of parties who otherwise might believe that they have a 'certain winner' on their hands. This process is used most commonly in court programs to encourage early settlement or withdrawal.

Investigation involves a third party undertaking an investigation (which may include interviewing the parties and meeting with them together) to determine, as far as possible, the facts of the matter and the bases upon which the claims and counterclaims of the parties are being made. The investigation process itself may resolve the conflict as the parties are required to engage in some analysis and reflection. The investigator is usually required to provide conclusions about the claims, and may make recommendations about options for resolution. The results of the investigation may be made available to the parties, or to someone else, and may be used as the basis for further action. In some cases, investigation may be undertaken as a preliminary (and even a prerequisite) for another process (for example, conciliation), and the latter process may or may not be undertaken by the same person who has undertaken the investigation.

A *mini-trial* is generally a formal process in which the parties to a conflict (or more often their advocates) argue their respective cases in the conflict before an impartial third party. The process of argument may in itself lead to part or all of the conflict being resolved as each party (or its advocate) comes to understand the other side's position. The third party provides advice as to the probable outcome should the matter go to litigation or adjudication. In this sense, a mini-trial is similar to case presentation, but it is often used exclusively for conflicts in which the matter could proceed to litigation and adjudication. Also, the third party in a mini-trial is usually legally qualified and gives advice on the basis of what he or she believes a court would determine.

There are also advisory processes in which a third party assists a party or both parties separately to consider the conflict and options for its resolution, including consideration of their respective rights in the matter. These processes include advising, advocacy, dispute counselling, grievance advising, and pre-mediation conferencing.

There are further third-party advisory processes in which a third party provides information and/or training to the parties (who may or may not be in conflict) in order to:

- enhance their skills in areas that will assist in the prevention or resolution of conflict
- enable them to understand the nature of conflict and the processes for its resolution.

These processes include the provision of information and training, and the use of games, role-play, and simulations. In addition there are processes in which a third party and/or parties to potential conflicts develop and implement processes that are designed to prevent, manage, and resolve future conflicts.

Complaint or dispute management involves the establishment of formal processes by which individuals (for example, employees or customers) can lodge complaints and have these investigated and resolved. In some cases, complaint management systems will include mediation, conciliation, arbitration, or adjudication. *Grievance management* involves the establishment of formal processes whereby individuals (for example, employees or customers) can lodge grievances and have these investigated and resolved. In some cases, grievance management systems will include mediation, conciliation, arbitration, or adjudication. Different organisations vary in their uses of the terms 'complaint' and 'grievance', and in some cases they are used interchangeably. However, 'complaint' is generally used to refer to a formal and potentially serious matter, and many complaint management systems require that complaints be lodged in writing, thereby initiating a formal process of investigation and determination. 'Grievance' can refer to something less serious, and notification of a grievance can be given informally, leading to a less formal process of resolution.

Determinative processes

Determinative processes are those in which a third party investigates and/or hears evidence and/or arguments regarding a conflict and provides a decision (which may or may not be binding on the parties).

Adjudication is the process whereby a decision is made by a third party who has the authority to intervene in a dispute—whether or not the participants request or desire such intervention—to make a decision, and to enforce compliance with that decision (or to impose sanctions for non-compliance).

Arbitration is the process whereby a decision is made by a third party who has the authority to intervene in a dispute at the participants' request and to make a decision. In some cases (for example, where the parties to the conflict have entered into an agreement to accept the determination of the arbitrator), the decision may be binding on both parties and may be enforceable (for example, by civil action in the courts). The essential distinction between adjudication and arbitration relates to the enforcement of the decision: the adjudicator can enforce compliance; the arbitrator cannot. In arbitration, a party can seek intervention from an adjudicatory body to ensure compliance.

Fast-track arbitration is defined by NADRAC as:

> a process in which the parties to a dispute present, at an early stage in the attempt to resolve the dispute, arguments and evidence to a neutral third party (the arbitrator) who makes a determination on the most important and most immediate issues in dispute (NADRAC 1997a, p. 11).

In *final-offer arbitration* the arbitrator is required only to determine which of the final offers made by each of the two parties is binding.

The most interventionist, formal, and enforceable form of conflict resolution is arbitration or adjudication—for example, the court system in which an outside authority considers the positions of the participants in the conflict and makes a determination. In some cases, the adjudication is enforceable by the State (as with the court system); in others it is enforceable by one of the parties (for example, where it has been subject to a pre-arbitration agreement to accept the determination of the arbitrator). Arbitration will be considered in detail in chapter 7.

Case management is the process of analysing a matter that is proceeding to litigation in an attempt to identify the underlying issues, and to promote the resolution of any of those issues that can more effectively be undertaken by other means (for example, by mediation or arbitration). Case management seeks to promote effective conflict resolution by clarifying the matters of conflict.

Expert determination is defined by NADRAC as 'a process in which the parties to a dispute present arguments and evidence to a neutral third party chosen on the basis of their specialist qualification or experience in the subject of the dispute (the expert) who makes a determination' (NADRAC 1997a, p. 11). In some cases, expert determination is used to ascertain issues of fact or law prior to further processes (like mediation) being undertaken. For example, in a dispute between two neighbours in which one issue relates to the position of the boundary between their two properties, it may be more effective for an expert (such as a surveyor) to make a determination of the fact before any discussion between the neighbours (with or without the assistance of a third party) takes place.

Voluntary and coercive processes

Processes involving a third party can also be divided into those in which the third party is involved at the invitation of the parties to the conflict (*voluntary processes*), and those in which the third party intervenes without such an invitation (for example, a parent intervening in a conflict between two children, or a manager intervening in a conflict between two employees)(*coercive processes*).

Action and inaction

Although taking no action may be seen to be, and may indeed be, a form of negative action, it need not be. There are times and circumstances in which a deliberate decision to take no action can be a positive one, particularly where it is conditional—for example, 'Unless this problem arises again within a month, I will take no action' or 'If it is still causing me anger this time tomorrow, I will take action'. Some conflict, while it appears significant at the time, may be best left alone.

Inappropriate and premature attempts at resolution may sometimes magnify a conflict out of all proportion to its real significance. The conflict may be a product of a particular situation that, if left alone, will disappear. Some basic analysis should disclose whether this is the case. A decision to avoid conflict is very different from deciding to defer resolution.

The number of parties to a conflict

It is frequently assumed that conflict involves only two parties; even when there are many more than two, they are often expected to divide and to take two opposing positions. Conflict resolution processes, therefore, are often divided between those involving only the two parties to the conflict (dyadic) and those involving a third-party resolution facilitator (triadic). In many conflicts, however, there are more than two parties, and more than two positions, and the positions are not necessarily fixed. For example, in a conflict within a local community, there may be a hundred parties, and these parties may broadly fall into several different groupings within which general positions are taken, but positions and allegiances are likely to have a degree of variability. Two participants who support each other on one aspect of the matter in dispute may be in opposition on another.

Intervention

In all systems of intervention, it is clear that the third party should be, and (probably more importantly) must be seen to be, impartial and competent, and must encourage the parties to the conflict to express their versions of events and their opinions on resolution.

Even within mediation and conciliation, which are minimally intervention-ist, there are different approaches to the amount of intervention that is appropriate or necessary. Questions can be raised, for example, regarding the role of the third party in encouraging assertive communication, in asking questions to elicit information, in forcing the addressing of issues that neither party has raised, and in determining which are key issues in a conflict. The third party may also have to consider controlling the parties (especially when angry) and controlling the process (for example, duration, breaks, agenda). Some media-tors would practise minimum intervention, avoiding any active participation in the content of the resolution and viewing their roles as relating to process alone; others would be prepared to put forward options for the consideration of the parties, and to raise issues that the parties did not raise.

Power balance

Conflict resolution involves an attempt to balance power between the parties. Power is not simply related to physical strength, authority of a position, or possession of resources. Personal power is usually more important than posi-tional power. Power includes both present power (for example, verbal skills) and future power (for example, the power to punish or disadvantage in the future). Power can derive from resources—for example, a party with the resources to keep the conflict running, or to take prolonged legal action, has a great advantage over someone who needs immediate resolution and cannot afford litigation. Power can derive from actual and potential threats (explicitly, or more usually implicitly, disclosed).

Mediation and conciliation are processes that depend very much on verbal skills, self-esteem, status and power, personal confidence and assertiveness, and negotiating abilities. If the parties are not equally balanced in their personal power and abilities, in their positional power, or in their possession of necessary resources (including information), and if the third party is not an advocate for either of them, how is a balance of power to be maintained in mediation? The issue of the rights of the parties, or the balance of power, is one that arises in all forms of conflict resolution, including the use of the court system (where some are disadvantaged by being unable to afford the best legal representation) and in alternative forms of dispute resolution (where some may lack the esteem, assertiveness, or verbal skills to cope effectively).

In any conflict, one party may be personally less able to participate: low self-esteem, 'learned helplessness', submissiveness, and lack of verbal skills (which may include low-level skills in spoken English) will all hinder participation. This is one reason why the model of the completely neutral and non-interventionist third party has been questioned, and why in conciliation (as opposed to traditional mediation), the third party may take a more active part in an attempt to ensure that some balance of power is maintained. It is also the reason that major criticism of non-judicial conflict resolution systems focuses on its dependence on the abilities of the parties to the conflict to represent and protect themselves, even if they are in positions of comparative disadvantage.

The power balance is not only affected by the personal skills and personality of the participants; the context can be even more important. For example, in a dispute between an employer and an employee (who wishes to continue in employment), the employer will have a usually unspoken but obvious power advantage. The conflict may be resolved, but the effect on the employer–employee relationship is likely to cause the employee some anxiety. Conflicts between the very powerful (including agents of the State) and the very powerless (often members of minority groups) create particular difficulties. But the balance of power is an issue even in interpersonal matters. The classic case of the 'battered wife' is a good example: a woman who has no employment outside the home, who is caring for small children, and who lacks independent means is not likely to have a strong base from which to resolve conflict with a husband who assaults her. As well as her feelings of powerlessness, she is likely to be, in real terms, significantly less powerful than her husband. If she wishes to continue living with him, her position is further weakened. Conflict resolution in such a situation faces obvious difficulties in dealing with the power imbalance.

Sometimes the balance of power can be addressed through the use of advocates or representatives, although the involvement of such people in the mediation process is often questioned. Certainly it is clear that effective conflict resolution requires the active participation of those involved in the conflict.

This does not preclude, but does severely limit, the role of representatives and advocates, particularly when they may be motivated by agendas other than the resolution of the conflict itself (for example, where a trade union representative may be pursuing a general attack on an employer and uses the specific conflict as a focus for this).

Planning for resolution

Once a conflict has been analysed, as outlined in chapter 2, and a decision taken to initiate some form of action for resolution, careful planning and preparation should be undertaken wherever this is possible. Planning for resolution needs to be undertaken separately by each individual, particularly the one who plans to initiate resolution, and by the participants together. The more collaborative planning for resolution that can be undertaken the more likely resolution becomes.

Practical considerations

Planning should include not only matters associated with the psychology or relationship of the participants, but also those matters that are basic and practical. Conflict resolution can be facilitated or obstructed by the provision or lack of resources. These resources can include information (for example, a dispute about a commercial matter is unlikely to be resolved without the availability of relevant documents and costings), 'tools' (for example, a whiteboard or notepad), and refreshments. The importance of the symbolism of hospitality should not be overlooked in conflict resolution: it can form a vital part of establishing positive conflict-resolving relationships.

The environment, which should be carefully planned, includes the physical circumstances: a comfortable, relaxing, secure situation is conducive to resolution. Interruptions, distractions, background noise, the possibility of being overheard, and physical discomfort may all unnecessarily interfere with the process. The importance of the choice of place cannot be overlooked. There are both advantages and disadvantages in having a conflict resolution process take place in the territory of one or other of the parties, or of a neutral third parry. 'Territory' is an important concept, particularly in determining where to attempt the process.

The venue should be 'comfortable', a term that is probably self-explanatory. However, the level of comfort involves not only the temperature, lighting, and the comfort of chairs and tables, but also the physical relationship between the parties. It is suggested in some studies that placing people in different physical relationships—for example, opposite each other, beside each other, diagonally opposite each other, at a square or round table—can either promote or damage different personal relationships. While this remains largely a matter of speculation, it is worth considering. For example, it is useful to explore the possible effects of placing two people in conflict immediately opposite each other with a large distance between them; closely beside each other at a small table facing a mediator; closely beside each other on a small couch; or at the opposite ends of a long table facing a mediator at another table (the 'courtroom scenario').

The context of resolution

The context refers both to the time and to the relationship to other events. Although conflict resolution is most effective when attempted as close as possible to the conflict concerned, to try to achieve it immediately, when the parties are angry or otherwise emotional, is unlikely to be successful. Part of the planning process may be to set aside time, to establish commitments that both parties undertake to meet, and to ensure a suitable environment.

Planning the appropriate context within which to raise issues that may lead to conflict resolution requires skill. For example, attempting to resolve a domestic conflict about putting out the garbage when one or both of the parties is angry and accusing the other of failing in her or his domestic responsibilities is unlikely to be successful.

Preparation

Preparation is essential for all those involved in conflict resolution: the parties to the conflict and the third party (if one is involved). Individual preparation should include looking at personal perceptions of the conflict (what I think it is about, and what I think happened), personal feelings about the conflict (what I feel), personal interests in the resolution (what it is in my interest to obtain), personal preferences in resolution (my preferred outcome), and personal limits to resolution (what I must have, what I would like to have, what I would not like to have, and what I cannot have).

Preparation should not consist of a script-flow in imagination: playing out scripts of what will happen is dangerous and usually counterproductive: the other person will rarely follow the script written in the imagination. It is much more productive to consider 'How would I feel if they said . . . and why would I . . . ?' than to consider 'What would I say if they said . . . ?'

Collective preparation between the participants to the conflict should include agreement on the problem, on the purpose, on the process, on the context, and on interests. Unless there is agreement on the problem, further discussion is unlikely to be productive: the agreement should be on a precise, specific, clearly defined problem or problems. Agreement on purpose, involving a mutually agreed aim in the process of resolution, may sound unnecessary, but it is very important. If one participant simply wants to have an opportunity to criticise the other, while the other wants to reach a solution, the process will not work. An explicitly stated, mutually agreed purpose, precisely defined, facilitates resolution. There may be a general purpose for the process as a whole, and sub-purposes for specific parts of the process. This is, essentially, agenda-setting.

Agreement on process

Agreement on the process is essential. If, for example, mediation is to be used, both parties must agree in principle, agree to the mediator, and to the specific form of mediation proposed. Agreement on context involves a mutual recognition of the circumstances within which the process is occurring—for example, the fact that the participants have a long history of mutual hostility, or that they want to go on living or working together. Reflection on interests involves the participants looking at their mutual interests: 'Since we are going to continue as neighbours for the foreseeable future, it's in both our interests to . . . '.

In preparing for conflict resolution, it is useful to analyse the conflict (jointly if this has only been undertaken by one party, or by the parties separately), set an agenda, establish an environment for resolution, establish dialogue, and promote trust. Thinking about the structure of a conflict is an important part of preparation; actually preparing a 'map' can be useful. In a sense, mapping is like obtaining an aerial photograph to analyse territory: looking down from a height to gain a broader perspective.

Before any conflict resolution meeting, an agenda—that is, a list of the issues to be dealt with—should be prepared by agreement between the parties. Setting the agenda is a very powerful tool in controlling a meeting (as good political strategists very well know). Items on the agenda need to be prioritised. A general, free-for-all discussion is unlikely to lead to a productive outcome. The agenda needs to be planned rationally so that it is workable and has some possibility of being dealt with in the allocated time.

Creating an environment conducive to resolution is essential, and should ensure that the parties feel safe, both physically and emotionally, and secure in terms of confidentiality and freedom from future punishment for the expression of feelings or perceptions.

Establishing dialogue and promoting trust

Establishing dialogue is often the most difficult part of conflict resolution, particularly when the participants are strongly and emotionally in conflict. The key skill of the mediator, for example, lies in facilitating such dialogue. Where no mediator is involved, it is often an inability to establish, or a sense of powerlessness in establishing, dialogue that hinders or prevents attempts at conflict resolution. Promoting an argument is not establishing dialogue, which presupposes communication—speaking and listening—between the participants.

One of the most effective ways of promoting dialogue before conflict resolution is to identify the mutual interests of the participants. Dialogue often needs to be first established at a fairly shallow and apparently trivial level (particularly in the case of long-standing conflicts) to allow the participants to tentatively explore each other's feelings and to develop trust. 'Getting down to the important issues' is not something that can or should be attempted in the first five minutes.

Case study 4

Michael is fifteen; he generally does little around the house unless he wants something from his parents. They have tried to establish a roster of household responsibilities so that they and their three children, of whom Michael is the eldest, each take a reasonable part in the housework.

Michael does not argue about his assigned duties; he just does not carry them out, often going out at the time he should be doing housework. His parents have tried withholding pocket-money or other privileges, but it seems that Michael can hold out longer than they can.

After analysing this conflict, undertake the preparation for attempting its resolution. This will involve considering a range of options that the parents might try.

Promoting trust is a more difficult part of the conflict resolution process. The longer and more bitter a dispute, the less ready or likely the participants are to trust each other. Where trust has been assumed in the past (particularly in inter-personal relationships with high degrees of intensity, importance, and invest-ment), the conflict will often involve a strong sense of betrayal. Once it is believed that trust has been betrayed, it is very difficult simply to re-establish it. Promoting trust will be explored in considering the conflict resolution process in chapter 8.

All processes raise questions; this is a positive and creative aspect of conflict resolution, provided that means of dealing with questions are included. It should never be assumed that every issue or question raised, either in prepara-tion or during the actual process, can be addressed immediately; obviously, where suitable, issues should be dealt with as quickly as possible, but not if this means that decisions are made without adequate thought, reflection, or infor-mation. Where questions or issues cannot be dealt with, a clear process and time-frame for resolution should be identified and mutually agreed upon: 'I will obtain the figures on comparative salaries and have them to you by next Tuesday'; 'I will consider that offer, and let you have my decision by tomorrow lunchtime at the latest'.

As in all resolution processes, the time-frame ought not to be an inflexible barrier, but should be worked to unless it becomes impossible, in which case an explanation should be provided (as soon as possible, and certainly not after the deadline) and a further time-frame established: 'I will not be able to provide the salary figures by next Tuesday because the union has to obtain them from head office; they say they will have them to me by Wednesday, and I will give them to you then'. Reasonable delay, properly explained, is different from stalling.

Direct communication between the parties to a conflict is, except in rare cases, an essential prerequisite to resolution (as opposed to management or settlement), largely because both conflict and conflict resolution involve each party understanding the feelings of the other. Communicating through representatives is rarely effective. In planning a resolution process, therefore, it is necessary to consider how the parties can be brought together most effectively and most productively.

Analysis is an essential initial phase in conflict resolution. It should be followed by careful planning to maximise the effectiveness of the resolution process. Once the analysis and planning have been completed, the process itself can begin. Obviously, there is no point at which analysis and planning must end; if the process is effective, the participants (and any third party) will be undertaking ongoing analysis and planning, and reanalysis and replanning.

5 Collaborative Problem Solving

In the process of conflict resolution, the ongoing collaboration of the participants in the conflict is usually essential if the process is to be effective. The participants need to move from perceiving each other as opponents to working together (at least minimally) as collaborators. This does not mean they must like, approve of, or agree with each other; but it does require that they recognise at least minimal common needs and common purposes, and accept, if only pragmatically, the need for some basic level of cooperation.

The most effective, sustainable, and satisfactory resolutions usually result from processes that maximise the direct participation of the parties to the conflict. Collaborative problem solving refers to any processes in which the parties work towards resolution without third-party intervention. This can include informal discussions, or more formal structured problem solving, and covers both formal and informal negotiation. The majority of people settle most of their disputes and resolve most of their conflicts through collaborative problem solving, although they would probably not refer to it by that name. It involves an element of mutual analysis and planning, and collaboration on identifying options and selecting an appropriate solution (even if not in a formal, structured process).

Although collaborative problem solving may appear to be informal and unstructured, it usually has an internal structure, whether or not this is consciously adopted. This chapter will outline ways in which collaborative problem solving can be made more effective, and will also discuss strategies for effective negotiation. Although negotiation as such is not necessarily involved, it is often a part of collaborative problem solving. When one or both parties to a conflict are planning resolution through collaboration, it can be very helpful to think about structuring the process, even if relatively informally, to maximise its effectiveness.

Planning for collaboration

As with all conflict resolution, collaborative problem solving should begin with analysis and planning. This should include careful thinking about the appropriate time, place, and context within which to initiate and carry out the process.

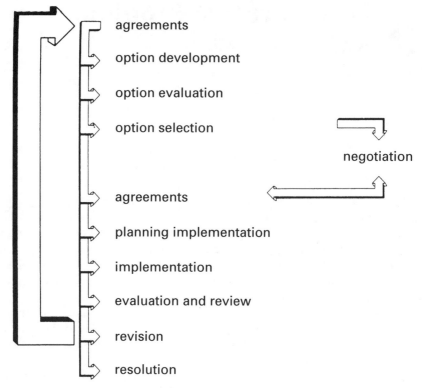

Figure 5.1 Process of collaborative problem solving

As far as possible, the initiating party should avoid anything that appears to be an ambush—that is, taking the other by surprise. Although raising the conflict may involve some element of surprise, or even alarm, this does not mean that the process of resolution should immediately follow. It is usually more appropriate to alert the other person to the fact that a subject needs to be discussed, and to encourage the parties to plan collaboratively the appropriate time and place for the discussion. Although it is often thought that giving advance notice takes away some advantage, and may give undue advantage to the other party, this will only apply if the aim is a fight in which a victory is the goal. If the aim is a process of resolution, providing maximum opportunity for reflection and preparation will greatly assist the achievement of this aim.

Agreeing on the problem

When the parties meet to begin the process of collaborative problem solving, the first step is to agree on a definition of the problem and of the aim of the process. This requires effective communication, including active listening, to ensure that each participant clearly presents her or his feelings, perceptions, and needs, and hears and understands those of the other. Sometimes this stage will disclose either that the problem is essentially a misunderstanding, which may dissolve as a result, or that what appeared to be a single conflict is a number of different conflicts.

Options

The second stage involves identifying options or possibilities for resolution; this can include the process of 'brainstorming'. Rather than presenting fixed solutions for which they then argue, the participants should simply identify a range of options as a preliminary to considering which of them is the most appropriate.

The third stage is the evaluation of the options; this should relate directly to the identified problem and to the aims of the process of collaborative problem solving. It is very easy for the parties to lapse into arguing for specific options simply because they originally suggested them, rather than considering them on the basis of their particular merit. It is important that open and honest personal assessment of options occurs, including expressing feelings about them as well as providing practical evaluations. The process becomes ineffective if either party fails to disclose strong feelings for or against particular options.

Once the options have been evaluated, the fourth stage is the selection of an option for implementation. Once again, this should be done on the basis of the parties' evaluations and feelings, and should be carefully measured against the problem and the aim of the process. The selected option needs to be carefully discussed and defined; the more clearly, precisely, and specifically it is defined, the more likely it is that the option will be implemented. 'We agree to be nicer to each other in future' is the sort of option that sets the parties up for future breakdown with renewed, and probably more intense, conflict. Any proposed behaviour change needs to be very carefully and specifically described.

Collaborative planning

The fifth stage involves collaborative planning for the implementation of the selected option. Once again, this must be done clearly, precisely, and specifically. The plan should describe what will be done and by whom, where and how, and by when. It is useful to commit this proposal to writing, if only in the form of rough notes, to ensure that both parties have the same precise understanding of what each is committed to doing. Conflict that appears to have been resolved often breaks down as a result of one or both parties believing that the other has failed to keep to an agreement for resolution.

Cooperative implementation

The sixth stage is the implementation of the agreed option. This should, as far as is practicable, involve collaboration by the parties, or at least activities that involve them in as much cooperation or communication as possible. If the implementation is to take a considerable period, then regular and frequent meetings to discuss and review progress are important.

Evaluation, review, and revision

The collaborative problem-solving process must include provision for a seventh stage: evaluation, review, and revision of the selected solution. Many people are hesitant to agree to something that appears to be a final, fixed, and immutable resolution; they often feel that a real resolution will not be possible. They are rightly concerned that any agreement may not work well in practice, may need fine tuning (or even major revision), or may in fact simply fail to work, and that any commitment to it is likely to lock them into an unsatisfactory situation. Establishing that the proposed solution will be reviewed and revised after its implementation will largely overcome this anxiety. This also recognises the fact that a solution that appears to be excellent in collaborative problem-solving discussions may in fact require modification, or fail to resolve the conflict.

The seventh stage is that of evaluating, reviewing, and revising the option that has been implemented. This requires that the parties openly and honestly discuss their perceptions of, and feelings about, the implementation, and the effectiveness of the option as a means of resolving the conflict. If it has been unsuccessful, the process may return to the stage of option identification. Or, indeed, it may return to the first stage of problem definition if the attempt at resolution his failed because it revealed that the problem being addressed was not the real problem. Review and revision sometimes amounts to little more than fine tuning, in which case a further period of implementation should be followed by a further review and revision. Sometimes this becomes a cyclical process: each implementation is followed by a review that identifies a further dimension or aspect of the problem, leading into the exploration of further options and the implementation of new solutions. Such a process is important in maintaining dialogue and cooperation between the participants, and in building trust and establishing a collaborative problem-solving approach to conflict.

Clearly defined goals

It is very important that the participants in the collaborative problem-solving process define in advance what will constitute resolution, and how they will know it has been accomplished. Without some such in-built success and/or failure standards, the whole process lacks a clear sense of direction and purpose. As with each of the other stages, it is particularly important that this definition be clear and precise. Working towards a vaguely described goal is difficult and has the potential for creating conflict as each participant interprets the definition in her or his own terms. For example, 'an improved relationship' may sound like an excellent goal, but it is so vague that it could mean whatever either party wishes it to mean. How would they know when the relationship had improved? What would characterise an improved relationship? An inventory of characteristics of the improved relationship will assist to provide a checklist against which to measure the effectiveness of resolution.

Resolution

The final stage is that of resolution. It is essential that, at some point, the participants reach an agreement that the conflict has or has not been resolved. This does not need to be a once-and-for-all decision, but there is little point in persisting with a seemingly endless resolution process. It may be, for example, that specific times for a review of the situation will be established. In some cases, there will be externally determined points at which a decision will have to be made. If it is considered that the conflict has been resolved, this needs to be almost formally stated; there are benefits to some form of symbolic recognition of this fact, and to what may almost amount to a 'declaration of peace', not necessarily in writing, but as a way of identifying the fact that the conflict is formally resolved. If this is omitted, the conflict can appear to continue and the process of resolution fail to provide the psychological satisfaction that should follow its completion.

Although similar conflicts may occur in the future, they should generally be seen as new conflicts, rather than repetitions of the earlier one. It can sometimes happen, however, that the repetition of a similar conflict is an indication either that the previous process did not in fact resolve the issue or, more frequently, that the previous process was addressing a focal or manifest conflict, but failed to deal with the underlying one. In that case, the process needs to return to problem identification, and to undertake a more detailed analysis than had previously occurred.

The environment of resolution

Although the participants in collaborative problem solving are the most important determinants of the effectiveness of the process, the environment, both physical and psychological, should also be taken into account. Environment includes the context—that is, the historical and psychological environment within which collaborative problem solving is being attempted. Choosing an appropriate time is important, not only in terms of the time of the day and day of the week, but also in terms of the time within the lives of the individuals concerned. People undergoing considerable stress, or even crisis, in other aspects of their lives may not be in the best frame of mind to participate in collaborative problem solving, and it may be more effective, wherever possible, to postpone the process until the other pressures have abated. Obviously, it is important to ensure that the time chosen allows for sufficient discussion, free from interruptions and distractions.

Environment also includes the physical environment—that is, the location of the collaborative problem-solving process. This involves both physical and psychological factors. The psychological factors relate to the significance of the environment for either or both of the participants. For example, if a couple are seeking to discuss a conflict in their relationship and have previously spent a lot of time arguing in their home, it may be inappropriate for them to undertake collaborative problem solving there. The home may be psychologically identified with conflict, and therefore be conducive to argument rather than collaboration. Place is also important and can relate to relatively obvious factors such as ownership (for example, the meeting taking place in the home or office of one party or the other, or in a neutral place) or to the physical relationship between the parties (for example, one sitting behind a desk).

To be effective, collaborative problem solving needs to take place in a secure and comfortable psychological environment. Part of the psychological security can be the relative formality of the process, including the use of an agenda and the establishment of basic rules and agreements. This is particularly important if the parties have developed hostility or distrust towards each other, or if the subject of the conflict is emotionally charged.

Negotiation

Part of the collaborative problem-solving process may involve negotiation. Negotiation can be, and often is, a part of conflict resolution, but it is important not to identify negotiation with conflict resolution. A conflict can be resolved without negotiation. In most conflicts, the resolution is a necessary prerequisite to effective negotiation; participants who are in conflict, who oppose and distrust each other, do not have a good basis for negotiation. Until there is at least a minimum level of resolution of the relationship between them, negotiation may be frustrating and ineffectual.

Negotiation will often follow conflict resolution as the process in which an option for resolution of the conflict is selected, and its implementation decided. It is important, however, to understand that negotiation as such does not resolve conflict, and may lead to an agreement that is satisfactory in the short term without the conflict being resolved.

Sometimes 'conflict management' is used to describe a process of negotiating 'around' conflict rather than 'through' it. Negotiation apart from conflict resolution essentially represents dispute settlement, and in some cases is an appropriate means of bringing about a short-term solution to a practical problem. For example, in an acute conflict it may be essential that some immediate, short-term agreement is reached as a preliminary to a more long-term approach to resolution. Where the parties refuse to participate in resolution but have to maintain some degree of cooperative relationship, it is sometimes necessary to manage, rather than to resolve, conflict. However, although sometimes useful, conflict management must be recognised for what it is, and not be seen as resolution. The conflict has not been resolved; it has been managed to minimise its effects. This may be the only realistic option under difficult circumstances, and may be the most appropriate option where no ongoing relationship exists between the parties.

Effective negotiation cannot occur if unresolved conflicts remain, since the parties to the negotiation will have unresolved issues outstanding, and are unlikely to have the degree of trust, commitment, and self-disclosure necessary for effective collaborative problem solving. Once an approach has been made to the resolution of a conflict, it may be appropriate for the parties to negotiate on the details of which option is to be chosen, and how it is to be implemented.

Almost every situation is negotiable, even when one or both of the parties state definitely that it is not. Negotiation involves only the agreement of the parties to negotiate. Once there is agreement, negotiation is possible. Statements such as 'This is not negotiable' or 'It's not our policy to discuss this further' or 'I consider this matter closed' can be, and often are, nothing more than parts of a negotiating process; it is often called 'bluff', and forms a central element in most negotiating strategies.

Negotiation in practice

Negotiation involves two (or more) parties, with competing or conflicting interests or needs, working towards an agreement on how they will cooperate. It often involves, particularly in commercial negotiation, attempts by each party to maximise the benefits and advantages that he or she obtains, while minimising the advantages and benefits to be received by the other. Negotiation essentially involves communication and bargaining.

Negotiation of different types and in different contexts requires different approaches. It can be personal, commercial, community, or international. It can involve two people, or two thousand people, direct negotiation between the parties, or negotiation through representatives or advocates. Very importantly, it can represent a single instance or be part of an ongoing process. Obviously, doing a deal with someone who need never be dealt with again is very different from negotiating with someone with whom one proposes to live or work or do business for the foreseeable future. Tactics that may be successful in one-off negotiation (for example, cheating, lying, misleading, threatening) can be preparations for disaster in an ongoing relationship. A negotiator who aims for a short-term victory, and who acts as if a negotiation is a one-off event, will inevitably face long-term losses if the negotiation is but one part of a negotiation process. Loss of trust, desire for revenge and/or justice, and other negative feelings are the likely outcomes of short-term tactics.

Approaches to negotiation

There are two fundamental approaches to negotiation, and these relate to short- and long-term aims. The first approach, which appears in books and training programs designed to provide strategies for gaining immediate maximum advantage over the other party, is essentially a 'grab-it-and-run' style. It has so many disadvantages, particularly in any attempt to resolve conflict, that it will not even be outlined here. It is the characteristic style of the stereotyped used-car salesman of television comedy (which is, like all stereotypes, unfair to the majority of such people).

The second approach depends upon the establishment of a positive relationship between the parties, and an attempt to identify and meet as many needs of both parties as possible. It presupposes the sort of analysis and preparation that are required for effective conflict resolution. Some basic principles can be defined that will assist in both effective collaborative problem solving and negotiation. Some of these may appear to be inappropriately cooperative and helpful to the other party; this is deliberately the case. Promoting cooperation, trust, communication, and self-disclosure are more likely to lead to a satisfactory long-term outcome than more heavy-handed and dishonest techniques.

Effective negotiation

The same principles apply in negotiation as in analysis of a conflict and preparation for resolution: without adequate preparation, success is unlikely. The preparation for negotiation includes all those elements essential to preparation for conflict resolution: careful identification of, and reflection on, the needs of both parties, and an evaluation of options, costs, and benefits. The preparation must include the establishment of a positive climate for negotiation. Although fear, intimidation, the exercise of power, blackmail, and other common approaches to winning may seem to be effective in negotiation, they inevitably either transform it from negotiating to fighting, or set up an agenda for future responses such as revenge or payback, threatening future relationships and negotiation. A positive climate includes a sense of openness, trust, communication, honesty, and preparedness to consider the other side.

Positions or demands of the parties should be distinguished from interests or needs. The difference between long- and short-term interests should also be identified: a short-term loss can sometimes lead to a long-term gain. What is called 'positional bargaining' has to be distinguished from interest-based negotiating. The former is based on taking a position and making demands, and then fighting to achieve as many of the demands as possible, while yielding as little as possible to the other person. Interest-based negotiation recognises that needs can be met in a variety of ways and that apparently conflicting needs may, upon careful analysis and discussion, not be in conflict at all. Open discussion of interests and needs, although self-disclosing in a way that is not common in negotiation (particularly commercial negotiation), is more likely to lead to an outcome that meets the needs of both parties and, equally importantly, to establish the basis for positive future negotiation and collaborative problem solving.

Each party should seek to understand the other, and to provide sufficient disclosure to be understood in return. Concealing relevant information, although very common in negotiation, is usually counterproductive. Mutual empathy positively encourages understanding. This does not mean sympathy or agreement with, but rather an attempt to understand, the position being taken, the reasons for it, and the feelings behind it. The more comprehensively the other party is understood, the more effective negotiation with them will be. For example, if they are making a difficult and apparently unreasonable demand, argument should be avoided. Instead, an attempt should be made to understand the underlying motivation and interests, and exploration should be initiated into other options for meeting the same need.

Roger Ury and William Fisher, in what has become a classic of negotiation technique, *Getting to Yes* (1981), emphasise the importance of avoiding positions and personalities in negotiating; that is, negotiating should be seen as a process that seeks to meet interests, not to win positions or to gain victories for people. This can be difficult, particularly when negotiation occurs in the context of conflict resolution. It is very easy to lapse into fighting the person, or fighting for a particular position or demand, essentially as a point-scoring exercise in which the aim is to win, almost regardless of cost.

Negotiation is rarely effective if it begins from two fixed, and theoretically immovable, positions: 'I won't sell at all for less than $500'; 'I won't ever buy for more than $250'. The more exploratory the process becomes, the easier it is for both parties to sound each other out about possible options. Tentative language—'it might be possible . . . '; 'Perhaps I could . . . '; 'If you were able to . . . '; 'I might be able to . . . '—and tentative non-verbal communication promote negotiation.

Offering clear and reasonable explanations for options being promoted encourages a perception that the negotiator and the negotiation are reasonable and fair. Unreasonable negotiators encourage unreasonable negotiation. If, for example, the real price sought is $5000, beginning with a demand for '$30 000 and not a cent less', when the other party knows that the market price is from $4000 to $6000, does not suggest 'fair trading'. Similarly, the ultimatum that 'Either you put the garbage out every Tuesday night or I will leave you' is not likely to be seen as reasonable, and seems designed to provoke a fight rather than negotiation on interests and needs. Honest negotiation presupposes that the parties neither lie to each other nor conceal essential information. Both lying and concealing (often dignified with the description of 'bluff' or 'ambit claim') are characteristic of much negotiation; the problems that can arise from such dishonest strategies, and some responses to them, are considered in chapter 10. Trust is important in conflict resolution and negotiating: an assumption that the other party is untrustworthy encourages suspicion, and is also likely to cause dishonest negotiation in return.

A good negotiator is visibly cooperative. Although often interpreted as weakness and 'giving in', being flexible, willing to explore options, and prepared to look at, and try to meet, as many of the needs of the other party as possible are attributes that positively promote effective negotiation. Being seen to be cooperative encourages cooperation from the other party and conveys the message of eagerness to deal effectively with the matter. Fixed positions and demands—

Compromise

Many approaches to negotiation and conflict resolution use language that suggests compromise is never necessary or desirable. Concepts such as 'win–win approaches' and 'negotiating without giving in' imply that, in every case, it is possible for all parties to obtain what they want. This is, of course, unrealistic in most cases. Negotiation cannot proceed without compromise. If one or both parties cannot move at all on their stated positions, there is no negotiation. In reality, most conflicts are resolved by some form of realistic and acceptable compromise. However, the word retains strongly negative connotations, implying 'giving in', 'yielding', and 'losing face'.

But people compromise every day simply in order to be able to function in the world. Employees compromise by going to work when they would probably prefer to stay at home or go fishing. Motorists compromise by travelling (more or less) under speed limits when they may well prefer to go faster. Members of families compromise in all manner of ways in order to live together in relative harmony and happiness. Compromise is giving up what is less important (for example, the opportunity to speed) in order to obtain that which is more important (for example, avoiding a speeding fine, avoiding injury to others, and keeping a driver's licence).

Participants in conflicts can benefit from reflecting on the practical necessity of compromise, and identifying it as a survival skill, rather than seeing it as some form of personal weakness. Compromise is movement, flexibility, and change; without these, situations remains static and conflict cannot be resolved.

'Unless . . . then . . . '—are not as effective as suggestions to consider options: 'If you could . . . then I might . . . ' or, better still, 'If I was to . . . could you . . . ?'

The key characteristics of effective negotiation include adopting a positive approach to solving problems and meeting needs, with adequate analysis and preparation. The focus should be on meeting the other's needs, as far as possible, both in terms of the outcome of the negotiation and of any personal interests as well. Effective communication, particularly active listening, is essential. Willingness to cooperate, to be flexible, and to adapt must be demonstrated. Final agreements need to be clearly and precisely defined. It is particularly useful to commit the agreement to writing, although not necessarily as a formal agreement.

Facilitated negotiation

Sometimes the process of negotiation will be enhanced by the assistance of a facilitator. The facilitator will work with the parties, often both separately and together. With each party separately, the facilitator will facilitate:

- critical, analytical self-reflection on subject matter
- focusing on subject matter
- clarification of essential issues
- elimination of non-essential issues
- identification of needs (as contrasted with wants, demands or positions)
- option identification (or even, with caution and where appropriate, option suggestion—for example, where options are externally limited)
- option evaluation
- reality testing.

With the parties together, the facilitator will:
- facilitate communication (not monologues, arguments, attacks, or defences)
- facilitate joint clarification of essential issues
- facilitate joint elimination of non-essential issues
- provide focused (and accurate) summaries throughout the process
- provide focused clarification of agreements and disagreements (without being unrealistically optimistic)
- facilitate joint identification of needs (as contrasted with wants, demands, or positions)
- facilitate joint option identification (with caution and where appropriate— for example, where options are externally limited)
- facilitate joint option evaluation
- facilitate joint reality testing
- facilitate negotiation towards agreement
- facilitate realistic, specific agreement
- facilitate resolution of blocks, problems, and obstructions
- maintain control of process
- provide appropriate pressure and focus in the process (but without putting pressure on the parties to settle inappropriately).

In preparation for the negotiation, the facilitator will have undertaken, as far as possible, an analysis and assessment of the matter, an assessment of the parties, an assessment of potential problems, and a preliminary identification of the agenda.

Useful 'tools' in facilitating negotiation include a visible and agreed statement of issues (points of agreement and disagreement), a visible and agreed agenda (for example, on a whiteboard), and the use of 'controlled communication' in situations in which hostility obstructs dialogue (sometimes even the use of 'shuttle negotiation', in which the parties are not brought, or kept, together).

Specialist negotiation

There are circumstances—for example, in highly technical areas—in which negotiators need special skills or expert knowledge, or immediate access to expert opinion. Negotiation involves not only process, but also content, and a negotiator who does not understand the content is unlikely to be effective. For example, in industrial relations negotiation, a good knowledge of industrial relations and employment law will be essential.

Case study 5

Christine and Josh share a small terrace house together; they were once lovers, but their relationship ended last year after three years. Each wants to continue to live with the other, but they are finding it very difficult to cooperate in the house.

Josh usually wants Christine to go out if he is bringing any women friends home, but if she brings men home, he likes to stay in and talk with them. Christine feels that she is expected to carry out many more household chores than Josh. If they are home together at night, he seems to assume that she will cook, serve the meal, and wash up the dishes. She has tried talking to him about this, but he just avoids the issue. Josh is much happier with a messy, dirty house than Christine is, and on the occasions when she has left housework undone in the hope that he would feel obliged to do it, he has simply ignored it.

Looking at this conflict from Christine's point of view, explore ways of promoting collaborative problem solving. It will be necessary to analyse the conflict first, and to consider appropriate ways of motivating Josh to take part.

Team negotiation is becoming increasingly common; it is used extensively by Japanese corporations in commercial negotiation. A negotiating team will usually include members with specific responsibilities and roles: one may do the talking; another may be concerned with analysis of the process, while another may do nothing but listen carefully to the other side. The team will meet regularly for debriefing and discussions, and for the planning of the next stage of the negotiation.

Collaborative problem solving, whether it involves negotiation or not, has the potential to resolve conflict effectively, to provide considerable satisfaction for the participants, and to promote positively the development of good communication and relations between the parties. In general, it is the most appropriate initial process for most conflicts and should be attempted in the first instance unless there are clear reasons for considering that it may be counter-productive. Alternatives such as arbitration and mediation should be chosen only when there is clear reason for doing so; appropriate reasons are considered in the following chapters, which deal with these processes.

6 Mediation

Although collaborative problem solving between the participants in a conflict is the ideal, it is often neither the reality nor even a realistic possibility. Some conflict resolution requires, or is facilitated by, the involvement of what is usually described as a 'third party', although this may, in fact, be more than one person.

Participants in a conflict—whether individuals, groups, corporations, or nations—will sometimes voluntarily seek the intervention of a third party to assist in the process of resolving the conflict; for example, they may ask a mediator or conciliator to facilitate. In other cases, third-party intervention may be imposed on the participants—for example, as a result of legal action. Such intervention—where it does not involve the third person making a decision about, or arbitrating in, the conflict—is described as mediation, conciliation, or facilitation. The term 'mediation' is used in different contexts and in different countries to mean slightly different things. Terms such as 'conciliation' and 'facilitation' are also variously used. However, the common principle underlying their usage is that of an independent, impartial third party whose intervention is concerned essentially with helping the process of resolution, and who is not primarily concerned with the content of the conflict.

Choosing mediation

The reasons for deciding to seek mediation (or conciliation or facilitation) rather than to use collaborative problem solving include a previous failure to resolve through collaboration, or a perception that the parties cannot resolve their differences alone. This situation may result from a breakdown in relations between the parties or from the existence of such distrust or hostility that collaboration seems unworkable. The complexity of the content of the conflict, or of the feelings about the conflict, can also indicate a need for mediation. If the conflict has existed for a long time—particularly if there has been no attempt to resolve it, or if periodic unsuccessful attempts have occurred—it may also be helpful to try mediation. The number of parties to the conflict can also be a factor determining the appropriateness of mediation: collaborative problem solving can be difficult if more than four participants are involved. The dynamics and logistics of communication and collaboration become complicated with greater numbers, and will essentially require that someone take the role of facilitator; it can obstruct the process if the facilitator is also a participant in the conflict.

To be most effective, it is preferable that all participants have agreed to mediation, as well as agreeing to a particular mediation process and a particular mediator. It is possible, however, for mediation to be successful even without the initial agreement of any or all of the parties. A skilled mediator should be able to encourage their participation and cooperation.

The mediation process

Mediation follows very much the same process as collaborative problem solving (chapter 5) or conflict resolution generally (chapter 8). The essential difference is that in mediation, a third party is present to control and direct the process. The mediator can, very importantly, provide some sense of safety and security for the participants, and can minimise the risk of the process being diverted or stalled.

Risks in mediation

Mediation is not—despite some of the overly optimistic marketing—always safe or always free of risks. There are risks to the participants, and there is a risk that the very process of mediation may not only fail to resolve the conflict, but also make it worse and less amenable to future resolution. The major risks in mediation are:

- *power imbalance*: There may be a power imbalance where one party is significantly disempowered in relation to the other, and therefore may appear to be participating in the process while, in fact, doing so with great caution or anxiety.
- *coercion*: One party may be coerced (whether explicitly or implicitly) by the other, whether directly (for example, by threats) or indirectly (for example, by effective but dishonest persuasion). Both parties may be subject to coercion (directly or indirectly) by the mediator.
- *lack of skills*: One of both parties may lack the skills necessary to participate effectively, and will therefore be disadvantaged.
- *trauma*: One or both parties may experience psychological trauma before, during, or after the mediation. Pre-mediation anxiety can be quite severe, especially if the mediation involves direct confrontation with someone who is feared. Trauma during mediation can occur as a result of abuse, the disclosure of traumatising information, or serious embarrassment. Trauma can occur after mediation; sometimes this results from distress at what has been disclosed, particularly if the other party has to be faced outside the mediation context. Of course, verbal and (threatened or even actual) physical

violence can occur in mediation, particularly when the conflict is highly emotionally charged.

- *conflict escalation*: The conflict can escalate as a result of the disclosures and the expressions of opinions and feelings that mediation tends to encourage.
- *position entrenchment*: Parties can feel that the mediation process is an adversarial one, in which they have to argue for and strongly defend pre-determined positions, as a result of which their positions can become entrenched.
- *injustice*: Because mediation is essentially (as one critic has called it) 'private justice behind closed doors', participants can be seriously disadvantaged (for example, agreeing to proposals on the basis of ignorance or insufficient information). Mediation can contribute to social injustice by concealing matters that it may be in the public interest to have disclosed (for example, an employer may be eager to settle workplace injury claims with employees individually in mediation rather than have unsafe work practices publicly disclosed).
- *misuse of process*: The process of mediation can be abused. Some parties will simply pretend to participate in order to be seen to be cooperating and to be working towards resolution, while frustrating any real resolution. In some cases, parties (particularly legal representatives) may view the mediation as an opportunity for a 'fishing expedition'—that is, an opportunity to acquire as much information as possible about the arguments or evidence that the other party has at their disposal. Regardless of whether such material can be used in any future proceedings, it provides a valuable basis upon which to assess the strengths of their case, and to prepare a defence. In other cases, parties may view mediation as an opportunity for the 'punishment' of the other party by subjecting them to verbal abuse, ridicule, personal attack, or intimidation.
- *dangerous disclosure*: Mediation can allow, and indeed sometimes encourage, disclosures that may be detrimental to the interests and well-being of parties. It may be that one party discloses some highly sensitive personal information that may be used by the other to cause embarrassment or distress in the future, and which may be passed on to others.

The mediator needs to reflect upon the possibility of risks and dangers, both generally and in regard to specific cases. Parties proposing to participate in mediation also need to be given adequate information on potential risks to ensure that they are aware, both generally and in regard to their particular case, of what the risks may be. In some cases (for example, in relationships in which violence has occurred), the mediator may determine that mediation is not an appropriate process even to attempt.

The mediator

The key variable in mediation is not the nature of the conflict or its participants, or even the approach or style of mediation being used. It is the mediator, who must possess appropriate personal and professional skills. The personal qualities required by anyone who wishes to help other people to reach resolution by mediation includes clear, rational, and innovative thinking. The mediator must be able to show empathy, humour, and flexibility, as well as assertiveness. To be effective, the mediator needs to be goal-oriented, even when the process appears to be stuck or is wandering. Self-awareness, creativity, self-control, and self-motivation are equally important. The mediator also requires basic organisational skills and an ability to analyse objectively. These personal characteristics apply regardless of the sort of mediation to be undertaken. There are some process-related skills that all mediators require, as well as specialist skills for particular types of mediation. For example, there are special skills that are necessary in relationship or marriage mediation that may not be required in commercial mediation, and vice versa.

The necessary process-related skills include interpersonal skills in communication, listening, and building trust and rapport. The mediator also requires skills in analysis, facilitation, and option development. Some basic counselling skills may also be necessary, particularly when mediating interpersonal conflict. Relevant legal knowledge and appropriate ethical standards are essential. In addition, some areas require specialist knowledge, and even specialist skills, for mediation in industrial, personnel, commercial, environmental, and ethnic conflict. Similarly, specialist issues may arise in neighbourhood, relationship and marriage, or family conflict. There are, of course, other areas in which specialist mediation would also be effective, and in which specialist skills would be required by the mediator. A sound working knowledge of any relevant legislation or legal issues is very important.

Co-mediation and team mediation

Mediation does not necessarily mean the use of a single third party: in some cases, co-mediation (that is, the use of two mediators) or team mediation can be particularly effective. The team will usually consist of no more than three mediators, who will have carefully planned their different roles in the process.

Team mediation can be most effective when the conflict involves more than two participants, and particularly when it involves groups of participants (for example, racial conflict between two divisions in a country town). It can also be beneficial if the conflict raises issues that require specialist knowledge or skills in addition to mediation skills. In some cases, co-mediation or team mediation is appropriate because the conflict may involve important symbolic issues. For example, a racial conflict between an Aboriginal person and a non-Aboriginal person raises questions as to whether the mediator should be an Aboriginal or a non-Aboriginal person. Likewise, a conflict relating to sexual harassment creates the problem of whether the mediator should be male or female. In such cases the implications (or the perceptions of the parties) of the characteristics and symbolic importance of the mediator need to be taken into account. Co-mediators or mediators in a team must have an effective personal and professional relationship, and be able to work in a cooperative, rather than a superior–subordinate, relationship. A team including mediators with different personalities and mediation styles can be most effective.

Issues for mediators

There are five important issues for mediators: the relationship between mediation and counselling; intervention; resistance; empowerment; and neutrality.
An effective mediator will, at times, take a role similar to that of a counsellor,
and indeed, there are times when it would be difficult to distinguish counselling
from mediation. There are four essential qualities of effective counselling—
listening, understanding, accepting, and being interested—and these qualities
apply equally in effective mediation. Participants in both counselling and mediation processes can and do detect failure on the part of the counsellor or the
mediator to achieve these standards.

Personal qualities of the mediator

The mediator, like the counsellor, must possess and be able to demonstrate a
number of basic qualities. One of the most important is empathy—that is, being
able to understand how someone else is feeling, and to show this by reflecting the
other's feelings. A quality often described as 'warm acceptance' is also important;
this means being non-judgmental, responding warmly and caringly, without criticism or argument. While this does not necessarily presuppose agreement or
approval, it does mean encouraging the other to continue self-disclosing,
suspending one's own opinions and values for the present, respecting clients'
rights to feel and say whatever they want, and not interrupting the process of
self-disclosure by verbal or non-verbal indications of judgment or disapproval.
This, necessarily, involves being aware of one's own professional and personal
prejudices, opinions, and values, and will be considered further when the issue of
neutrality is examined. The mediator, like the counsellor, must be able to show
genuineness and the ability to consistently maintain an open and sincere
approach, to resist playing roles or being defensive, and to be able to concentrate
both time and attention on the participants. This involves not being manipula-
tive or patronising, but showing sincere concern for the client.

Both the mediation and the counselling processes tend to be divided into
three stages: exploring, understanding, and acting. The mediator usually helps
the parties to explore and understand both their separate situations and the
situation that brings them together. The mediator, like the counsellor, is not
there to interpret or diagnose for the parties, but to encourage and help them to
do so for themselves. In the final stage, the mediator works towards assisting the
parties to formulate a plan of action for the resolution of the conflict. In some
mediation processes, these three stages—although not necessarily called by
those names—are very clearly defined and worked through.

The mediator or the counsellor needs to be aware of her or his responsibilities to, and power and influence over, the client. This includes sensitivity to
the problem of clients becoming dependent on the mediator or the mediation
process, and trying to abdicate personal involvement and responsibility for

decision-making. It is also important that the mediator and the participants address their expectations of each other and of the process: unspoken and undefined expectations and projections can cause major problems, particularly if the parties have different, or even contradictory, expectations. For example, one or both participants in mediation may expect the mediator to arbitrate, and will become disillusioned or angry if this does not occur, even though they may not explicitly identify this expectation.

Mediation as a helping relationship

The role of the counsellor and the mediator, and of other professionals working with people in situations of conflict, is often described as a 'helping relationship'. A considerable amount of research has been done on the effectiveness of such relationships in a range of professions, including medicine, counselling, psychology, and psychiatry. Carl Rogers (1961), who has written extensively on the helping relationship, has summarised the considerations that, on the basis of the available evidence, he believes are most important in promoting an effective helping relationship—and which, incidentally, he considers to be more important than formal qualifications or professional skills. The most essential characteristics are those of being perceived as trustworthy, dependable, and consistent, and of being able to communicate unambiguously. It is also essential that the helping professional has the positive attitudes of warmth, caring, interest, liking, and respect towards the other person.

The professional must have the strength to remain separate from the client or clients, and also be confident enough within him- or herself to let the other people retain their separate identities. The temptation to impose solutions or changes on others should be identified and overcome. It is also essential that the professional be able to allow him- or herself to enter fully into the world of the other person's feelings and personal meanings, and to see these as the client does; this is the quality of empathy. It also involves being able to receive and accept the other person as he or she is (that is, not conditionally or judgmentally) and to communicate this acceptance to him or her. The mediator or counsellor should be able to meet the other person as someone who is in the 'process of becoming' and who is therefore capable of change and growth. This ought to exclude the use of labels or stereotypes, which define people on the basis of specific characteristics or the past.

Intervention

Counsellors and mediators differ widely in their views on intervention. What is the role of a third party in intervening in conflict and conflict resolution? Should the third party remain detached and only observe or facilitate, or should he or she actively intervene with either or both of the participants? If so, what sort of intervention should be involved? Obviously, these questions also arise for a range of people who may be involved in observing conflict: employers, managers, and supervisors; school teachers; parents; neighbours; and family members. Similarly, most people take different positions on when and how, and indeed if, they should intervene in personal conflict in which they may be involved either personally or professionally, directly or indirectly. Should they wait until a crisis, until the other participant takes action, until something compels them to become involved, or should they take the initiative in seeking resolution?

There are two aspects of intervention that require consideration: intervention with an individual and intervention in the conflict or the conflict resolution process. Intervention with the individual usually means providing advice, support, or assistance to an individual; this is what counsellors and other people (including parents, friends, teachers) who play a counselling role often do. Questions arise about the degree of their intervention: Should they tell individuals what to do, suggest options, encourage one action as against another, or disclose their own feelings and preferences? Or should they carefully avoid anything that might be taken as advice, only seeking to assist in clarifying the individuals' own thoughts, feelings, and decisions? What should be done if individuals actually ask for advice? Common questions are: 'You understand these things; what should I do?'; 'What would you do if you were in my situation?' 'What answers should be given?' This can become a particular problem when individuals are disempowered, helpless, confused, ill-informed, overwhelmed, or likely to be disadvantaged. Can a counsellor or a mediator stand back and ignore what he or she recognises to be a mistake about to be made, one that will ultimately be to the client's disadvantage?

Intervention in the processes of mediation or counselling also raises some difficult questions. When and how should a mediator intervene: to prevent argument? to stop a fist fight? to force the parties to talk about an issue they wish to avoid? to criticise the behaviour of one party? or to stop the process? The mediator usually has a great deal of power in the control of the process and often of the outcome. How this is to be exercised requires considerable reflection. The counsellor faces similar problems: how much to intervene; when, how, and for what purpose; and how much to disclose.

Self-disclosure

Self-disclosure raises important questions: how much should mediators disclose of themselves? There are both appropriate and inappropriate occasions for, and means of, self-disclosure. It may be appropriate when it helps the participants consider options, promotes a more direct relationship with them, or assists them in understanding their situation and themselves. The important qualification is always that the focus should remain on the participants and not be shifted to the mediator, and that it should not be assumed that the disclosed experiences of the mediator are identical, although they may be similar. Sometimes demands for self-disclosure ('What are your qualifications for being a mediator?'; 'Are you old enough to understand these situations?') can be attempts to undermine the control of the mediator, rather than genuine requests for relevant information.

Confrontation

Confrontation is intervention at its strongest, and mediators often face a difficult decision in determining whether and how to confront participants directly with issues that they have avoided, either consciously or unconsciously, but that the mediator believes to be crucial to the mediation process or the resolution of the conflict. Should the mediator try to force the client to face issues, questions, or feelings that they have suppressed or refuse to recognise? Like self-disclosure, confrontation can be handled appropriately and inappropriately. It may be appropriate when it is helpful to the client, promotes the process, and is not an accusation or a challenge. Badly handled, confrontation can be damaging, both to the process and to the relationship with the participants. Confrontation needs to be tentative—using statements, for example, such as 'It seems to me that . . . ' or 'Perhaps it would be helpful if . . . '. Confronting participants with options or real situations, if done carefully and thoughtfully, can be helpful, and can sometimes overcome blocks in the process.

Process analysis

Process analysis is a form of intervention that is often a useful means of addressing problems in mediation. It is related to confrontation and refers to situations in which the mediator needs to discuss with the participants what is happening in the mediation process, particularly when it seems not to be working or is stuck. Like confrontation, this needs to be done carefully, with tentative rather than accusatory language: 'I feel that . . . '; 'It seems to me that . . . '; 'I feel as if we are . . . '; 'Let's think about how this is going'. Asking questions about the relationship and the process is helpful.

Empowering

One of the most important roles of the mediation process is to empower the participants to understand their situations, both individually and collectively, to make informed personal and, preferably, mutual decisions, and to carry out those decisions. The mediator's role is one of empowering and facilitating. Empowering must be distinguished from decision-making and from manipulation, whether direct or indirect. In a helping relationship, indirect, subtle manipulation can occur, of which the mediator may not even be consciously aware. One way in which participants can be disempowered, while the mediator may believe he or she is empowering them, is by labelling, categorising, or typecasting people or problems: 'This is a typical working-class domestic crisis'; 'Aborigines always need help when this sort of thing happens'; 'The Greeks always get their families involved in these sorts of conflicts'. Purporting to show understanding by labelling—for example, 'I really get on well with blind people, so I understand how you feel'—suggests a lack of understanding, and a lack of respect for the individual.

Control in mediation

The mediator controls the process, not by any special or 'magical' powers, and certainly not by coercion, but by using a number of 'tools' and techniques. These include the use of a mutually defined agenda and mutually defined goal(s), to which the mediator makes frequent reference, assisting the parties to keep their focus on the goal of their discussions.

The mediator also makes sure that, from the beginning (if not before), the parties have a clear understanding of the process of mediation and the role of the mediator, and of their own roles within the mediation. The mediator will conduct him- or herself in an appropriate style, maintaining control very often simply by assuming and demonstrating it. Effective use of technology (for example, whiteboards) can assist in giving a focus to the discussions, and this focus is controlled by the mediator. The mediator is also responsible for effective process management and effective time management, both of which enable control to be exercised over and during the process.

Neutrality

Mediators are often described, and describe themselves, as 'neutral'. It is, however, quite difficult to identify what this means in practical terms. It clearly cannot mean a person who has no opinions or feelings on any matter that may arise in the mediation process. There is no such thing as a value-free person; those professions that strive for objectivity, professional detachment, and neutrality can only hope to move along a spectrum from involvement, subjectivity, and partiality towards the other extreme, but they cannot hope to reach it. It is essential that mediators recognise that they, like all people, have preferences and prejudices, tastes and distastes, likes and dislikes, strong emotional commitments and passionate objections.

It can certainly be questioned whether the objective and detached person, even if one could be found, would be particularly helpful in conflict resolution or mediation. What matters is the mediator's ability to be aware of values and beliefs, to recognise when they may or do get in the way—and when they are unhelpful in a particular situation (which is not the same as saying that they are wrong or false)—and to know when personal values and beliefs are interfering with the process or the relationship with one or both of the participants. This can be particularly difficult in matters involving value conflict, in which the mediator may have very strong personal views that support one participant and oppose the other.

Mediation usually involves helping people to make decisions. This is decision facilitating or assisting, not decision-making. Making a decision on behalf of other people, or telling them what to do, is often much easier than facilitating their own decision-making. However, neither in conflict resolution nor in mediation is it usually appropriate to make decisions for others, even when they ask that this be done.

Resistance

Mediators need to recognise also that resistance can be a block to the mediation process. 'Resistance' is a term derived from psychoanalysis, and essentially denotes a defence mechanism that appears when the process begins to delve into or raise issues that are sensitive or painful to the individual. Resistance is often a sign that a key issue is being approached and that the participant feels threatened. Resistance can manifest in a wide variety of ways, including all the defence mechanisms considered in chapter 10. It may lead to late arrivals, cancelled appointments, early departures, sudden raising of procedural problems, preoccupation with the issue prior to that which the participant wishes to avoid, or an urgent need to deal with the issue to follow that which the participant wishes to avoid. It can be manifested by a sudden outburst over an issue that had previously seemed resolved, an urgent need for legal or other advice, or the need to have other people approve of some decision. Although potentially very frustrating and demanding, resistance usually does suggest that the process is moving into the deeper structure and approaching the real conflict or problem.

There are three approaches to resistance that can often be helpful in the mediation process. The first is effectively confrontation—that is, dealing directly with the issue. This involves describing the situation as it appears to be and asking the participants what they believe is happening. This should be done as objectively and non-accusingly as possible: 'It seems to me that every time we approach the fourth item on our list, something happens that prevents our discussing it: how does it seem to you?'; 'I have the feeling that you may not want to talk about your relationship with your father-in-law; am I correct?'

If directly identifying the problem is considered to be too confronting, a second and less direct approach is to raise it obliquely and very gradually, trying to help the individual to become desensitised to the subject. Sometimes even this may be too confronting, and a third and gentler approach is to raise directly the general area of subjects with which the participants appear to feel uncomfortable, or about which they seem unwilling to speak. The mediator should confirm that this is normal, that everyone has some subjects with which they are uncomfortable, that it is important that these be approached at some stage, and that the participants might like to set their own pace. For example, it can be useful in relationship counselling to help the participants to draw up a list, often in ascending order of sensitivity, of things to discuss.

The mediator's role is not to reprimand people for not wishing to talk about subjects, and nor is it to force them to do so. There is often a need to help them to understand what they are doing and to recognise that they can make a conscious choice not to deal with an issue. There certainly is a role for the mediator in providing support, encouragement, and reassurance when resistance is overcome and disclosure follows. The fear of disclosure is often a fear of ridicule, and of personal loss, including actual loss and loss of esteem. The development of a trusting relationship with the mediator will gradually demonstrate to the participants that disclosure is less risky than it might at first have appeared.

Emotion in mediation

Feelings almost inevitably play an important part in conflict and conflict resolution, and in the mediation process. Resolutions that appear to involve no expression of feeling are usually those that will not succeed. Participants in mediation, no less than mediators, will often feel uncomfortable in expressing their feelings, and in having others express feelings to them. It is therefore not uncommon for participants to conceal their feelings, being conscious of some degree of risk in disclosing them. The mediator needs to be sensitive to this, and to feelings that may not be openly expressed. The skill of active listening is very important in this area; it may be what is said, the way it is said, or what is not said that identifies underlying feelings. For the process to be effective, it is important that participants are encouraged to express their feelings, as well as their opinions, and that they feel secure in doing so.

Feelings that become obstructions to the mediation process need to be identified, sometimes directly, and sometimes indirectly. The mediator needs to be aware, however, that sometimes even emotions such as anger or aggression, or fear of rejection, can have a positive role, provided that they are part of a process through which the participant moves, and not a state in which he or she become fixed. The expression of strong negative emotions is not, as such, an obstruction to the process; it can be therapeutic and cathartic.

Mediation, whatever form it takes or process it uses, can be a positive way of seeking to resolve conflict in which the collaborative problem-solving process has not been successful, or where it is inappropriate. The key variable in mediation is not the nature of the dispute or the personalities of the participants, but the mediator, who brings to mediation both personal and professional skills. It is these skills that, essentially, determine whether mediation is effective. The

---

Case Study 6

The Utopia Welfare Centre is in a state of crisis: one of its paid employees, Mark, the newly appointed Volunteer Coordinator, has had a major disagreement with Jenny, one of the centre's longest serving volunteers. Each has indicated to the committee that he or she considers the other to be incompetent, uncooperative, and disruptive. Jenny insists that she will not deal with Mark, and wants another member of the staff to be available to supervise her volunteer work. Mark insists that, as Volunteer Coordinator, he is responsible for supervision of all volunteers, and for deciding who serves as a volunteer. He argues that Jenny should be removed from the roster, even though she has worked at the centre for five years.

The committee wants to keep both Jenny, an exceptional and dedicated volunteer, and Mark, a highly skilled coordinator. They decide, therefore, to bring a mediator in to try to resolve the conflict.

As the mediator, analyse the conflict and prepare for attempting resolution. Consider when, where, how, and with whom mediation would be undertaken.

---

fact that a matter may not be resolved in mediation is not a sign that either the mediation process or the mediator failed; the realisation that no immediate resolution is possible may be a realistic outcome in some cases, or a basis for a more realistic approach to resolution in the future.

Sometimes, however, a conflict may require more external intervention than mediation provides, and some form of arbitration might then be considered.

7 Arbitration

Although collaborative resolution by the parties to a conflict is usually the most effective form of resolution, in some cases third-party intervention is helpful or necessary. The least interventionist forms of third-party involvement are facilitative processes (such as mediation), but there are circumstances in which a more interventionist approach is appropriate or even necessary. These processes involve a third party making a determination (which may or may not be enforceable) of the matter.

NADRAC defines determinative processes in the following way:

> Determinative processes involve a third party investigating the dispute (which may include the hearing of formal evidence from the parties) and making a determination, which is potentially enforceable, as to its resolution.
>
> Processes which are determinative may be divided into those which are internally enforceable, those which are externally enforceable and those which are neither internally or externally enforceable (NADRAC 1997a, p. 10).

The main divisions of determinative processes are adjudication and arbitration, which NADRAC classifies in the following ways:

> Adjudication is a process in which the parties present arguments and evidence to a neutral third party (the adjudicator) who makes a determination which is enforceable by the authority of the adjudicator. The most common form of internally enforceable adjudication is determination by state authorities empowered to enforce decisions by law (for example, courts, tribunals) within the traditional judicial system. However, there are also other internally enforceable adjudication processes (for example, internal disciplinary or grievance processes implemented by employers).
>
> Arbitration is a process in which the parties to a dispute present arguments and evidence to a neutral third party (the arbitrator) who makes a determination (NADRAC 1997a, p. 10–11).

Arbitration refers to the use of a neutral third party to make a decision regarding a conflict. Although, broadly, it can include the process of adjudication—in which the arbitrator is a judge whose decision can be enforced by the power of the State or some other authority (such as an employer)—the term arbitration is more often used to refer to a private process through which an independent arbitrator, usually chosen by the parties to the conflict, determines the outcome. In arbitration the determination of the arbitrator is often binding upon the parties, in some cases because the law provides for this, in others because the parties have entered into a contract to this effect.

It is sometimes suggested by those who promote conflict resolution and alternative dispute resolution (ADR), that adjudication and arbitration are poor options, and unlikely to resolve a matter effectively. This is often, but not always, true. There are matters that are best dealt with by adjudication or arbitration directly, and in which non-adversarial processes may simply increase the level of conflict, and decrease the prospect of resolution.

Sometimes arbitration can be very helpfully used in dealing with preliminary matters prior to a collaborative or mediated attempt at resolution. For example, if some elements of the conflict relate to questions on which an expert determination could be obtained, and the parties are willing to agree to a suitable expert, the arbitration (by expert determination) of these questions can facilitate subsequent discussions. Take, as a simple example, a dispute between neighbours that includes the issue of the precise location of the property boundary between their blocks. Since the position of the boundary is a matter of fact and law, it is not, essentially, determined by mutual agreement. It may be useful for the parties to identify and employ a mutually acceptable (and suitably qualified) surveyor, and to agree, in advance, to accept her or his determination as to the location of the boundary. Disputes about what are essentially facts rarely resolve the matter (being likely to lead to endless 'It is . . . ' / 'It is not . . . ' exchanges), and may both strengthen the fixed position of each party and further damage the relationship between them. Sorting out those matters that can be determined (as matters of fact or law) through preliminary (and usually arbitrational) processes assists in establishing a more realistic framework for collaborative conflict resolution.

The arbitrator, unlike the mediator, is concerned with the content of the conflict as well as with the process of resolution. He or she must, like a judge, assess the evidence and the arguments of the parties and reach a decision that he or she believes to be correct, fair, equitable, and just.

In some jurisdictions, legislation provides for arbitrators to deal with some disputes (for example, the NSW *Arbitration (Civil Actions) Act 1983*). Similarly, some courts have provisions in their rules for disputes, or aspects of them, to be referred to arbitrators or referees.

It is probably more common, however, for the parties to a dispute to decide to have the matter arbitrated and to select a mutually acceptable arbitrator. In recent years, some commercial contracts have included clauses specifically requiring that disputes be referred, in the first instance, to mediation or arbitration, and preventing them from going to litigation until that has been attempted. Such contractual provisions are promoted and encouraged by organisations such as the Australian Institute of Arbitrators and the Australian Commercial Disputes Centre.

Although some writers imply that either arbitration (including adjudication) or mediation is the only effective means of resolving conflict, it is obvious that either or both processes, or combinations of aspects of each, can be effective in different situations and with different conflicts. Until a conflict has been analysed, it is rarely possible to identify the process that will be most effective for its resolution, and part of the process of planning for resolution involves the identification of the most appropriate process.

There are some conflicts that are particularly amenable to one process, and some for which the other is most effective. In some cases, the potential for a judicial decision or arbitration, if mediation is not successful, can assist in promoting resolution; in other cases, the threat or promise of arbitration will hinder mediation.

Types of arbitration

As with mediation, there are different types of arbitration. Arbitration ranges from fairly informal decision-making processes to quasi-judicial processes that imitate those of the court. The nature of the arbitration process depends on the context within which it is occurring; for example, in some cases it is within the legal system and defined by statute. It may also vary according to the needs of the parties and the style of the arbitrator.

Specialist arbitration, sometimes called '*expert determination*', is a process in which the arbitrator is chosen on the basis of her or his specialist qualification or experience in the subject matter of the conflict. Sometimes expert determination is used to determine preliminary questions of fact or law in a conflict, prior to further processes. In some cases, a form of arbitration known as '*private judging*' may be employed. This is sometimes (perhaps unfortunately) also known as 'rent-a-judge'. This process utilises an arbitrator chosen on the basis of her or his experience as a member of the judiciary (the 'private judge') who makes a determination in accordance with her or his opinion as to what decision would be made if the matter was judicially determined. In essence, this process is said to offer the advantages of going before a judge in a court, without the disadvantages, including cost, delay, and public exposure. This can include a variant, often called a '*mini-trial*', in which the parties present the cases they would anticipate presenting in litigation, and as a result of each party hearing the evidence and arguments of the other, some form of mutual agreement may be reached. In some cases, this may be combined with private judging.

Fast-track arbitration involves the presentation of the conflict to an arbitrator who makes a determination on the most important and most immediate issues in dispute. In *final-offer arbitration*, the arbitrator is involved at the conclusion of negotiations between the parties, and only determines which of the final offers of the parties will be implemented. The theory behind final-offer arbitration is that the parties, knowing that whatever they offer may have an equal probability of being selected, will put forward the most reasonable proposal possible. This approach to arbitration has the advantage of speed, and requires minimal investigation or hearing by the arbitrator. Its major disadvantage is that it does not allow for flexibility; the arbitrator may believe that the best possible outcome is a combination of elements from both proposals or, in fact, a new third proposal that he or she can identify, but the arbitrator is not able to offer these as options.

A relatively new form of arbitration developed in the USA in recent years is called 'med/arb': it involves a third party acting as a mediator, but having the power to move into the role of arbitrator at such time as he or she concludes that mediation is not succeeding. In some American jurisdictions this has a statutory basis. It poses some particular problems for the use of mediation since there is necessarily an element of coercion; the parties are aware that if they are not prepared to reach a mediated settlement, they face the risk of arbitration.

Many commentators on mediation consider that if mediation is deemed to have failed and the parties decide, or are compelled, to move into arbitration, a different person should undertake the arbitration. One of the essential elements of mediation is the ability of the parties to discuss the conflict freely and frankly, and to know that the mediator is not essentially concerned with the content of their conflict. In other words, ideally, they are not being judged or evaluated by the mediator. Knowing that the mediator may transform into an arbitrator is likely to cause the participants to be more hesitant in making frank and open disclosures, and more inclined to present cases in which their separate positions are vindicated. This almost by definition precludes the possibility of effective mediation. There is, however, nothing intrinsically impractical about the concept of moving into arbitration if mediation is not successful; this is already the process in a number of Australian jurisdictions (for example, human rights and equal opportunity legislation). In those cases, however, the mediator or mediating agency generally refers the participants to a different and separate arbitration process.

Types of conflict suitable for arbitration

The types of conflict generally more amenable to the process of arbitration include disputes solely or principally on a question of fact or legal interpretation (for example, a dispute over the location of a property boundary, or the legal requirement for the height of a fence). In such cases, discussions about the question will be of limited value, and the parties would be better to seek a formal ruling. Similarly, disputes in which both parties agree that complex questions of fact or legal interpretation are central to the conflict often require arbitration, at least to determine some of the basic questions in dispute. It may be, for example, that an expert arbitration on key questions of fact will facilitate collaborative resolution of the conflict as such.

Arbitration is usually more effective when no ongoing relationship is involved, so that the parties (even if they reject or are resentful of the arbitrator's determination) do not have to deal with each other directly in future.

A conflict over the division of resources or property in which there is no primary, underlying emotional or value conflict, and in which the parties have been unable to reach a collaborative or mediated agreement, will often benefit from arbitration. (Indeed, the more quickly the parties go to arbitration, the less the likelihood there is of serious emotional conflict developing.) This is very different from a conflict over the division of property in which there are deep underlying emotional factors; the best, or worst, examples of this involve marital break-ups. In those cases, arbitration is more likely to promote ongoing conflict because it cannot address the real conflict and is concerned only with the surface dispute.

Arbitration can he particularly effective with long-standing conflicts in which there appears to have been an irreconcilable breakdown in relations between the parties. Conflict resolution, other than by arbitration, requires at least a minimal degree of mutual cooperation, communication, and trust on the parts of the participants. If this is not possible (particularly if the relationship has become characterised by a reverse situation), it may be appropriate to move quickly into arbitration once mediation has been attempted. In such cases, arbitration is unlikely to resolve the conflict, because it cannot compel cooperation, communication, or trust, but it will be able to deal with any disputes that have resulted from the conflict.

Conflict is usually characterised by ongoing disputes. If it is leading to the termination of a long-term relationship, it can sometimes be effectively dealt with by arbitration, particularly where there is a need to resolve practical problems (for example, the division of property or money). People who are facing the ending of an important, intense relationship in which they have previously made a considerable investment will often find the process of conflict resolution, which requires them to collaborate, extremely confronting and emotionally painful. While this may, in fact, be therapeutic and ultimately beneficial to them, it is likely to be a situation from which they wish to withdraw, or with which they will cope badly. In some cases, interim arrangements are necessary to allow both parties to get on with their lives, and these may be effectively undertaken through arbitration. In such cases, it is assumed that arbitration establishes a temporary arrangement, and that once the parties feel more comfortable with each other and with their situation they will seek to address the real conflict. Unfortunately, this can have the adverse effect of providing them with a sense of escape from the real issues and may lead to an increased reluctance to seek resolution.

Arbitration is particularly effective with conflict that is solely or principally of a commercial nature; the less personal importance the participants place on a conflict, the more amenable they are likely to be to arbitration.

Just as there are conflicts in which an arbitration process can be very effective, so there are those in which arbitration may be the least effective means of resolution. The most obvious is conflict that is solely or principally based on feelings, values, or interpersonal relationships, in which it is not possible to arbitrate. It is possible to hand down decisions or rulings about behaviour and, to varying degrees, to coerce people to comply with them. Feelings, however, cannot be directed in this way, and where values are involved, it is unlikely that parties will comply, in more than a superficial way, with any arbitration that contradicts deeply held values. The same holds true for almost any conflict between people whose relationship is personal rather than commercial or legal.

Conflicts between people who wish to continue in a stable, long-term personal relationship after the resolution of the conflict are usually not suitable for arbitration. The imposition of a decision that is seen to favour one party and to disadvantage another is unlikely to strengthen or support their relationship. Similarly, disputes in which there are other matters causing conflict between the parties, apart from those that can be dealt with by the legal process, are rarely resolved in arbitration. If a conflict is a compound of issues, then dealing with one or two of them, particularly if the outcome is not acceptable to one of the parties, will not resolve the whole. In some cases, the arbitrator, who may be a judge in a court, will be precluded from dealing with anything other than a narrow part of an overall conflict; this is often so unsatisfactory that it has the effect of increasing the magnitude of the conflict as a whole.

Arbitration also has difficulty in dealing with conflicts in which there is little or no objective evidence to support the claims of either party, or in which there is nothing that can be awarded to one party or divided between the parties. If one of the parties seeks vindication or 'justice', the arbitration process may not be able to meet that need; if the party seeks an award of damages or a determination on fact, the arbitration process can usually deal with that quite effectively.

Advantages and disadvantages of arbitration

There are both advantages and disadvantages to the process of arbitration, and whether or not any particular characteristic is advantageous or disadvantageous will depend largely on the nature of the conflict and on the participants, including the arbitrator. Arbitration allows both parties equal opportunity to present their views, and places the power to make a decision with an impartial adjudicator. This has the effect of minimising the need for decision-making by the participants, either or both of whom may view this as either an advantage or a disadvantage. Arbitration allows for expert evidence, an advantage particularly in matters involving complex technical information. It also provides what is usually intended to be a final, and sometimes enforceable, resolution.

Arbitration generally attempts to maintain the objectivity of process, avoiding issues of feeling and minimising the role of the person. It has some potential to redress any imbalance of power (in theory) since the outcome is not necessarily dependent on the skills of the parties. In many cases, the parties can be represented by advocates accustomed to presenting arguments. Arbitration also avoids one of the great problems of collaborative problem solving: it does not depend on the goodwill, trust, or cooperation of parties. It is also a finite, usually fixed-time process; the participants cannot simply continue without restriction, and therefore may be forced to focus on the problem. Arbitration, apart from the court process, is generally private.

Arbitration does have a number of identifiable inadequacies. It can favour the wealthy and disadvantage the poor if it involves substantial costs or requires the use of advocates (for example, in the court system). Although non-judicial arbitration can be very quick, court-based adjudication often involves extensive delay, and associated costs.

Arbitration generally does not consider, and may even suppress, the feelings of parties, and therefore is usually incapable of addressing the emotional elements of a conflict. Much arbitration, especially the court process, positively promotes an adversarial approach, requiring parties to oppose one another and often, at least implicitly, forcing them to take strong positions that they defend while attacking the position taken by the other participant. If the process is rigid, it may also be limited to formal, inflexible solutions; this is particularly the case in the judicial system, where options are limited by law and precedent. Arbitration, because it takes the process away from the parties, can damage an ongoing relationship.

It is important to recognise that just as there are advantages and disadvantages in arbitration and the traditional judicial process, so there are in the non-arbitrational forms of conflict resolution and dispute settlement. As with arbitration, whether or not a characteristic is advantageous or otherwise depends very much on the matter concerned.

The major advantage of non-arbitrational processes is that they maximise involvement by participants, and further maximise their decision-making. This encourages individual responsibility and commitment to any outcome, and can positively strengthen an ongoing relationship. Such processes also avoid legalistic arguments. They should be able to encourage innovative, flexible solutions adapted to meet the needs of the specific situation and the particular people involved.

The major disadvantage of non-arbitrational processes is that the participants are generally required to rely on intellectual and verbal skills, and on assertiveness. The inarticulate, non-assertive, and shy may be disadvantaged. There is a heavy reliance on the parties' knowledge, and in cases involving complex technical information this may be very limited. Hence one party can dominate the process, particularly in collaborative problem solving, in which there is no third person to control the process. It depends on goodwill, communication and the cooperation of the parties, which, in times of conflict, may be severely lacking. Because no one is independently involved in controlling the process, it may be delayed, stalled, diverted, or interrupted by one party, or by both parties. Resolutions are usually unenforceable, and therefore the outcome may simply fail, reinstating the conflict and bringing about a loss of faith in the process.

The arbitrator

In mediation the key variable is the mediator, and similarly in arbitration it is the arbitrator. The arbitrator should be characterised by being impartial and competent, and acceptable to the parties to the conflict. In those cases in which the participants do not select the arbitrator (for example, the court system), it is important that they either accept the arbitrator appointed or accept the authority of the system that appoints the arbitrator.

Arbitration is generally based on a number of key principles: fairness, impartiality, equity, good conscience, the merits of the case, and natural justice. The arbitrator should be, and should be seen to be, both fair and impartial, both in the process itself and in the final award, and should make her or his determination on the merits of the case and not on any extraneous matter.

In some cases, the matter in dispute may be of a complex technical, legal, or scientific nature. Although it seems to be assumed in the court process that a judge without any specialist knowledge can, on the basis of expert evidence, make a decision, arbitration will often involve the use of a specialist arbitrator chosen for her or his knowledge of the area concerned. For example, in a dispute regarding a construction project, it may involve an expert builder. The advantage of an expert arbitrator is that he or she is qualified and competent to make a decision on the content of the dispute. Some contracts now include clauses providing that, in the event of a dispute, an expert arbitrator acceptable to both parties will be appointed to determine the matter.

Arbitration, like mediation, does not necessarily involve only one arbitrator; sometimes a team of arbitrators will be more appropriate. The same basic principles of team mediation (outlined in chapter 6) apply to team arbitration.

The stages of arbitration

There are normally a series of stages in arbitration, just as there are in collaborative problem solving and mediation. In all three approaches, the stages tend to be similar. Arbitration normally begins with the parties agreeing to the process and to an arbitrator, and with the arbitrator undertaking preliminary discussions to ascertain the nature of the dispute and her or his appropriateness as an arbitrator. This is followed by a stage of investigation or information gathering; normally, the arbitrator will expect the parties to provide adequate information about the dispute, as well as written material on their respective positions. This will often be followed by a hearing, which can be formal and court-like, or informal, depending on the style of the arbitrator or the system of arbitration in which he or she works. This stage involves both parties presenting their arguments, responding to the arguments of the other, and answering the questions of the arbitrator. They may also be presented with options by the arbitrator, and be asked to comment on them.

The arbitrator alone then enters the stage of decision-making, during which he or she will have to consider the material provided, the arguments, and the options, and will make a determination. This is then handed down to the parties. It will normally deal specifically with the matter referred by the parties to the arbitrator; the amount of explanation and commentary accompanying the decision will depend on a number of factors, including the style of the arbi-

Case study 7

Janice has a particular interest in home building, although she has no formal qualifications in the field. She designed her own house and, as an owner-builder, organised its construction. She had one special problem with the completion of the project: the construction of a concrete driveway beside the house. The block sloped at a difficult angle and posed considerable difficulties for the company that built the driveway. In the hope of minimising any problems with her house, Janice drew up very precise specifications for each contractor.

The concrete on several sections of the driveway is now badly cracked, and Janice wants it taken up and replaced. The contractors refuse to do this saying that they have complied precisely with her specifications and that the problem results from these being faulty. The contractor has commented that Janice was foolish to rely on her own inadequate knowledge of building.

A range of conflict resolution processes might be applied in this situation. Assuming that arbitration is to be used, analyse the conflict from the perspective of the arbitrator. This should involve determining the sort of person who should be arbitrator and the sort of arbitration process that will be used.

trator and the requirements of the parties. In some cases, they may simply seek a brief decision (for example, X to pay Y $50 000); in others, a detailed explanation of, and rationale for, the decision may be required.

Arbitration can be a very effective means of resolving certain conflicts or particular parts of conflicts. But, as with a decision to attempt collaborative problem solving or mediation, it is important that sufficient analysis and preparation is undertaken to ensure that arbitration is the most appropriate process for the specific conflict.

8 The Conflict Resolution Process

Although conflict resolution may make use of a number of approaches, methods, and styles, including collaboration, mediation, and arbitration, it is possible to outline a basic process through which the resolution of conflict usually works. This is not to suggest that there is a rigid set of rules for resolution; there is no magical formula that works always, everywhere, and for everyone. There are, however, some basic principles underlying the resolution process, just as there are in analysis and preparation.

In this chapter the basic process of resolution will be outlined. This may, or may not, include a formal conflict resolution meeting, and may or may not involve a form of mediation.

Agreements

The conflict resolution process can be divided into a number of stages (various commentators describe these differently and offer different sets of stages) which fall broadly into at least three areas of agreement, without which resolution is unlikely if not impossible. All conflict resolution depends on agreements between the parties. While this may sound like a statement of the obvious—and in part it is—the concept of *agreements*, as distinct from *agreement*, is often overlooked.

The agreements that begin the process of conflict resolution are not, initially, agreements on the resolution of the conflict. That may be the aim of the process, but it is rarely achieved at the beginning, or even during the early stages of the process. Conflict resolution is facilitated by an ever-increasing number of agreements between the parties; even agreements on matters that seem to be of relatively little importance assist in establishing communication, trust, and effective collaborative problem solving. Each time the participants reach another agreement, they have extended the area of their mutual interests and common commitment and enhanced the process of working towards resolution.

Any agreement may be tentative, conditional, and subject to all manner of reservations; only a working agreement is required. The agreement may be subjected to statements such as, 'Well, if I accepted that . . . then I might . . .'. Tentative language and non-committal words—'might', 'could', 'possibly', 'perhaps'—can be used to promote working agreement. The initial use of 'soft' language and style is generally more likely to encourage resolution than the use of 'hard' language. It may be necessary, as the discussion proceeds, to harden the approach, but an initial hard statement will provoke defensiveness and encourage fighting rather than resolving. Gentle questioning and the suggestion of possibilities, is more effective than hard demands: 'Would it be possible to . . . ?'; 'Might we be able to . . . ?'; 'If I was to . . . do you think you might be able to . . . ?'. Blatant demands are much more likely to provoke immediate resistance than serious, rational consideration. Most people do not respond positively to attempts at coercion or threat: 'You have got to . . . '; 'Unless you do . . . then I will . . . '; 'I'm not accepting anything less than . . . '.

Agreement on the problem

Conflict resolution requires, essentially, agreement in three major areas, and the agreement almost always has to be reached in this order: agreement on the problem, agreement on the process, and agreement on a plan for resolution. The participants must agree that there is a conflict (or are conflicts), and on essentially what the conflict is (or the conflicts are). This was considered in detail in chapter 2.

Recalling that the conflict will usually include both manifest and unmanifest dimensions, and that either or both parties may be unaware of some of the dimensions, agreement on the problem is not always easy. It is rather too simple to fix on the focal conflict and try to resolve that, usually without long-term success if the focal problem is but a symptom of an underlying conflict that remains unresolved. Unless there is mutual agreement on the conflict (or conflicts), any attempt at resolution is likely to be frustrated; if one party is seeking to resolve conflict A and the other conflict B, but they are both able to describe the conflict in imprecise terms as C, then the outcome, though apparently satisfactory, is unlikely to be a long-term resolution.

In what may be described as one conflict, there may be, in fact, a number of different conflicts. Although the parties involved may describe the situation as a single conflict (for example, 'our working relationship', 'the division of tasks around the home', or 'how the contract is working out'), each party may have a different, and individually specific, definition of the conflict. To use the example of 'our working relationship', for one party this may be a perception that too much work is being allocated by a supervisor, and for the other it may be that work allocated is not being completed efficiently.

Until and unless the conflict is defined precisely and specifically, resolution is impossible. Indeed, dialogue about the conflict may make the relationship between the parties worse since each will be seeking the resolution of the conflict as he or she perceives it, rather than as it is defined by the other. Initial specification of the precise details of the conflict as seen by each participant is essential. One of the particular roles of any third party is in facilitating this through skilled questioning and focusing.

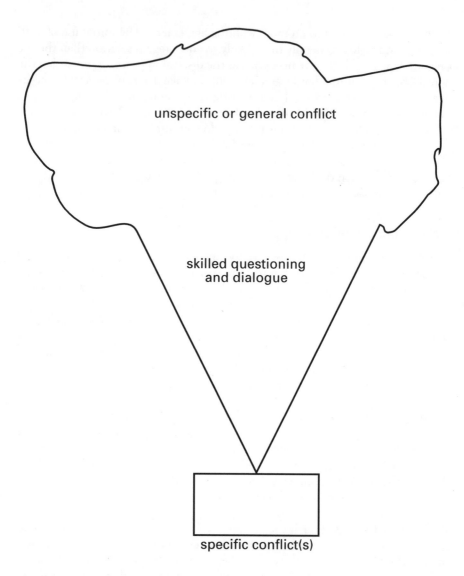

unspecific or general conflict

skilled questioning
and dialogue

specific conflict(s)

Figure 8.1 The focusing process

Conflict is very often initially described in vague and imprecise terms. This is usually not so much a result of wilful refusal to disclose details as a sense of being overwhelmed by the conflict and an inability to see it in terms of specific components. A parallel can be drawn with depression: those who are depressed will often feel as though they are surrounded by a 'black cloud' and will find great difficulty in precisely defining the causes of the depression. So those who feel themselves to be engulfed by a highly emotionally charged situation of conflict will often find it difficult to describe the situation specifically and precisely. This is one of the reasons why the intervention of a skilled third party can be of assistance. By gentle, but skilful, questioning, the third party can assist those immersed in 'the cloud of conflict' to identify and specify the precise details of the situation.

In some cases, there is a sense of anxiety or embarrassment about disclosing specific details. This may be because they are thought to be trivial or 'out of date'. If a central issue is a passing remark that was made a long time ago, the party for whom this is important may feel that it cannot be raised because it will be seen (by the other party) to be insignificant. However, if a comment made ten years ago is still generating emotional conflict, it is not trivial and needs to be worked through.

Likewise, some issues are not openly identified because of a (sometimes realistic) perception of risk. If, for an employee, the central conflict relates to the behaviour of a supervisor or manager, that employee may believe that identifying the behaviour will place him or her in danger, either of loss of employment or of some other form of retribution. Failure or refusal to disclose the concern about the behaviour makes it unlikely that the conflict will be resolved. The third party's role may be in assisting in identifying an appropriate, but less risky, way of expressing the concern.

Until and unless the real conflicts are identified and specified, no real resolution is possible. All sorts of agreements and settlements can be reached—often as vaguely worded as the imprecisely defined conflict—but these are highly unlikely to lead to a resolution of the real conflict(s). For example, if the conflict is defined as 'our working relationship' and the agreement is defined as 'We agree to have a better working relationship in future', the situation is unlikely to improve except in the very short term. Since 'our working relationship' can mean almost anything (from mild disagreements to serious harassment), the proposed 'better working relationship' can also mean whatever either party assumes it to mean. Not only does it not address the real conflict, but it also sets up a situation in which a breakdown of the agreement is almost certain. Each party will probably understand the agreement to mean different things, and therefore he or she will conform—not to what the other has assumed to be the undertakings, but to what he or she assumed to have been undertaken. Each will measure the other's compliance with the agreement in terms of her or his own assumptions, perceptions, and expectations; since these have not been made explicit, the risk of failure, and of a consequent assumption that the agreement has been breached, is very high.

Specification of the conflict(s) is thus critically important for effective resolution. This often involves the fractionation of what is initially defined as a single, imprecisely described conflict into multiple, precisely defined conflicts. Although this process can sometimes appear unhelpful (with parties sometimes complaining that 'We thought we only had one conflict, and now we've ended up with a dozen'), it is, in fact, necessary. A dozen precisely specified conflicts are much more amenable to effective resolution than one vaguely defined conflict.

Sasha and David

David is the manager of the section in which Sasha works; they have a poor workplace relationship, characterised by frequent conflicts.
Original definition of conflict: 'We have a poor working relationship'

Specification:

Sasha	David
David allocates too much work to me.	Sasha doesn't complete tasks quickly enough.
David simply dumps files on my desk without explanation.	Sasha often fails to do precisely what is required.
I find it difficult to get time with David to discuss what is required in particular tasks.	Sasha often addresses the wrong issues in writing reports.
I have had problems with my computer for the past three months, and despite repeated requests, it has not been serviced.	The layout of Sasha's reports is often not of an appropriate quality.
David returns files to me with brief notes that I often do not understand.	When asked to correct work, Sasha rarely does what is required.

Agreement on the process

Agreement on the process involves accepting a means of working towards a possible resolution: how can we approach the conflict, which we agree exists, in the hope of resolving it? This may include agreement that the parties will try to work it out together, or that they will seek the assistance of a third party (for example, in mediation). It should include some definite proposals for a process of resolution: when they will meet, where, how they will arrange the discussion, and what ground rules will apply. Selecting the right time, or even making an appointment, is an important part of establishing agreement on the process, and avoids the difficulties of being seen to 'ambush', or of trying for resolution at a time of high emotional tension.

It is not necessary for a single process to be used; it may be that different elements of a conflict require different processes, either sequentially or concurrently. For example, it may be necessary for some preliminary investigation or determination of fact to be made before further discussion occurs.

Agreement on a plan

Agreement on a plan for resolution is the desired outcome of the process. Note that this refers to a plan rather than a solution. The plan is to be seen as a possible or probable resolution requiring implementation: what they are going to try to do to solve the problem. Some conflicts, of course, are resolved by the agreement on the problem—that is, they are discovered to have been based on misunderstanding: 'Now that I know you didn't in fact do what I believed you had done, we have no conflict'. In those sorts of conflicts, however, it is important that some discussion about strategies be undertaken for the minimisation of future conflicts: 'To make sure we don't get caught up in this sort of situation in future, perhaps we could . . . '.

The more tentative and conditional the plan, the more likely participants will be to accept it. If they fear it is set in concrete, immutable and unchangeable, there will be much more hesitation and anxiety. Particularly in situations where trust in each other is low (or even non-existent), definitive mutual agreements will usually be assumed to be unlikely to succeed. Tentative, staged proposals are necessary if a working trust is to be re-established. Plans should be presented as proposals rather than as absolute, guaranteed solutions. If it is presented as the solution, the participants are given unrealistically heightened expectations and, should things not work out, unrealistically dashed hopes. A proposal that the participants are going to try is more realistic and allows flexibility. The plan should provide for review and revision.

Models and stages

There are numerous models of the conflict resolution process; many published works list series of stages through which they suggest the process should flow. These stages are more often than not the same or similar, but differently named. Obviously, models and stages are imperfect ways of representing the process. No model applies universally. In some conflicts, stages will be missed, or repeated, or the process may be begun in the middle. Models or stages offer a useful checklist of matters to be considered, rather than inventories that must be worked through if the process is to be successful. They should always be critically assessed.

As a practical guide to the process of conflict resolution, the stages suggested below are something of a composite from a wide range of writers and theorists, mixed with experience in the process of conflict resolution.

In general, the following stages will be worked through:

- agreement on conflict(s)
- agreement on purpose(s)
- agreement on process(es)
- sharing perceptions
- responding

- defining objectives
- exploring options
- evaluating options
- choosing preferred option(s)
- projecting outcomes
- negotiating
- selecting option(s)
- planning implementation
- implementing
- evaluating and reviewing
- revising
- resolving.

Purpose

Agreement needs to be reached on what the participants want to do: the nature of their mutual aim in conflict resolution. This should be defined as precisely as possible. In the short term, the purpose may not deal with what is seen as the central conflict. For example, deciding whether or not to build a smelter outside a particular town may be a long-term issue; the immediate issue may be deciding on what preliminary matters need to be taken into account—for example, common ground rules for environmental protection.

The larger and more complex the conflict, the more likely it is that a series of purposes will be defined and worked through, with the conflict resolution process in fact consisting of a series of conflict resolution processes. In any conflict resolution process there needs to be, however, a clear understanding of what outcome is being sought. Without that, amiable and endless discussions may proceed without anything being accomplished.

The purposes of a resolution process will usually be different in conflicts involving ongoing and terminating relationships. In ongoing relationships, the purposes necessarily include ensuring that the future relationship between the parties is at least minimally workable. If the resolution of the current conflict (however effective it may be in dealing with the immediate situation) damages the ongoing relationship, leading to further (and possibly worse) conflict in future, it has served only to make things more difficult between the parties. Thus, in ongoing relationships, the issue of future conflicts and how they will be dealt with is of critical importance. At its best, effective conflict resolution will enable the parties not only to deal with the immediate situation, but also to develop insight, skills, and motivation to deal more effectively with future conflicts, and to reflect on and implement conflict-minimisation processes within their relationships. This is what John Burton refers to as 'conflict provention' (see p. 188).

Where the relationship is not ongoing (for example, where it relates to the termination of employment), it should aim at enabling both parties to conclude the relationship both externally and internally. Unfortunately, many such processes produce an external resolution (for example, a division of property after a relationship separation) but, in fact, greatly increase the internal conflict felt by both parties. In some cases this will indeed prevent the external resolution—no matter how apparently willingly agreed to by the parties at the time—from being effective as either or both return to the external conflict in an (often unconscious) attempt to work out the inner conflict.

This is seen at its most obvious in relationship conflict (including marital breakdowns), in which the parties participate in processes for the 'ending' of their relationship. This 'ending' usually refers not to any serious attempt to work through the emotional and psychological issues, but to a process of negotiation about property (and, sometimes, children) in which the emotional and psychological issues are very carefully avoided. Although an apparently rational and workable agreement may be the result of the process of negotiation, it will rarely work in practice if the real conflict has not been addressed. Thus, ongoing disputes may arise; every opportunity may be taken to reopen negotiations; terms of an agreement may be repeatedly broken; attempts may be made to sabotage agreements; and a high level of emotional conflict may arise over apparently minor matters.

Such behaviour is indicative that the real conflict has not been addressed, let alone resolved. This is particularly the case when parties are led (at least implicitly) to believe that the process of resolution is about the relationship, rather than about (for example) their possessions. It is less problematic when the parties explicitly understand that they are not dealing with the relationship conflicts (which they may or may not wish to deal with on some future occasion) but only about practical matters related to the division of property.

However, even in such cases (which are, in Burton's terms, the settlement of disputes rather than the resolution of conflicts), for the agreements to be workable the parties need to reflect on and take account of the underlying, often highly emotionally charged, conflict that remains unaddressed. If two people, who previously had a highly positive emotional relationship, now have a highly negative emotional relationship, how can they work effectively together to implement agreements that require some form of ongoing relationship (for example, in regard to custody and access to children after a marital breakdown)? Is it realistic (as opposed to idealistic) to expect them to be able to separate the implementation of the resolved conflict (for example, an agreement about payment of maintenance and access to children) from the (probably much more personally important) unresolved conflict arising from the breakdown of their relationship? In most cases, it is not. An endless series of disputes often arises as a manifestation of the underlying unresolved conflict.

The conflict

The definition of the conflict needs to be carefully undertaken: to say that the problem is 'You swindled me', 'Your workmanship is shoddy', or 'Your company cheated me' will more likely provoke defence and argument than agreement. The agreement on the conflict should be phrased in neutral, objective terms: 'I

was told my car would be repaired by four o' clock and it isn't' rather than 'Your shoddy workmanship means my car isn't ready'. The first description can be examined objectively:
- Was I told my car would be repaired by four o'clock?
- Has my car been repaired by four o'clock?

The conflict—'The car was not repaired at the time I required it'—can then be agreed on and dealt with.

The agreement regarding the conflict should be a statement of fact or personal feeling, not phrased as an accusation or charge. This involves the principles of effective communication considered in chapter 3—for example, 'The Multi-galactic Company wants to build a smelter in Coastville; some local residents object', rather than 'Your multinational capitalist conglomerate wants to vandalise the environment, destroy our beautiful area, and pollute the coast, and everyone here is opposed to it'.

The conflict should also be defined, as far as possible, in terms that presuppose a possible resolution. That is, from the description of the conflict, it should be possible to see what might be done to resolve it—for example, 'My car was not repaired by four o'clock. I had to attend a meeting at half past four, and therefore had to take a taxi to and from the meeting'. Conflicts that are not defined in what might be called 'resolvable terms' often lead to endless, and unproductive, discussion (or argument).

Many of the concerns and anxieties about the conflict will come out during the conflict resolution process, but they are about the conflict, and are likely to be highly contentious. For example, in case of the smelter being built outside the town, the concerns may include whether or not the smelter will pollute, and what percentage of residents actually object. Some concerns can be objectively assessed; others can be the subject of specific agreements about appropriate means of evaluation. For example, if the question of the percentage of residents who object to the smelter is an important issue, it should be dealt with not by repetitively disputing contrary claims ('The majority object '; 'No, they don't'; 'Yes, they do'; 'No, they don't') but by agreeing on a process whereby the factual question can be determined.

Problems of facts need to be distinguished from problems of feelings; once again, clear thinking and assertiveness are key skills here. The conflict may arise from a feeling ('I feel upset when you come home late without letting me know') rather than a fact ('You come home late without letting me know, and you know that this upsets me'). Where negative emotions are strong, attributions of deliberate intent and even malice are common, but it is most helpful if the conflict is defined to avoid terms that imply 'guilt'. Most people, when accused, immediately attempt to defend themselves; what the subject of the complaint hears is 'attack', rather than the substance of the statement. The response is to the style, rather than to the content. If the content can be presented in a non-accusatory style, it is much more likely to be heard and understood.

It is necessary that the participants agree on how the resolution of the conflict will be approached. This includes agreement on time-frame, location, participants, time, place, degree of formality, presence of third party, agenda, and rules (for example, about interruptions or breaks). Obviously, these factors are rarely worked through as a formal agenda, and may be dealt with indirectly.

Disclosing perceptions

It is important to consider the effect that perceptions or interpretations have on feelings. For example, is the problem late home-coming, or is it how the late home-coming affects me? Is there anything objectively problematical about the late home-coming? Was it late arrival or the fact that I had not been informed in advance that upset me? That the conflict is about feelings does not make it any less real or important. Particularly in close relationships, feelings are almost always more important than facts. Feelings and perceptions need to be presented as feelings and perceptions, however, rather than (as often happens) being disguised as facts. Misrepresenting feelings or perceptions as facts usually occurs when a person believes that her or his feelings are inappropriate or likely to be demeaned, or that personal emotional needs should not be admitted.

One of the keys of the conflict resolution is that of enabling the participants to understand each other—not simply what each person claims, but what each believes happened and how each feels about it. Once again, it is necessary to distinguish the facts from the feelings, to recognise that both are important, and indeed to acknowledge that feelings and perceptions are often more important, although participants are usually less comfortable talking about them.

It is useful to have the parties express their perceptions of what has happened, and how they feel about it. This needs to be done without interruption or evaluation; only real questions of clarification need be asked. It is valuable if the rules of this part of the process are spelt out explicitly and enforced—for example, no accusations, attacks, name-calling, blaming, or 'dumping'. If there is a third party, this is one of her or his important roles.

This stage requires both effective communication and assertiveness (being able to express feelings and perceptions) and active listening (being willing and able to listen to and hear what the other participant is saying). The principles outlined in chapter 3 need to be applied with care and skill. Often in a situation of conflict, people are not willing to say what they mean, to listen to the other (particularly if they do not like what is being said), or to make sure that they understand what they are hearing.

Active, supportive listening is essential: each participant must actively try to understand the perceptions and feelings of the other. This is not done with accusations. Each participant needs to understand what the other perceives and feels; he or she should not accuse or have to face accusations of being irrational or mistaken in their feelings.

Understanding the other does not mean agreeing with, approving of, or even accepting what he or she says. This often needs to be made explicit before any mutual disclosure. It is often assumed that even allowing another person to make statements without interrupting, arguing, or rejecting them is some form of tacit agreement. Where third parties are involved in resolution processes, they need to assist the participants to understand that this is not the case. The aim is understanding; this may involve understanding but still rejecting, disagreeing with, or disapproving of what is being said. The process is intended to enable each party to understand how the other perceived and felt about the situation. If done effectively, this can have a powerful diffusing effect on the negative emotions involved in some conflicts. It is important to understand that the other party may not have acted out of wilful malice and deliberate intention to cause distress (which is commonly an initial assumption) but because, given the way he or she saw the situation, this behaviour seemed logical. Such an understanding can assist in reducing the level of hostility, even if such perceptions are rejected and the behaviour is still believed to have been wrong.

Take the example of late home-coming: if the person who came home late (without telephoning in advance to advise that this was likely) is understood to have behaved that way because he or she did not believe it was necessary to telephone unless the delay was more than an hour, the allegation that it was done deliberately to cause anxiety, or was indicative of indifference to the other, will be diffused. It may be that the conflict is then identified as being based (as are many conflicts in interpersonal relationships) in assumptions about rules. If one party's rule is 'If you are going to be more than twenty minutes late, you should telephone' and the other party's rule is 'If you are going to be more than an hour late, you should telephone', the potential for repeated conflict remains until both parties explicitly discuss this particular rule in their relationship.

Responding

Each party needs an opportunity to respond (but preferably without counter-accusation or argument) to the perceptions of the other. This should not be in terms of defence, denial, and counter-allegation. Where the conflict has been based almost entirely on misunderstanding or misinterpretation, an exchange of perceptions may actually resolve it.

One participant, having heard the perceptions and feelings of the other, needs to respond with her or his own perceptions and feelings. Conflict is rarely resolved if there is no response from the other side: a detached indifference to what the other is saying suggests (although it need not mean) an indifference to the conflict (and therefore to the relationship between them). The response does not have to be agreement; disagreement need not be argument. Once again, assertive communication, involving clear expressions of personal belief and feeling, is required rather than accusations or defences. If one person feels that he or she is being accused of something, the normal reaction is defence or counter-attack; it is more difficult to respond effectively.

The responding phase should include as much clarification of, and agreement on, the facts of the conflict as possible. Those matters on which the parties agree should be clearly identified, as should those on which they disagree. Resolution does not depend on agreement on all (or, indeed, of any) the facts for resolution.

Approaches to conflict resolution that seek to avoid identification of disagreements and to maximise—even to exaggerate—the extent of agreements can be effective in the production of short-term settlements. This is, to some extent, a dishonest process. It relies on persuading the parties that they agree on most things, or on all the important things, and that their disagreements are of minimal importance. It is always easy to fabricate apparent agreements through the use of vague and artificially positive language. 'We all agree that we want things to be better between us' is a statement that is unlikely to produce dissent (in part because expressing disagreement may be seen to be unacceptable), but which is so vague as to be largely meaningless. The parties are in conflict, not because of the points on which they agree, but because of those on which they disagree. Although agreements should be precisely identified, they must now be allowed to mask disagreements.

It should also be recognised that people can and do live and work together with varying degrees of disagreement. It is sometimes necessary for a third party in conflict resolution to remind the parties of this obvious, but often over-looked, fact. If the assumption is either that there will be agreement on absolutely everything, or that the conflict cannot be resolved, it is almost certain that real resolution will not be possible. The extent to which disagreement can be accepted should be explored. Are there matters on which agreement is essential for the resolution of the conflict and for effective working relationships in the future? It is rare that every element in a conflict requires such agreement.

Objectives

Objectives are different from, but related to, purpose. The objectives will be defined for a meeting or for a part of the process: what it is that the parties need to do, and what limits or boundaries apply (for example, 'We want to go on living together' or 'We want to go on working together'). Objectives should be specific, practical, and achievable. It is often useful to include relatively unimportant and basic objectives that can be easily met: this promotes a sense of collaboration and mutual achievement. If there is only one objective, achieving it may seem impossible; if there are ten, achieving four or five of them (even if they are relatively easy) gives a sense of accomplishment, which encourages a sense of being able to achieve the other objectives.

Collaboration in accomplishing a number of objectives promotes a sense of control, mutual achievement, and success. A large, potentially overwhelming conflict should be divided into a number of small parts arranged in a sequence, preferably from least to most difficult. This process, called 'fractionating', assists resolution by presenting the conflict in the form of a number of more manageable segments. For example, the objective 'We agree to save our relationship' is very difficult to work on: it may mean many different things to each party, and success or failure is likely to be very difficult to define. If the problem with the relationship is defined in a series of more specific terms, it is more likely to lead to a sequence of practical steps towards resolution.

One major difficulty in conflict resolution is the assumption by many people that a situation of conflict can only be resolved in three ways: win–lose, lose–win, and compromise (which is usually understood to be lose–lose). The assumption that there are two options for resolution—one for each party—traps the participants into 'fight-or-submit' modes rather than a 'resolve' mode. Discovering that there are numerous options, including (but not limited to) those originally put by the participants, empowers people to explore problem solving rather than maintaining their positions. In reality, almost all problems, disputes, and conflicts are dealt with by varying degrees of compromise. This does not usually involve 'losing' in any significant sense, but recognising that in conflicts, as in most of life, it is necessary to adjust to reality.

Brainstorming to explore options

Probably the most effective means of identifying options or possible solutions is through 'brainstorming'—without evaluation, argument, or criticism—to produce a list of possibilities (including the 'impossible' or improbable). What are all the options? Brainstorming not only encourages the discovery of options, but also promotes communication and understanding between the participants, and the sense of collaborative problem solving. Better options are usually identified through collaborative and creative discussion than by an individual participant trying to find solutions separately and then presenting them to the other.

During brainstorming, no evaluation or assessment should occur: it is a simple listing (preferably in writing, visible to the participants) of every option that can be considered, including those that may be inherently unlikely—there are some psychological benefits to suggesting a few crazy proposals as well. Brainstorming often acquires an intriguing momentum, and after an initial hesitation—caused by an assumption that there are only a few options—participants usually begin to discover possibilities. The process positively promotes communication and collaboration.

There are very, very few conflicts in which options are severely restricted: any suggestion that there are only one or two options needs to be examined in case this perception results from rigid, uncritical, and uncreative assumptions about the situation. If the participants can find no options, a skilful facilitator or mediator should be able to offer some that are imaginative. However, the third party needs to be very cautious in presenting options: they will often be taken up by the parties with a sense of relief that someone else (possibly identified as 'an expert') has come up with the solution. If the parties have reached a point where they really cannot see multiple options, a third party might suggest several at once (rather than just one), or suggest options that are inherently improbable or known to be unacceptable to both parties.

Option evaluation

Once the options have been recorded (and this does not formally end the option-generation process, as new options are often raised later during the process), the list should be worked through to evaluate the options in terms of how effectively they meet the objectives—not according to personalities, history, or politics. Evaluation is in terms of problem solving, not of winning, point-scoring, or political advantage. This may, of course, be difficult for some participants, and requires some change to the normal mode of thinking. It presupposes that at the beginning the participants have actually agreed (as opposed to appearing to have agreed) that they want to resolve the conflict.

In a first round, options can be eliminated that are mutually agreed to be potentially ineffective, and others can be identified by either or both of the participants as realistic and desirable options. In a second round, the participants can look at those options on which they differ, explaining why, and seeking agreement. New options may emerge during this process and should simply be added to the list. This stage will usually end up with two or three options that the participants agree could resolve the conflict. Once again, it is important that the participants select options on the basis of their effectiveness in resolving the conflict, not because of vested interests in their selection.

Option selection

After assessment, the participants should choose the option that they jointly prefer. This may involve negotiation, including negotiation on the description and terms of the preferred option. The aim, however, is consensus in terms of the interests of the parties. This is almost always going to include projection— that is, the carrying out of some sort of cost–benefit analysis, either jointly and openly, or by each of the participants privately. It is useful for the participants either to work together through the chosen option or, if there is a difference between them, to look at possible and probable outcomes, and at the costs and benefits, of two or more options in order to facilitate analysis of the relative advantages and disadvantages of each. The 'if . . . then . . . ' process can be applied—'If we select this option, then . . . '—and an assessment made of the advantages and disadvantages in terms of resolving the conflict (once again, this needs to be emphasised). Projection often takes the form, whether consciously or unconsciously, of personal cost–benefit analysis—'If I agree to this, it will look as if I have given in, then . . . '—rather than evaluating the effectiveness of the option in achieving a resolution.

Negotiation may be an important part of these stages, either in terms of which option is adopted or in terms of how it is defined. Negotiation is most effectively undertaken by talking of possibilities and proposals in language that is tentative, using words such as 'possibly', 'perhaps', 'could', and 'might'.

The participants need to select a preferred solution, and to agree on it in precise terms. Each participant must clearly understand what the other means by 'the solution'. It is useful to have this in writing, although not necessarily in the form of a legal agreement. Future conflict will arise if each participant has a different perception of what was agreed or what the other meant. Precision in agreement may sound pedantic, but it is essential. If something is to be done, it must be specified when, by whom, and how it is to be done; 'I'll do something about that some time' is not a helpful response. Third parties often find that their real work begins here. The parties have reached an agreement and may feel that the matter is now concluded. They may feel a sense of relief, and a sense of exhaustion, that encourages them to hope that the process is concluded. They have, after all, reached an agreement. But they must now be guided to work through a precise and detailed identification of what the agreement means in practice.

Implementation

Implementation of the solution should be planned: Who will do what? How? When? Where? And with what resources? When will the implementation be reviewed? What will be taken to mean success, and what to mean failure? In-built standards of success and failure are an important means of facilitating subsequent evaluation. Any plan for implementation must include a definite time-frame and, if possible, incorporate a proposal to review.

Implementation can very usefully involve a trial period during which both parties try out an option and then review and evaluate it; this goal is often achievable when what is seen to be a final, immutable decision is not. Participants need to understand and accept that they can return to further discussion and resolution in the future.

The final decision may be committed to writing, and may even be in the form of a legally binding contract. It is essential that both parties clearly and precisely understand what has been agreed, what they are required to do, and what they can expect from the other party. The proposed solution, obviously, must then be put into effect.

Evaluation, review, and revision

The implementation and the solution should be evaluated and reviewed, either at a prearranged time or when the things agreed to have been accomplished— for example, 'We'll meet again at the same time next week' or 'We'll meet again when the next account arrives'. The evaluation and review will consider whether the proposal was implemented effectively, and whether the implemen-tation has worked. If it has not, reasons should be identified. If the proposed solution is not working, the participants should go back to looking at options again, or review the implementation and revise it.

If the resolution process has been successful, the fact that the solution did not work to the participants' satisfaction will not necessarily mean a breakdown in relations: the process has incorporated review, revision, and re-implementa-tion mechanisms, and therefore incorporates a means of solving problems. The review and evaluation may lead to revision and renegotiation. Aspects of the solution may require fine-tuning, or one or other of the participants may have discovered problems. It is important that problems are discussed and resolved; otherwise the solution may appear to fail because one aspect of implementation fails. The participants need to discuss not only how effective they believe the solution to be, but also how they feel about the situation.

Resolution

It is essential that a defined test for resolution be developed, and that, at some point, the parties agree that resolution has occurred and that the matter has now been resolved. This does not mean that a similar problem may not arise again, but unlike the original issue, it will not be allowed to go on indefinitely. The participants need to define at what point they will accept that the present conflict has been resolved. If this is not done, the conflict can be, as it were, recycled over and over again.

Agreements

Agreements between the participants can be formal or informal, written or oral. The more complex the agreement, the more hostile the participants, and the less trust there is in their relationship, the more important it is that the agreement be written, whether it is in the form of a legal contract or not. If there is a written statement, of which both participants have copies and on which they have agreed, it is more difficult for misunderstanding or arguments to arise about what was, or was not, agreed. Any written agreement should be precise, specific, and detailed—for example, 'ABC Pty Ltd will on Tuesday 2 March, between 9.00 a.m. and 4.00 p.m., replace the rear fender of Mr Smith's motor vehicle registra-tion XZY 123 with a fender identical to that presently on the vehicle, and will meet all costs involved, except the amount of $50, which Mr Smith will pay when he collects his repaired vehicle'. Participants considering signing docu-ments that may be legally binding should take legal advice before doing so.

The process outlined in this chapter generally applies regardless of whether the parties to a conflict are working collaboratively on its resolution or using a mediator to assist the process. It is not generally followed in arbitration. The stages in the process provide a useful checklist for an effective resolution. It is

---

Case study 8

Dale and Peter jointly purchased an expensive sports car; before buying the car, they had worked out a fairly complicated written agreement outlining when each would be able to use the car. This agreement is now clearly not working. Each often finds that the car is available when it is not convenient, and not available when required. They have had disagreements over the costs of repairs and maintenance, each arguing that the other must bear more than half the cost of some work. They have also argued about the care of the car: Dale believes such an expensive car should be professionally washed and polished with the cost shared equally, while Peter wants them to take turns in washing and polishing. Neither wants to sell the car, since neither can really afford another.

Having analysed this conflict, outline in detail the process that should be followed in attempting resolution.

---

not, as was emphasised at the beginning of this chapter, a magical formula that brings about resolution. It will need adjustment and modification to meet the specific needs of particular people in particular conflicts. And even then, problems and obstructions can arise. Some of the common problems in the smooth flow of the process are considered in chapter 10.

9 Practical Conflict Resolution Skills

Conflict resolution essentially involves a set of practical skills; it must work in practice if it is to have any real value. The skills involved are not esoteric or complex; they are basic intellectual and interpersonal skills that everyone possesses, but that are often largely underdeveloped and unapplied. Particularly in situations of great personal importance or strong emotions, most people lose the ability consciously to apply skills that they possess. It is thus easier to see what skills ought to be applied by other people in dealing with their conflicts than it is to identify and apply those skills in your own conflicts.

There are many basic skills that can and should be applied in the resolution of conflict. A range of basic psychological principles can be used to help facilitate conflict resolution. They include skills that assist individuals to understand themselves, to understand others, and to understand interpersonal relations, and skills that enhance the individual's ability to overcome problems in interpersonal relations.

Conflict analysis

Analysis and planning—involving a consideration of a range of psychological issues—before attempting conflict resolution will increase the effectiveness of the process. Similarly, being conscious throughout the process of what is happening will keep it flowing productively. Conflict resolution, like listening, is not a passive process: simply being there is not enough. Active, conscious participation is necessary. This requires the individual to remain aware of her or his own behaviour and that of others, as well as any problems and difficulties that may be obstructing the process, either within or between the participants. This awareness should promote resolution, not victory. 'Winning through intimidation' (as the title of one American book puts it), or through the use of other psychological tactics designed to dominate others, should not be the intention. The rejection of such methods is less on ethical than practical grounds. Intimidation, coercion, manipulation, and dishonest persuasion, however effective they can sometimes be in the short term, are rarely effective in resolving conflict in the long term, and often have destructive consequences.

Even where conflict is nominally between groups, corporations, or nations, it will be acted out in the behaviour of individuals. Therefore a basic understanding of interpersonal behaviour, about which there are many theories, is essential in conflict resolution. Michael Argyle's *The Psychology of Interpersonal Behaviour* (1975) is particularly useful in providing a basic knowledge. It is necessary, however, to be wary of popular studies that claim to provide simple keys to totally understanding, controlling, or dominating other people. The psychological and sociological study of human behaviour is a complex area, from which simple, universal rules can rarely be derived.

The key areas of psychology that are directly relevant to conflict resolution include cognition, affect, motivation, perception, human needs, and cognitive dissonance. Those seeking to develop effective conflict resolution skills should undertake at least some basic reading in these areas.

Just as analysis should be undertaken before attempting conflict resolution, so it should be continued throughout the process. Analysing and reflecting on the behaviour (including verbal and non-verbal) of the participants is important. The analysis should be concerned with trying to understand why people are behaving in a particular way, rather than judging their behaviour. Understanding promotes empathy, which in turn promotes effective communication and response. It will also help in identifying and understanding (and often in meeting) needs, pressures, and projections.

Simply responding to the behaviour (for example, responding to an attack with a defence, becoming angry in the face of anger, or becoming impatient with procrastination), however understandable, is generally unhelpful. Action and reaction can go on indefinitely without any creative resolution, and often with a predictable escalation of the conflict. The 'she/he hit me first' approach to conflict does not promote resolution, but incites escalation, recrimination, and breakdowns in communication. 'Why did she/he hit me?' is the question to be asked, and the further question ought to be 'How can I most effectively respond?'

By deliberately taking an analytical approach, a degree of objectivity and rationality can be attained that is otherwise often missing, particularly in highly emotionally charged conflicts. If the aim is resolution, the method is positive and creative action, not emotional reaction. That is not to say that the expression of feelings, even strong and negative feelings, is an undesirable thing; emotion, however, needs to be balanced with reason, and if the emotion is so overwhelming that no rational response is possible, it is better to defer the attempt at resolution. The presence of a third person, who is essentially concerned with the process of resolution, can assist in highly charged emotional situations by allowing the participants to express themselves freely while keeping them moving towards a goal that might otherwise be lost in distress and turmoil.

The ability to predict behaviour is obviously a useful element in conflict resolution, but the accuracy of such prediction should not be exaggerated. Probably the most effective approach is to identify needs and to consider a variety of possible behavioural outcomes, rather than attempting to apply simplistic rules about what people must and will do. Human beings are often unpredictable, and proceeding in attempts at conflict resolution on the assumption that a person will inevitably respond in a particular way is likely to be ineffective. Simplistic (and often pseudo-scientific) models for predicting how people will behave and what their behaviour means should be avoided; they simply do not work in practice.

Motivation

Appropriate and sufficient motivation is essential for effective conflict resolution. Motivation to win is not motivation to resolve, the latter being more difficult to develop. Motivation does not mean optimism or a positive sense of knowing how a conflict can be resolved. It does, however, mean both willingness and a degree of energetic commitment to the attempt to bring about resolution. Despair, helplessness, disempowerment, the desire for revenge or punishment, and anger are usually feelings that exclude motivation to attempt resolution; they are also feelings very commonly found in parties to a conflict, particularly where the conflict is highly emotionally charged or has continued for a long time.

Not only is it necessary to try positively to motivate participants, but it is also important to address and to attempt to overcome any negative feelings that may obstruct participation in resolution. Openly discussing feelings can assist in this, as can encouraging the other participant to recognise that feelings of hopelessness and helplessness, no less than anger or the desire for revenge, are common and can be overcome. There are many psychological theories of motivation, and consideration of some basic texts on the psychology of motivation will help to identify the key issues.

Human needs theory

Human needs theory has a particular relevance to motivation in conflict resolution. Abraham Maslow (1987) suggested that all human beings have common needs, and that human needs fall into a hierarchy: at the top are self-actualising, altruistic needs (such as self-esteem); below these are social needs (such as affiliation and affection), and at the base of the hierarchy are safety and security needs (such as shelter, clothing, and warmth), as well as survival needs (such as water, food, and air). Maslow suggests that, generally, each level of need—from survival up—has to be met before the next level can be met. This principle has been subject to questioning, but in conflict resolution, if basic survival needs are threatened (for example, if there is a threat of dismissal from employment), it will usually be pointless to try to deal with social needs until the survival needs are resolved.

Two participants in a conflict may be dealing with different levels of need: the employer may be concerned with self-esteem, while the threatened employee is concerned with survival. The clear identification and recognition of the needs of all the participants in a conflict provide a basis for resolution, and for the motivation of the participants to work towards that resolution.

William Glasser and Victor Frankl also agree that all behaviour is an attempt to meet certain basic needs: biological, emotional, and social. Glasser (1985) suggests that identifying the particular needs of the particular individual in the particular situation is the key to understanding behaviour, and is therefore the key to motivation. It is important to recognise that *needs* are not necessarily the same as *demands*, and to note that sometimes a real need will be presented in an indirect way. Individuals may express a demand or a desire for something other than a real need, either because they do not believe it is appropriate or acceptable to express the real need, or because they do not believe it is possible to have the real need met. For example, many employees may have difficulty expressing a need for recognition, acceptance, and respect in employment, and may therefore make demands for more money and improved conditions. Tangible demands are often easier to express than intangible, but often more important, needs. However, many surveys of what employees see as their primary needs in the workplace relate to intangibles (such as recognition, creativity, and work satisfaction) rather than to tangible rewards (such as money).

It is necessary to understand individuals' perceptions of their world and of their needs in order to motivate them to participate in the conflict resolution process by directing the process towards meeting those needs. The real question (for a participant or a mediator) is: what are the real needs of the participants, and how can the process be directed towards demonstrating the possibility of meeting (at least the most important of) those needs, thereby motivating the participants to become involved most effectively?

Perceptions and cognition

Motivation is related to perceptions of the conflict resolution process: if a participant feels powerless, does not trust the process, or does not believe the conflict can be resolved, he or she will not be motivated to work for resolution.

An understanding of cognition is also important in conflict and conflict resolution: cognition refers to the way in which individuals perceive the world, themselves, and the conflict, and how they think about these things. This perception may or may not relate closely to 'reality' or to the world as perceived by other. Thus, behaviour interpreted as friendly and supportive by one person may be perceived to be hostile and threatening by another. Perception is much more important in conflict and conflict resolution than what is sometimes called 'objective reality'. People tend to deal with the world as they perceive it; conflict exists when they perceive it to exist regardless of, and in some cases despite, the objective situation. Trying to prove that the perception is mistaken is usually counterproductive (although the discovery that the perception is not the reality may be a by-product of resolution).

Cognition refers both to thinking about a specific situation (for example, a particular conflict) and to thinking processes generally (for example, how an individual thinks about relationships with others). Considering how the participants to a conflict perceive the world, themselves, each other, and the conflict is very helpful, not only in being able to motivate them towards resolution, but also in bringing about resolution. Conflicts begin in the mind; they start with thoughts, and these thoughts may be rational or irrational, and based on facts or on misinterpretation, insufficient data, or poor judgment. Quite often, thinking creates the conflict in the mind of one participant before it is acted out or communicated to the other.

One helpful, and visual, technique for identifying different perceptions is life-space mapping. This involves taking a defined area—for example, a circle—and having each party to a conflict divide it up according to her or his perceptions of the relative importance of its different aspects. For example, a workplace conflict may involve differential perceptions of the relative impor- tance of different duties in a given position. If the position involves six duties, a manager and an employee may perceive their importance (and thus the priority, and the amount of time, energy, and resources that will be given to each) differ- ently. Unless the differential perceptions of the position, and the relative importance of each duty, has been explicitly discussed, conflicts are likely to arise over the way in which specific tasks related to each duty are approached. The real conflict is probably less about any given task than about the way in which the position is perceived.

Thinking skills

Few people receive any training in thinking; it is usually assumed that it is a skill, like listening, that occurs naturally and either requires no training or cannot respond to training. Most people do not think as effectively and effi- ciently as they might, and in approaching conflict resolution, it is a good idea to undertake some work on thinking processes. A number of challenging, enter- taining, and well-written books are available in this area, and many include exercises and games that assist in the development of innovative and more effective thinking. Several of these are listed in the resource guide; since differ- ent works take different approaches, it is a good idea to explore a number of them to find the one or two that have particular personal appeal and relevance. Thinking for conflict resolution will ideally be rational, analytical, innovative, flexible, creative, and problem-solving.

Some theorists, most notably Albert Ellis (who developed Rational Emotive Therapy, or RET), have argued that human beings are primarily rational, think- ing organisms, and that irrational thinking is the cause of most emotional distress and conflict. Ellis (1989) suggests that if the thinking process is re- ordered, the emotional distress or conflict will diminish. He notes a number of common irrational values or beliefs that can lead to neurosis or conflict: for example, the belief that there is a right or perfect solution for every problem, and that it must be found or the results will be catastrophic. This belief can have dire consequences for any attempt at conflict resolution, since it presupposes only one solution, and predicts disaster if any other is attempted. Throughout his works, Ellis lists other common irrational beliefs, and these should also be considered since they often cause problems in conflict and conflict resolution. Even though they may readily be identified as irrational and unrealistic, they still have powerful effects (Ellis 1989).

The sort of rigid 'simple rule' thinking to which Ellis refers must be addressed in conflict resolution, not so much in the strong confrontation that characterises RET, as with more gentle and tentative questioning, in order to present the participant with the notion that, for example, there may be multiple options, and that any one of a number of them could be adopted for a trial period without disaster. Noting and questioning irrational beliefs can be more helpful in conflict resolution than direct confrontation, although confrontation is sometimes an appropriate strategy (Ellis 1989; Grieger & Boyd 1980).

Jay Folberg and Alison Taylor (1988) note the importance of linking thought (cognition), feeling (affect), and behaviour in conflict resolution. It is important to identify the behaviour, affect, and cognition of all participants to a conflict: what each did (behaviour), what each thought (cognition), and what each felt (affect). It is often very useful to discuss all three in the conflict resolution process: What happened? What did you think about it? How did you feel about it? This process also helps to identify the relationships between behaviour, thought, and feeling, for example, in order to understand why particular behaviour led to a particular feeling, rather than assuming a causal connection. Encouraging parties to a conflict to discuss which of their thoughts led to which of their feelings has a positive role in enabling understanding both of self and of others.

Empathy

Empathy is essential in conflict resolution. It must be distinguished from apathy and sympathy. Apathy is sometimes represented as professional detachment, but is really lack of interest. Sympathy involves a degree of committed identification, which usually hinders effective conflict resolution. The participants in conflict resolution need to be able to understand the feelings of the other parties, as does any mediator: they need to be able to recognise, to be aware of, and to be able to identify with those feelings. It is not a matter of saying 'I can understand that you're angry', but of being able to understand the anger, not in the critical sense of saying 'Well, if I were you, I wouldn't be so emotional', but of trying to share the feelings, without necessarily accepting that the feelings are right or rational or justified. Empathy does not depend on agreeing with or approving of the behaviour of the other person; in fact, it may be concluded that the person's response is irrational and unjustified and that her or his behaviour is wrong or inappropriate. It is important, however, to be able to understand how the other person feels.

Empathy is not simply a form of altruism: it is also a skill that assists in conflict resolution by allowing the situation to be seen from the other party's perspective. For example, having some idea of how others are feeling and think-

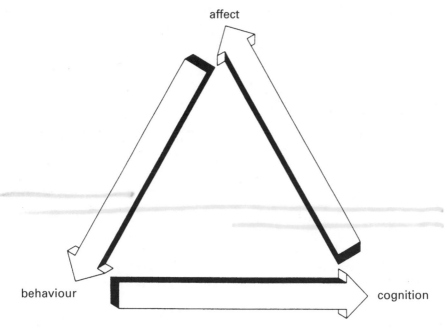

Figure 9.1   Factors in the conflict resolution process

ing makes it easier to present options and approaches that will meet their needs and encourage them to view resolution as possible. It is to the advantage of participants in conflict resolution to be able to have more than one perspective.

Self-disclosure

If conflict resolution begins with communication, it also requires the promotion of self-disclosure to make communication effective. Self-disclosure is promoted by all the communication skills discussed in chapter 3. It requires active listening, encouraging questioning, an atmosphere of trust and security, positive rather than negative responses, empathy, and positive reinforcement. Encouraging self-disclosure in one person is facilitated by self-disclosure by the other; sharing perceptions is more effective than seeking to force disclosure.

Conflict and conflict resolution are very much about the interpretation of words and behaviour: what people did and said, or did not do and say, is very often at the centre of disagreement. Other people's behaviour needs to be interpreted with care. Esoteric systems of interpretation—for example, some of the more rigid schools of body language ('folding your arms means you are being hostile')—are unlikely to be helpful.

Conflict resolution and counselling

Although conflict resolution is not counselling, and *vice versa*, there are situations in which both approaches can benefit from, or even demand, the skills of the other. Certainly, the mediator will often find it necessary to provide what amounts to counselling to assist the conflict resolution process; this is beneficial and healthy provided that it does not become the primary role of the mediator.

There is a difference between internal (intrapsychic or intrapersonal) conflict and interpersonal conflict. Conflict resolution is essentially concerned with the latter, while counselling (like psychology and psychotherapy) can be applied to both, but is primarily concerned with the former. Internal conflict can both be caused by and cause interpersonal conflict. Sometimes the causal flow is not clearly understood by the individual: is the inner conflict the cause or the product of external conflict? Is it necessary first to resolve the inner conflict before approaching the external conflict, or must the external conflict be dealt with first? In different cases, the relationship between inner and outer conflict will vary: in some, interpersonal conflict is clearly the result of inner conflict, while in others the inner conflict is the result of interpersonal conflict.

Role-play and games

Conflict can be played out not only in 'real life', where it often tends to be spontaneous, unplanned, and undesirable (partly because of the element of shock and unpreparedness), but also in hypothetical situations. Such situations include fiction, drama (including television drama), and moral-dilemma exercises. Conflict can be worked through in role-playing, games, case studies, and simulations; these have many advantages over merely considering conflict in the abstract. They enable participants to play through conflict situations, to explore options for behaviour, to consider issues of values and ethics, and to examine— in a non-threatening situation—the actions, language, and feelings of themselves and others. They can also provide some experience that relates to real life conflict, both through playing out conflicts that are similar to those being experienced in reality and through role-playing the real conflicts.

Some traditional games (for example, chess) are based on conflicts in which strategy, analysis, planning, and the ability to predict an opponent's actions are important elements in successful playing. Essentially, games, role-plays, and simulations all involve allowing participants to take part in the acting out of a conflict situation with varying degrees of proximity to reality, with maximum security and minimum personal discomfort, and with the opportunity for self-analysis and analysis of others. They also provide an opportunity for feedback from other participants and (in some cases) from professional trainers. In all approaches, there are both experiential learning components and personal sensitising and desensitising components.

Roles

Everyone plays different roles all the time; in everyday life, throughout careers, and throughout personal life, individuals will play a multiplicity of different, even conflicting, roles. Sometimes people choose roles, and sometimes roles are imposed on them. Some roles are very clearly defined (for example, some employment positions, which may have written duty statements and clear rules of behaviour), while others are only vaguely defined (for example, the role of the consumer). Some roles may be perceived differently by different people. For example, if a patient and a physician have different views of the role that each has and how it should be played out, there is likely to be conflict, just as there is if husband and wife, teacher and student, or consumer and supplier perceive their roles differently. Some roles are general (for example, that of parent) and others are highly specific (for example, the father of a particular child).

Some roles have imprecise definitions because they lack clear places in the social structure—step-parents are a classic example of this. Many adults and children face conflict over a lack of understanding of just what the roles are; for example, what are the limits of a step-father's power in relation to a step-child? Some roles change over time; for example, the role of parent changes as the child grows up (and the child's role changes also), and there is often conflict if parties in a reciprocal role relationship do not agree on the nature and rate of change. Some roles are part of reciprocal relationships: husband and wife, parent and child, employer and employee, doctor and patient. Conflict often arises in these relationships if there is disagreement on the nature of the roles, how they should be acted out, how they interrelate, and how they change. Conflict as a result of role disagreement is very common: it includes a large proportion of family and relationship conflict, and of generational (particularly cross-cultural generational) conflict.

Roles often assume slightly different characteristics in relationships, and these differences often pertain to status, power, deference, and precedence. The personal characters of the role-players affect the roles and their relationship. There is both role or positional power and personal power, and it is personal power that tends to be the most important.

Culture generally defines behaviour in terms of what is appropriate to particular roles—a father's behaviour as distinct from a mother's, for example. Different cultures may define the same roles differently, and conflict can result in cross-cultural interactions when parties behave according to different cultural definitions. Society's expectations and rules change over time, but usually slowly (for example, the role of the 'house-husband'). Role confusion or conflict can occur when a person has two discrepant roles—for example, a parent who is also a teacher of her or his own child. One role can clash with another—for example, the public service 'whistle-blower' who believes that the role of concerned citizen takes precedence over that of public servant loyal to the department.

Roles from one context can also be carried over (inappropriately) into different situations—for example, the army officer who continues to play the role of Colonel at home or, for that matter, the father who plays a paternal role when acting as a Colonel in the army. Conflict can arise if a person adopts the characteristics and behaviour appropriate to and assumed in one role while holding another—for example, when a junior clerk assumes the role characteristics of the managing director.

Rules about roles are very rarely formally defined in any detail. The person who takes up a new role (for example, the woman who becomes a wife, the man who becomes a father, or the employee promoted to manager) will have some explicit rules to follow, but there exists a vast number of unwritten, informal, often unconscious rules about role behaviour. Most of these are learnt by observing others. Media portrayals of particular roles can be influential in defining the rules applying to them.

Role-play

Although most of the roles that people play are not deliberately taken on and thought about, it is possible, for the purposes of expanding one's experiences and learning new skills, to consciously assume roles that may not be held in the external world. Role-playing can be particularly useful in developing skills associated with conflict resolution (for example, to help communication or listening or assertion). It can also assist in training for conflict resolution (for example, role-playing the resolution of personally relevant conflicts) and in preparation for conflict resolution (for example, role-playing elements of a specific conflict in which an individual is involved). Role-playing can also be a valuable part of the conflict resolution process (for instance, having parties to a conflict role-play elements of the conflict, including playing opposite roles).

Very simply, role-play involves individuals imagining that they are another person, or themselves, in a particular situation, and behaving (trying to think, feel, speak, and act) as they believe the other person would, or as they would, in that situation. This enables them to gain some experience of the person and/or the situations involved. The role-play may require individuals to play another person generally, or to play another person in a specific situation. It can include individuals playing themselves generally or in a specific situation, and can involve one or more people, with varying amounts of preparation, 'props', and scripting. The situations may be simple or complex, short or long, carefully planned or spontaneous, or based on real past experiences, real projected experiences, or wholly imaginary situations.

Role-play can be designed to develop specific skills (for example, active listening), general skills (such as communication), and self-confidence (often by desensitising), or to explore options of style (for instance, opening approaches in initiating discussions). It can help in analysing past situations and in preparing for future situations. Role-playing can both sensitise (for example, by role-playing active listening) and desensitise (for example, by role-playing uncomfortable or threatening situations).

Role-playing is a powerful educational method since it is often highly motivating and enables the individual to gain a breadth of experience that is simply not possible in 'the real world' (for example, by running through the same situation with different approaches, by making mistakes that have no effect, by obtaining ongoing feedback from other participants, and by playing the part of another person). In conflict resolution, role-playing can have the added benefits of allowing the expression of otherwise undisclosed thoughts or feelings. It can help one participant to understand the other by role-playing that person. It also allows participants to play through the conflict, or aspects of it, in a fictional and therefore tentative and less threatening form—in a situation that is supportive and safe. They can desensitise themselves to situations that are perceived to be difficult. Role-play often promotes a sense of being able to participate in resolution by demonstrating the exploration of options in a practical way.

There are, however, disadvantages in role-playing. It can unrealistically simplify complex situations, or it can lead to inner script-writing and promote inflexibility. It may increase sensitivity and discomfort, or develop an inappropriate lack of sensitivity. It can raise unnecessary doubts and fears, or inspire inappropriate overconfidence. Feedback is very important if role-play is to be effective. Solitary role-play probably risks more of the disadvantages since the individual receives no commentary on performance. Role-play is therefore most effective when it involves at least two people, with one role-playing and the other observing, or with both role-playing but then commenting on the experience. If the role-play involves two or more participants, it is particularly helpful if there are one or more observers. This allows the participants to give each other feedback, and for them to receive more objective feedback from a detached observer. Most people are unable to 'see' themselves clearly, and a video tape can sometimes provide an opportunity for them to see and hear how they behave. Even an audio tape of a situation can assist with feedback.

Case studies

Case studies, used as a form of role-play, are particularly useful for training in and preparation for conflict resolution. For example, conflict resolution in a workplace may be enhanced by giving people an opportunity to play through case examples that are either based on past real cases or specifically written to parallel real cases. In many situations, similar or virtually identical conflicts present repeatedly, or the same or similar issues arise in different conflicts. It is possible to prepare case studies based on past experience that draw out these similarities and common qualities, or that focus on the key difficulties and questions. By working through such case studies, both by analysing, planning, and role-playing, participants have an opportunity to work through the key elements of future conflicts, to identify personal and group problems and needs, and to develop necessary skills.

By using actual cases, adjusted for reasons of confidentiality, the actual outcomes can be known: how the matter was worked through and what consequences followed. Participants in a case study can therefore explore alternatives, and can speculate on better strategies and outcomes.

Simulations are a particular form of role-play designed to be as realistic as possible for the specific situation of the participants. For example, this may involve the use of real cases from the particular context, or case studies based on the real situation of the participants. Simulations differ from case studies in the degree of effort put into making them appear realistic, including the amount of background information given to the participants. This enables them to increase skills in a context that is directly and demonstrably related to their needs.

Games

All conflicts can be modelled as games. The advantages of doing this include the desensitising effect of being able to look at the conflict more objectively, with the opportunity to analyse and plan strategy. A game model will usually be used to undertake a number of 'what if' projections: 'If I did this, they could . . . then if they did that, I could . . . '.

Everyone plays roles all the time, as has already been noted. In conflict resolution, it is important to avoid becoming trapped into a fixed and rigid role that does not allow for the flexibility necessary in resolution (for example, always playing the role of 'aggressive demander'). Playing fixed roles is something that some people do generally in all their interpersonal relationships; others may play fixed roles in particular types of situations or in relation to particular people.

In looking at a particular conflict as a game, it can be possible to identify what role (and what style) particular participants take (or are given by others), and what rules are applied. People in situations of conflict can often simply maintain roles and apply rules that are ineffective, or even dysfunctional, without critically analysing whether or not they wish to go on 'playing this game' or participating in the way that has been determined by past experience or prescribed by other people. A recognition that the individual's role (with its accompanying behavioural and, often, cognitive style) is rarely fixed and immutable, and that the rules (that is, prescriptions as to what is or is not done) also depend to a large extent on mutual consent, can empower an individual to break out of rigid patterns of thought and behaviour, and to try (or at least think about trying) something new.

Acceptance of the rules of the game is often uncritical: people will often define their behaviour as being determined by the situation. For example, an individual who says 'He shouted at me and so we had to have an argument' presupposes a necessary causal connection between his shouting and the individual's participation in the argument. It assumes that participation in the interaction is reactive, and beyond the conscious control of the individual. Asking 'Why?' in such situations can promote analytical reflection: 'Why did you have to engage in an argument? What were some other options? Is it necessary for you to behave in a particular way just because someone else does something?'

It can be empowering to reflect on the possibilities of trying new roles and applying different rules. Such innovative behaviour can bring about significant change in the behaviour of others. Where arguing is habituated (that is, where two individuals argue because that is what they always do when they meet), if one party decides to break out of the role of 'arguer' and not to abide by the (implicit) rules ('when I meet him, I argue'), what will happen? Often, after some initial attempts to enforce the old role and rule, the other party will begin to adapt to a new 'game'.

Having participants in conflicts (particularly long-standing and often habituated conflicts) consciously analyse the conflict as a game can assist in the development of useful insight and options for change.

Scripts

Scripts are often 'written' by participants in conflict resolution to help them in taking part ('I will say . . . And then when she says . . . I will say . . . '). Scripts are sometimes worked and reworked in anticipation of the actual discussion, often as a consequence of anxiety about a meeting. The problem with writing scripts is that they may be played through inflexibly even when the other party is unaware

---

Case study 9

Edwina and Chris were married for five years and have two children. Their marriage broke up six months ago after a year of bitter arguments that eventually involved both their families and various friends. Chris developed an alcohol problem, and it seemed that whenever he visited Edwina to discuss anything to do with the children, he had been drinking. Chris has been seeing the children on alternate weekends under an informal agreement with Edwina.

Although she has consulted a solicitor and been advised to have custody and access arrangements formalised, Edwina fears this will provoke Chris, who has frequently been arriving late to collect the children, or returning them late. He sometimes shows considerable anger towards Edwina, even when the children are present.

Edwina very much wants to improve her relationship with Chris, mainly for the sake of the children.

This conflict raises a number of extremely difficult issues, one of which is the question of whether anything other than the court process is an appropriate means of dealing with the custody and access matters. Analyse the conflict and consider appropriate processes for approaching its resolution. Assuming that Edwina still wishes to deal with it herself, explore ways in which she might best do this.

of the script and is not playing the same script: this causes confusion and tends to promote conflict rather than resolve it. Thinking about and planning ways of presenting certain information, particularly of initiating a discussion about a conflict and a proposal for resolution, can be positive and helpful. Learning a script, however, imposes a degree of rigidity that is more likely to be unhelpful.

A broad, basic understanding of key psychological issues is crucial to effective conflict resolution. The basic issues are not complex, and the skills needed to deal with them are essentially practical interpersonal skills, which can be consciously developed, improved, and applied.

10 When Things Go Wrong

Even if all the appropriate analysis and planning have been undertaken, the process of conflict resolution does not necessarily run smoothly. This chapter will consider some of the problems that can occur to obstruct the process and hinder resolution. Some of these can be relatively easily dealt with, using basic techniques that usually enable them to be overcome. There are, however, no magical methods for solving all problems all the time.

It is important to recognise that some conflicts may be extremely difficult to resolve, or even be beyond resolution, and that some people may, at certain times, simply be unwilling or unable to resolve. The fact that a person is taking part, even enthusiastically, in a process of resolution does not mean that the person really seeks resolution. Consciously, or more often unconsciously, the person may not want the conflict resolved. It is also important to recognise that time can be a crucial factor in the success of resolution: the parties may require time before attempting it. Those who are, as Jay Folberg and Alison Taylor describe it, 'actively bleeding'(1988, p. 97) (that is, suffering grave emotional distress) may find any attempt at resolution too painful.

Problems in conflict resolution

Problems in conflict resolution usually fall into two categories: problems of process, and problems of people. Problems of process arise when the process is defective, or fails to meet the needs of either the participants or the conflict. It may be, for example, that the conflict has not been clearly defined, and that the participants are, therefore, dealing with what they understand to be the conflict, but not with a conflict that has been mutually defined. They may be using the same words, but with different meanings. The process may have failed to allow one participant to express her or his feelings; this will often result in frustration and anger, or psychological withdrawal from the process. If problems arise, it can be useful to check back over the process to evaluate its effectiveness. This is not to suggest that any particular formula has a magical power to bring resolution regardless of the participants or the conflict, but ensuring that the major steps have been worked through eliminates some common causes of obstruction.

The second category comprises those problems relating to the participants in the conflict resolution process, and can result from individual psychological responses, or from the relationship between the participants. They can be the effect of unconscious responses (such as defence mechanisms) or deliberate tactics (such as games). This chapter will give an overview of blocks, defence mechanisms, games, resistance, and personal attack.

Blocks

While trying to work towards conflict resolution, it is not uncommon to come up against blocks—that is, to reach points beyond which it seems impossible to proceed. These may be deadlocks, states of exhaustion, or an inability to solve a minor problem despite endless discussions. Blocks are sometimes the natural outcome of exhaustion or a sense of being overwhelmed, in which case they can usually be overcome by taking a break and returning to the matter when the parties are refreshed. Sometimes the most effective response is to put the blocked matter to one side, and to proceed with other issues, returning to it later. A block may indicate fixation (which is discussed later in this chapter) or may be a deliberate game of power; this is likely to be the case where the issue concerned is not particularly difficult, or where the other party refuses to allow it to be postponed.

Sometimes a discussion about why the block exists (as opposed to how it can be overcome) is helpful: 'We seem to be stuck on item 6 on the agenda: why do you think that is?'

Defence mechanisms

Conflict and conflict resolution almost inevitably provoke defence mechanisms. These are reactions by which people seek to protect themselves from situations that are perceived (consciously or unconsciously) to be unpleasant, uncomfortable, or threatening; the term originated in psychoanalysis. The defence mechanism usually blocks the unpleasant matter from the conscious mind. Such mechanisms can be normal and healthy, and necessary to maintain well-being; they are often automatic and involuntary. They help to protect individuals from trauma that might otherwise overwhelm them, to deal with stress, and to help avoid feelings of guilt and depression. A defence mechanism may be adopted consciously, when it is usually referred to as a coping mechanism; for example, a person faced with a sense of overwhelming threat may consciously choose to put it to one side until he or she feels better able to deal with it. There is a wide range of defence mechanisms, and it is useful to be able to recognise them, and often equally useful to be able to draw the attention of the individual to the fact that they are being used—this is sometimes called 'behaviour nomination'.

Although in the traditional sense of the term, defence mechanisms are unconscious responses to perceived threat, the behaviour that follows is usually identical to some forms of conscious defensive behaviour found in situations of conflict.

Thus, for example, an individual may deny the existence of a conflict (or of a particular issue in a conflict) because he or she has (unconsciously) blocked the matter from conscious thought; alternately, the individual may consciously deny the existence of a conflict (or of a particular issue in a conflict) as a tactic to protect a position, to avoid a discussion, or to distress another person.

The term '*defence mechanisms*' is reserved for responses that are not conscious (that is, where the individual is not consciously aware of what is occurring), and the term '*games*' can be used for behaviour that, although often identical to the manifestations of defence mechanisms, is consciously adopted. In many cases, it will be very difficult to determine whether particular problematic behaviour is a defence mechanism or a game: the person employing it as a game is unlikely to be willing to disclose that fact, and the person for whom it is a defence mechanism will be unlikely to be able to disclose that fact.

Denial

It is helpful to understand the key defence mechanisms that are likely to be encountered in conflict resolution. In denial, the individual refuses to acknowledge or is incapable of recognising the unpleasant situation or behaviour. The participant may refuse to talk about the situation or her or his feelings, and may even deny that a situation exists, or that he or she is involved. In some cases, individuals will accept that there is a problem or a conflict, but they will deny that it involves them, and may direct responsibility to another. Anger may be redirected unproductively, as in projection. Denial is essentially 'covering up' or concealing.

Denial may be dealt with by giving permission for self-disclosure, and endeavouring to make an individual feel comfortable and safe about disclosing thoughts or feelings, or revealing a situation that has otherwise been concealed. Sometimes this can be encouraged by showing that other people—including the person talking to the individual (such as a mediator or counsellor)—have experienced similar situations. Occasional direct confrontation may be necessary, but this should be undertaken with great caution since its effect may be even stronger denial.

Story-telling, role-playing, games, and simulations are useful in overcoming denial in that they allow individuals to act out situations in a manner that is not threatening or personally identifying. Denial can also be overcome by allowing the individual to describe the feelings or behaviour of other (unnamed) people, thereby actually reporting on his or her own behaviour, thoughts, or feelings without admitting this: 'What do other people here think about . . . ? What problems are your colleagues finding? What sorts of things do you think people who have experienced this sort of situation may have felt or done?'

Repression

Repression is a form of denial in which the denial is so successful that the individual is unable to recall (consciously) the threatening subject matter. Repression 'hides' or 'puts the lid on' the undesirable material. Thus, an individual may feel strong hostility to someone, but be unable to recall the origin of the hostility. This often relates to the unconscious 'deep structure' of a conflict, in which the participant is unconscious of the origins of the conflict but rationalises them to provide explanations.

Projection

In projection, the individual places responsibility for the unpleasant situation or conflict onto someone or something else. It often involves 'victim talk', in which the individual emphasises that he or she is the victim of someone else who is doing something over which the individual has no control. At an extreme level, this leads to an obsession with conspiracy theory or the belief that everyone in a particular situation (or, in extreme cases, everyone in the world) is out to get the individual, and sometimes leads to paranoia (in the popular sense of the word). It is rarely effective to argue against or present facts disproving the projection; it is more effective to demonstrate to individuals that accepting some personal responsibility for the situation will also assist them to bring about positive change.

Diversion

In diversion, the individual (often very skilfully) changes the subject to avoid the threatening topic. Alternatively, this may involve a change of approach (rather than topic) so that the attack is turned on the person raising the undesired subject. Responding to what is perceived to be an accusation, an attack on the 'accuser' (a standard tactic among politicians, in which personal abuse is used as a response to an unwanted question) is sometimes used: 'Who are you to criticise me about that sort of thing?' 'Let me remind you that you . . . How do you explain that?' Creating a crisis to divert attention away from the subject can also be very effective: the immediate problem cannot be dealt with because a crisis has suddenly arisen that threatens to overwhelm everything and everyone.

When a person is seeking to divert the discussion, only persistent, firm, and directive identification of the specific problem at hand will force the person back to the original topic. Any conflict resolution must begin with a clear and mutually agreed-upon identification of the specific problem or conflict to be dealt with; this is probably the most important stage of conflict resolution. A clear, mutually agreed-upon (and sometimes written) agenda or process is also helpful in minimising the risk of diversion. If other problems are raised, they can be put later on the agenda, or set aside for attention at a later meeting, while the central problem is kept in focus. Diversion is probably more often a conscious coping strategy than are most other defence mechanisms; it is, more simply, finding an excuse as to why this matter cannot be dealt with now (or, in some cases, ever). Diversion can allow an individual simultaneously to complain about a situation of conflict, while ensuring that the process necessary for its resolution cannot proceed, and avoiding all responsibility for the process failing.

Displacement

In displacement, the individual's suppressed anger is directed at the wrong person. This often occurs when the real problem is a person whose power and status is such that the individual feels helpless to deal directly with him or her. Attacking someone powerless may be a mechanism adopted to vent the anger aroused by someone else who is very powerful. Initiating strong conflict with a co-worker may be a means of displacing a conflict against an employer. Displaced conflict usually occurs when the expression or acting out of the conflict in one location is perceived to be too dangerous; the conflict is then expressed or acted out in another, presumably safer, location.

An obvious example is the work/home division: an employee who is angry with her or his manager may assume (consciously or unconsciously) that there is high risk in expressing this anger to the person concerned in the workplace. But the anger—and the conflict that provokes the anger—is not simply resolved as a result. It is most likely to be expressed in the home, where it is assumed (again, consciously or unconsciously) that there is minimum danger. A similar situation is observed with children who are angered or frightened by behaviour (including abuse) in the home: they may act out their conflict and anger in the classroom, where the consequences are almost certainly less painful. Effective conflict analysis can assist in identifying conflict that is displaced. In some cases, assisting an individual to find appropriate and effective means to reducing the stress and tension that apparently unresolvable conflict produces, without trying to force them to deal directly with the cause of the conflict, will enable them to discuss what is really happening.

Rationalisation

Rationalisation involves the individual making excuses, usually reasonable, that are more acceptable than the real reason for what has been done or said. This is especially common when the individual recognises that what was done was wrong, or may have unpleasant consequences, and that a justification is necessary. Rationalisation is often very difficult to deal with since it has the appearance of being reasonable, factual, and satisfactory. Looking for the 'real reason' behind rationalisation requires either breaking down the rationalisation barrier to identify real feelings, or locating sufficient independent evidence to show that the rationalisation is not the explanation, although this will often lead to further rationalisation. This mechanism is adopted especially by highly articulate and assertive people (including 'professional talkers' such as lawyers) and tends to overwhelm the inarticulate or non-assertive, or those with poor self-esteem.

Rationalisation often occurs in order to provide explanations about why a particular action (or, in some cases, any action) cannot be carried out. Rather than simply saying 'I don't want to do that' or 'I don't want this conflict resolved', people will sometimes offer complex explanations about why it is not possible.

Intellectualisation

Intellectualisation, like rationalisation, is a particular problem for highly educated and articulate people, and for 'professional talkers', and has a negative effect on the less articulate and less assertive. In intellectualisation, the individual recognises that a problem exists but talks about it in a detached, philosophical manner with no expression of personal feeling or involvement. In some cases, this approach may be used to distinguish the 'rational' and 'intellectual' individual from the other party, who is represented as emotional, even hysterical and irrational: 'Let's try to talk about this rationally and intelligently, and not let our feelings get in the way'. However, conflict and conflict resolution are very much about feelings, and intellectualisation is usually a defence mechanism to avoid feelings or emotions.

Fixation

In fixation, an individual refuses to move from a particular point, often out of fear of the future, which is unpredictable, or to avoid a particular subject that is to be considered shortly. Thus, a particular and apparently trivial matter may be focused on in an obsessive manner, to the exclusion of more important matters. This can often cause blocks to conflict resolution: 'If we can't resolve this, I'm not prepared to go any further' often means 'I don't want to go any further because we're moving towards an issue I find threatening'. In discussions, it often requires firm and directive techniques to move a fixated individual on from a single issue. Conflict resolution should begin with a mutual agreement that issues will be worked through, but that any issue that cannot be resolved immediately will be put to one side and looked at again later.

Minimisation

In minimising, the individual tries to make the problem appear much less serious or significant than it actually is. A minimisation generally implies that the matter is probably not worth considering, and that any discussion is a waste of time and should be forgotten. The difficulty can be distinguishing between matters that *are* trivial and those that are being minimised as a means of avoidance. Minimisation can be effective in persuading the other parties that they are being unreasonable or silly in seeking to pursue something that is not worth the trouble.

In some cases, the conflict really does involve matters of greatly disproportionate significance for different parties. For example, a customer who has spent (what is to him or her) a great deal of money on a washing machine is likely to view its breakdown as being of great importance and its repair as being of great urgency. The company that sold the washing machine may view the customer as someone of no great significance (being only one of thousands with whom it deals, and someone unlikely to purchase a great number of its products), and the repair as of minimal urgency. Minimisation by the company in this case is not

what is mean by minimisation as a defence mechanism: it is a matter of differential perceptions of the problem.

Hostility

Hostility manifests with the individual becoming argumentative, angry, aggressive, or threatening when reference is made to a sensitive problem, issue, or
related behaviour. This tends to encourage other people to avoid the issue or often
to avoid discussion of any potentially sensitive issues with the person. It is sometimes said of people who regularly manifest hostility: 'Don't upset X; he has a
violent temper'; 'You mustn't raise that with Y; she gets upset'. The person who
reacts with hostility is not simply responding with normal emotions to something
distressing. The effect of the hostility is not cathartic or therapeutic in releasing
pent-up feelings. Hostility is a barrier defending the individual from what he or
she sees as a hostile world or a threatening subject. Individuals who respond with
hostility will also often claim that the issue is one affecting their personal
integrity, competence, and honour; it must therefore be viewed as a personal
attack. This diverts the issue from being, for example, a question of management
or workplace practice, to being an attack on the integrity of the manager.

It often requires firm, persistent, and directive techniques to overcome
hostility. The authority of a mediator, for example, is often challenged by hostility, and once that authority is weakened, it is very difficult to re-establish.

Conversion and fantasy

In conversion, the repressed psychological effects manifest in physical symptoms. In fantasy, the individual retreats into a world of imagination to avoid
unpleasant reality. This may include playing through imaginary situations in
which the real problem is dealt with successfully, those identified as responsible
are humiliated or punished, and the subject of unjust treatment is vindicated.
The major problem with fantasy arises when it has persisted for such a length of
time that the individual loses the ability to distinguish clearly between fantasy
and reality, between the world as acted out in the imagination and the drama
occurring in the real world. The individual may describe as fact events that
occurred only in the imagination. For example, it may be reported that things
were said that were only said in fantasy. This can sometimes occur if the individual has been playing through scripts in the imagination and has lost the ability to distinguish these from reality. This can be particularly the case if
substantial periods have elapsed between the event and the report of it. If there
has been extensive brooding on events, especially on what someone should
have done or said, the final report may not distinguish between what actually
happened and the fantasy of what happened or ought to have happened.

One characteristic effect of strongly felt unresolved conflict is an almost
obsessive process of thought whereby the conflict, and incidents related to it,
are 'replayed' in the mind. People sometimes describe it as 'tape-playing', as if an
audio or video tape of incidents in the conflict are played and replayed without

the individual possessing any ability to control the playing. Repeated recollection of and reflection on incidents in a conflict often lead to the incidents and the conflict being reconstructed in the perception and the memory of the individual, with the 'tape', as it were, being 'edited'. Thus, after the conflict has been 'replayed' repeatedly, it may be virtually impossible for the individual to recall accurately the circumstances as they occurred. The 'edited tape' has become the reality. And, because this has not been a conscious and deliberate reconstruction or misrepresentation, the individual sincerely believes it to be accurate; the person is not lying, but neither is he or she telling the truth in the sense of accurately reporting what was experienced at the time.

It is important to recall that in conflict and conflict resolution, perception is much more important than what is often called reality, and that what people say cannot simply be divided between that which is the truth and that which is a lie. Individuals only know the truth (that is, objective fact) in so far as they understand and remember it. Thus two people in a conflict may both be telling 'the truth' in their versions of what each did and said, but they may be completely wrong in terms of what a detached observer would have seen and heard. Because each genuinely believes her or his version to be the truth (that is, an objective statement of objective fact), the assumption is almost always that the other is lying (that is, deliberately misrepresenting what happened). Continued discussion of 'the facts' will thus tend not only to fail to produce agreement, but also to reinforce negative perceptions of each party in the mind of the other. This is why the language of perception, rather than the language of facts or reality, needs to be employed.

Identification

Identification means that the individual vicariously identifies with the source of the conflict or problem. An employee who is being treated badly by an employer, but who has no way to escape the situation, may develop excessive and irrational loyalty to the employer as a way of explaining (to him- or herself) that what is happening is really good and that the individual accepts and welcomes it. The identifying individual, in this case, may lose the ability to separate the personal from the corporate. In responding to dysfunctional identification, it is necessary to assist the individual to develop some sense of self-worth and to recognise that unpleasant situations can be experienced without any personal ability to overcome them.

Regression

Regression manifests in an individual who returns to childhood behaviour, and may include irrational anger, the throwing of tantrums, exaggerated tears, or refusing to speak. Regression can sometimes be dealt with by behaviour nomination (that is, by describing to the individual what is happening) or by playing a particular role (for example, taking on the parent role and acting towards the individual as if he or she is a 'naughty child'). Obviously, not all expressions of anger or all tears are regressive; they are often normal reactions to emotional stress. But where a particular behaviour is repeated (for example, where the individual bursts into tears every time a particular matter is mentioned), it may be a manifestation of a defence mechanism and an indication that the subject is threatening.

Flight

Flight is running away from a conflict. It does not mean strategic withdrawal, which can sometimes be highly beneficial. If the situation is believed to be too hostile, too painful, or impossible to resolve, a participant may regard the only solution to be escape. This can be physical escape (as in literally running away) or psychological escape in the sense of withdrawing from any active participation. The response to flight or the desire for flight is to encourage the individual to perceive the resolution process as positive and effective or, at the very least, worth a try. Projections of possible (but usually improbable) disastrous outcomes often lead to the desire for flight: 'What's the point of trying that; he'll only . . . '. Talking explicitly about such projections, and gently demonstrating them to be less potentially disastrous than may be assumed, can be helpful. Flight can lead to walkouts, although walkouts or the breaking off of dialogue are also often conscious power games.

Resignation and apathy

A feeling of powerlessness, helplessness, and hopelessness often leads to resignation or apathy and submission. Nothing is worth trying since nothing will work. Sometimes the sense of powerlessness and helplessness is based in reality: it may be that the individual's situation offers little hope for improvement, or even appears likely to deteriorate. However, in many situations this is not the case, and the negative feelings can be addressed by gentle analysis of the situation and possible ways of improving it. Unless self-esteem and a sense of personal power can be developed, resignation and apathy will prevail.

Games

Defence mechanisms are unconscious reactions to unpleasant situations; there are, however, also conscious strategies for avoiding pain or for dominating others. These can be referred to as 'games' or 'tactics', and they include a number of techniques commonly used in negotiation to try to coerce the other party into yielding. Some of the more common games are outlined in this chapter.

Threats and promises

Threats and promises are often traded in the resolution process. One party will demand something and threaten consequences if it is not given. This is sometimes presented as good negotiating. It is important, however, to project outcomes before making promises or demands. What will happen if the offer, threat, promise, or demand is accepted? Can it be fulfilled? Is it what the party making it wants, and is it a desirable outcome? If one participant says, 'Either you pay me $50 000 or I go elsewhere', what happens if the other says, 'So go elsewhere'? The greater the potential cost in taking a position, the greater the risk.

Making demands that the other side cannot—as opposed to will not—meet is not likely to be successful; it is likely to damage the whole conflict resolution process and the relationship between the parties. If they absolutely cannot spend more than $49 999, there is little point to demanding $50 000. Sound conflict analysis and preparation should ensure that parties have some understanding of what is realistic and what is not.

The most effective negotiating style includes a careful consideration of risk-taking. The old bargaining style supposedly effective in the market places of the developing world (the seller demands $1000; the buyer offers $200, and they both shout at each other until the seller settles for $350) is not sophisticated or flexible enough to take account of the multiple variables involved in conflict resolution. Very few real-life negotiations in conflict—except, perhaps, for an item in a market—involve only one consideration. Even in the developing world, the negotiator who works on the most–least principle is likely to lose out every time. The assumption that, because the seller started at $1000 and was 'beaten down' to $350, the buyer 'won' is flawed, particularly if the item could have been purchased for $100 elsewhere, or only cost the seller $20.

The question 'What if . . . ?' is a key to any planned offer or demand: What if they accept? What if they refuse? What if they break off negotiating?

Withdrawals

Withdrawals or walkouts are not uncommon in conflict resolution. Sometimes they are the outcome of stress, distress, or exhaustion. Sometimes they are part of a game. Conflict resolution is sometimes punctuated by threats to end the process. Sometimes this is by a verbal threat, but it can include physical movements towards walking out, or indeed actual walkouts: 'Well, if that's the best you can offer, there's no point to our talking any more' (as the speaker rises and moves towards the door), or 'I'm not going to stay here and have you make those sorts of demands; you'll be hearing from my solicitor'.

Sometimes this is bluff: it is supposed to intimidate the other participant into reducing the demand or increasing the offer, and is aimed at making him or her submit, therefore giving the threatening party a powerful advantage in future discussions. The threat of walkout thereafter hovers over the proceedings, and rarely has to be re-spoken. Sometimes the walkout or threat of walkout is a response to a real perception that no further discussion is possible, and may come in the face of an unreasonable demand from the other side. If it is assumed that the other side is unrealistic, uncooperative, and hostile, a walkout or threat of walkout may be appropriate, either to provoke them into a more realistic position or because negotiation actually has broken down. However, if walkout is to be used as a real response, rather than as a threat, it should be carefully explained: 'I'm sorry but I simply don't think we're getting anywhere: I offered to . . . but now I think we're just not going anywhere so . . . '.

Forcing confrontation is sometimes an effective technique in conflict resolution. It should not, however, just be calling bluff: if it is to be announced that one party cannot go any further, this should be true.

The most effective response to walkout or threat of walkout by one party is a clear reassertion by the other of a commitment to resolving the matter, and of a willingness to reopen discussions. Once someone has walked out, it is very difficult for that person to return; often, unless the other party re-initiates contact, both parties will remain in a stalemate and the matter will never be resolved. Although it is easy to become locked into the view that 'They walked out; if they want to talk to me, they know where I am', this prevents resolution. If the aim is resolving the conflict, rather than scoring points, the stalemate has to be broken.

Delaying or doing nothing

Deliberate delaying is sometimes used by one party when that person knows, or believes, that the other is under pressure of time, or just as a 'water torture' tactic to wear down the other side by extending the process unnecessarily. This can also involve doing nothing—taking no action, making no offers, giving no real responses—in an attempt to force the other party to 'show her or his hand' or give in, ensuring some sort of decision.

Other games

Bracketing involves adding two, often unrelated, items together—one of which the other party wants and one that is not wanted—and trying to obtain a single resolution on both. The game of *implications* is played by obliquely referring to the possible or probable indirect consequences of something: 'OK, well, you can do that if you like [rising inflection, followed by a pause] and you'll just have to endure the consequences'. The implications are not specified, but there is an underlying tone of threat. *Ghosts* is not unlike *implications*: one player refers obliquely to some hidden item from the past relationship (sometimes a personal relationship) with the other player: 'I really didn't expect you to take that approach after what happened in . . . '. The playing of *ghosts* is sometimes a form of blackmail, with the implication that the ghosts will become visible unless the other person gives in. *Secrets* is also a variant on *implications*: one party hints at knowing something vital that radically affects the conflict and its outcome, but about which he or she cannot or will not speak.

Good cop/bad cop is an old negotiating tactic; two negotiators are involved (in some variants, only one is physically present, but the other is referred to). One negotiator is pleasant, apparently communicative, and eager to negotiate; the other is hostile, aggressive, threatening, and uncooperative. The extreme difference between them is intended to make the other party eager to deal only with the 'good cop', and to avoid having to deal with the 'bad cop', therefore yielding to the 'good cop' wherever possible.

Changing negotiators is a tactic intended to exhaust and confuse the other party; it often means going back to the beginning by informing the new negotiator of everything that has gone before, although the new negotiator usually has, in fact, been fully briefed, and only pretends to be unaware of what has happened.

In *Bleeper*, one party arranges to be suddenly interrupted with an urgent message or crisis, which causes him or her to leave the room at a critical moment. The cause is not explained to the other party, but the effect is to disrupt proceedings and, coincidentally, give the departing party an opportunity to reflect or take advice. *Interruptions* is a variant on this: arranged interruptions occur throughout the discussion, the intention usually being to disturb the other party.

Overwhelm is a game that involves presenting the other side with masses of 'evidence' to 'prove' something. The material will often be given quite late, at a time when the other party will be unlikely to have an opportunity to consider it. Unfortunately, many people will feel the need to pretend that they have read and considered the material rather than risk appearing incompetent. This has a variant, which might be called '*Expert*', in which one party presents material that is overwhelming because of its technical complexity or obscurity: 'Given that the extrapolation factor has diminished by 5.433 per cent, Einstein's seventh law of desensitisation makes that option impossible'. This also tends to work because most people are unwilling to admit that they do not understand something.

Appearing helpless and pathetic can be a very effective ploy and often indicates the game '*Poor little me*'. Many people will not wish to take advantage of someone who is less intelligent, less competent, or less assertive than they are, and who appears afraid and powerless. '*Dumb little me*' is a variant of '*Poor little me*' but has the added dimension of appearing to demonstrate stupidity or ignorance: 'I simply cannot understand what you are saying or what is happening'. Both these games are usually played by those who are both well informed and quite powerful. A further variant is '*Powerless little me*', in which the other party claims to be trying to resolve the conflict under some sort of personal threat and without any real power to make decisions. For example, such individuals may claim to have been sent to do the negotiating with clear orders from a brutal and inhumane superior who has threatened them with dire personal consequences if they do not succeed, but who has given them no power. They may therefore enthusiastically agree with the other party, but then point out that they cannot do anything and will suffer personally if the outcome is not as they were directed it should be.

Sometimes people play the game of *Obnoxious*: obnoxious people sometimes achieve success because people are anxious to get out of their presence. A variant of this is *Mad and dangerous*, which also involves the added dimension of unpredictability and threat, and involves shouting irrationally, hitting tables, and sweeping documents onto the floor. Even talking about an uncontrollable temper often has a salutary effect.

Water torture is a strategy involving going on and on and on, often in relation to one small, sometimes trivial, matter, refusing to be side-tracked, insisting on clarification and agreement. This makes it seem as if the whole process will take forever and so the other side needs to give in now or they will never escape. This game depends on the fact that most people are polite, and are reluctant to bring discussions to a close simply because they appear to be circular and unproductive.

Game-playing often occurs during conflict and conflict resolution; recognising what is happening usually gives a sense of empowerment, and being able to give a name to an unhelpful response will often assist in defusing the hostility or despair that it may provoke.

Resistance

In addition to blocks, defence mechanisms, and games, resistance is also a problem often encountered in conflict resolution. 'Resistance' is a term used in psychoanalysis to refer to opposition to attempts to make unconscious processes conscious. Resistance is also met in conflict resolution through defence mechanisms and also through less obvious and more subtle responses. It can be expressed through symptoms of anxiety, verbal withdrawal, late arrival, physical withdrawal, attempts to reopen closed issues, and hostility aimed at other participants or any third party involved. Resistance is usually the result of a perception that conflict resolution is opening up personally threatening issues. It is likely to be a result of fear of having to expose things that have previously been hidden, or of having to face change.

Sometimes, the real fear is that resolution will, in fact, occur: a person who has an investment in the maintenance of the conflict may find its imminent resolution very threatening and may therefore find ways of resisting the conclusion of the process.

Resistance can be dealt with by positively reinforcing participation in the conflict resolution process by openly discussing concerns about the process before and during the process, by ensuring that proposals are put tentatively rather than absolutely, and by encouraging positive commitment. Where resistance is obstructing the process, it needs to be discussed, not accusingly but analytically: 'It seems that every time we arrange a meeting you arrive late and have to leave early; that seems to be . . . '.

Direct confrontation, however tempting it may be (particularly in the face of ongoing refusal to deal with what may appear to be obviously important issues) is rarely effective and, indeed, is more likely to increase the level of resistance.

Resistance is not necessarily an individual response; sometimes both parties in a conflict will resist consideration of a certain critical issue. This is particularly the case in relationship conflict, where what is almost a 'conspiracy of silence' may occur, with both parties consciously or unconsciously resisting discussion of what may be the key matter of their conflict. They will have reached a tacit agreement that some things are too sensitive and threatening.

Personal attack

Personal attack often occurs in conflict and conflict resolution. Sometimes it is a consequence of a defence mechanism; sometimes it is a deliberate strategy to unnerve and upset. Most people respond defensively to personal attack and, without thinking, are diverted into personal defence. This can very quickly shift the process away from the resolution of a particular conflict to a defence of the individual or a fight. As a diversionary tactic, personal attack is usually highly effective.

Personal attack usually involves questioning of competence, suggestions of immorality, comments about personal characteristics, or reference to an individual's past. The more personally sensitive a matter is to an individual, the more likely it is to be used by someone wishing to personally attack that person. This is common in personal relationships (where there is greater likelihood of one partner knowing the other's 'weak spots'), but it also occurs in other settings.

The only effective response to personal attack is not to respond. The exception should be where a criminal action is alleged or implied, and in such cases a clear, brief denial is all that should follow. The standard methods of dealing with problems in conflict resolution, which are outlined at the end of this chapter, should be applied, however difficult this may be because of the sensitivity and personally threatening nature of the attack.

Refusing to respond to personal attack does not involve making that refusal explicit in aggressive terms: that would be, in fact, a response to the attack. It is usually most effective to acknowledge the attack gently and without defence or confrontation, and then, equally gently but firmly, to return to the subject of the discussion: 'Yes, I understand that you do not think I am competent in my job, but what we're here to discuss is . . . ', or 'I understand that you would prefer not to deal with a woman, but I am the person handling this matter, so . . . '. Sometimes a gentle question about relevance can be employed, although this needs to be done with care in case the discussion is then diverted into an argument regarding relevance: 'I don't quite understand how my hairstyle relates to the subject of our meeting'.

Fighting

Conflict resolution can easily degenerate into fighting (that is, essentially unproductive exchanges), particularly where the issue is emotionally charged and the participants do not feel that resolution is a likely or even a desirable outcome. It is very important to understand that fighting and conflict resolution are not the same thing: fighting is not necessarily bad or destructive, and can sometimes be part of a conflict resolution process. Fighting, however, is often an alternative to conflict resolution: people may fight because they enjoy fighting rather than because they want a conflict resolved. If this is the case, the fighting should be identified and recognised, and not presented as conflict resolution. Fighting can sometimes precede resolution, and fighting can sometimes punctuate the resolution process. If this happens it is important that the fact is clearly identified, not in a judgmental way, but as a statement of fact. The parties may wish to fight for a time, and then return to resolution.

Responding to problems

There are a number of strategies that can be adopted to respond to the problems created by blocks, defence mechanisms, games, resistance, and personal attack. The skills involved in communication and assertion, including firm persistence, are very helpful. It is necessary to have a clear sense of the purpose of any discussion, and to reiterate it continually. It is very difficult to divert someone who has a clearly identified goal. Where attempts are made to divert, the discussion should be brought back to the original topic. This should be done quietly and gently, but persistently, sometimes by a technique referred to as 'broken record': regardless of the attempts by the other person to change the subject or provoke defensiveness, gentle persistence should be used to maintain movement towards the defined goal. The attempted diversion should be gently acknowledged in a non-accusatory manner, and the conversation brought back to the original topic—for example, 'I understand that you are angry about . . . but at the moment we are discussing . . . '.

Behaviour nomination

One particular strategy for dealing with these problems is behaviour nomination—that is, describing (in a non-accusatory manner) to individuals what their behaviour appears to be and, in some cases, asking them why they are engaging in it, (for example, why they are shouting, or why they keep diverting from the issue). It is important not to give instructions that behaviour should change; an order such as 'Don't shout at me!' will not be as productive as a statement such as 'I do not understand why you are shouting at me' (in a questioning, rather than accusatory tone). This draws the individual's attention to the behaviour and, if done firmly and repeatedly, often leads to behaviour change. It may also be useful to describe, as impartially as possible, how the behaviour is preventing the process of conflict resolution. For example, a mediator might say: 'If you continue to shout at X, then she is not likely to want to talk to you about resolving this matter.' The emphasis all the time must be on problem solving: 'How can we resolve this?'

Rules and procedures

It is important in conflict resolution to begin by establishing clear, mutually agreed rules and procedures, and to ensure that these take account of some of the defence mechanisms. This has been outlined in chapter 4 as part of preparation for conflict resolution. For example, it may be important to establish clearly that each party will have an opportunity, without interruption, to express her or his point of view, and that each party will have an opportunity, also without interruption, to respond to the other. If this begins to break down in a destructive way, it is possible to refer to the rules by requesting that they be adhered to. However, constant reference to the rules agreed to at the beginning, and attempts to suppress expressions of feelings, are not necessarily helpful; it depends very much on the effect of such expressions on the process.

A clear agenda, mutually agreed in advance, also helps to minimise problems. If problems arise, the agenda can be referred to; issues that may divert from the purpose of the meeting can be added to the agenda (although if they are only attempts at diversion, they are unlikely ever to be discussed). This is a more effective means of dealing with them than entering into arguments about whether or not they should be discussed. A written list of issues can be particularly helpful, and may be especially useful when dealing with a person who is known to avoid or divert. Similarly, an agreed and fixed period of time for the discussion will often assist in keeping participants to the agreed subject matter. Open-ended meetings encourage free-ranging and undirected discussions; this has some advantages, but can lead to unproductive and diversionary conversations.

Control and self-control

One of the most effective ways of dealing with problems is for the individual to demonstrate control and self-control. This involves both verbal and non-verbal behaviour. The more self-control and control of the situation that is demonstrated by one party, or by the mediator, the more influence this will eventually have on the other party. Remaining calm and non-aggressive, and indicating this in body language and speech, is important. This control must be established at the very beginning of a meeting, and must be maintained. Once lost, it is very difficult to regain.

The mediator or the parties must be prepared for challenges to control and self-control. Making people angry and making them lose control is one way of undermining their position and ability to participate in the conflict resolution process. These attempts will often be little more than power games in which one of the parties tries to demonstrate that he or she can exert control over the other (and over any mediator), and thereby dominate the whole process. This is often the case with professional advocates or negotiators and 'bullies', or people who are accustomed to getting their own way. It is important to encourage people to focus on the problem and not the personalities.

Case study 10

Richard manages a small printing business. One of the supervisors in his employ, Steve, has asked him to dismiss Kathy, an employee who has only been with the company for a few months. Steve says Kathy has repeatedly failed to carry out very clear instructions and, as a result, several jobs were spoilt and had to be repeated. Kathy tells Richard that she has always carried out Steve's instructions to the letter, but that he often gives her instructions and subsequently denies having done so. She says he will sometimes tell her to do something, and when she does it, reprimand her for doing it, and deny ever giving the instruction.

Richard calls both Steve and Kathy into his office in the hope of being able to resolve their differences. Once Kathy has described how she sees the situation, Steve walks out, saying he will not remain in the room with someone who calls him a liar, and that if Richard wants to keep Kathy he will resign.

Look at this conflict from Richard's perspective, and consider what skills and strategies he would need to use in an attempt to keep both Steve and Kathy, and to resolve the conflict between them.

Identifying problems is the beginning of responding to them. Clear, agreed process, purpose, and rules help to minimise the effect of problems, but often it will be necessary to identify and address them during the process. Ignoring blocks, defence mechanisms, games, resistance, and personal attack is likely to allow them to become part of the pattern of behaviour; the longer they continue, the more difficult it is to deal with them.

11 Interpersonal and Relationship Conflict

Conflict can be thought of as existing in a series of concentric circles radiating outwards from the individual. Some conflict is very close, intimate, and personal; some is more objective, distant, and impersonal.

This is the first of five chapters focusing on specific areas of conflict. Although general theories and principles of conflict resolution, as outlined earlier in this book, can be applied to all conflict, specific areas of conflict raise particular questions, problems, and issues that require attention in the resolution process. As previously noted, there is no simple, universal procedure whereby all conflicts of all types in all areas can be resolved in all circumstances.

These five chapters will outline the particular issues and problems that arise in conflict of different types, from the interpersonal to the environmental. They need to be read in conjunction with earlier chapters on general approaches to conflict.

Intrapersonal conflict

Intrapersonal (or intrapsychic) conflict is conflict that arises within the individual, is usually not obvious to another person (unless disclosed by the individual), and does not depend upon a relationship with someone else (although it is often a result of a relationship). It includes personal decision-making ('Will I take this new job?'), moral questions ('Will I be honest in my tax return?'), and decisions about initiating a relationship ('Will I go up and talk to that person?').

Other types of conflict almost inevitably provoke intrapersonal conflicts. For example, a person in an interpersonal conflict is likely to face a range of intrapersonal conflicts arising from her or his relationship with the other person. Conflict at work, for example, can provoke intrapersonal conflict relating to career and future options.

It is important to note that intrapersonal conflict, because it is usually private and undisclosed, can cause particular problems in other types of conflict, especially if the individual experiencing the intrapersonal conflict is erroneously interpreting the behaviour, motives, or needs of others, is thinking irrationally, or is basing her or his feelings on misunderstandings.

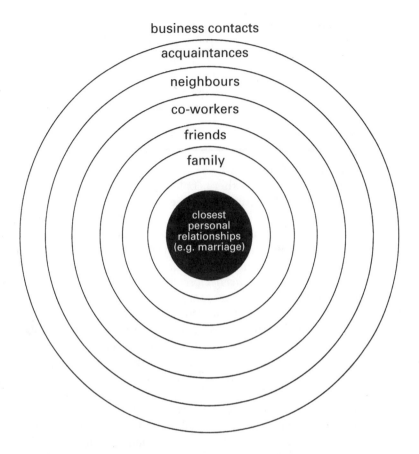

Figure 11.1 Interpersonal relationships

For example, one person in a conflict with a friend may be undergoing intense intrapersonal conflict on the basis of what he or she assumes the friend has done or said: 'Because X did or said that, I can no longer trust him/her, so I must treat everything he/she does and says with suspicion, and therefore I have to consider whether or not to continue the friendship'. Unless X knows what the friend believes he or she did or said, and has an opportunity to clarify or discuss this, the whole interpersonal conflict may be arising out of an irrational intrapersonal conflict.

Intrapersonal conflicts often relate to moral and ethical issues. Individual decision-making about if and when to undertake certain actions—for example, to lie or to tell the truth, to steal or not to steal, to have sexual relations or not to have sexual relations—can cause considerable intrapersonal conflict, and if this is not effectively resolved, the process of decision-making can be confused and confusing, leading to distressing outcomes and future regret.

An important approach both to intrapersonal conflict and to conflict generally is to seek to develop personal skills in effective thinking, problem solving, and decision-making. Many intrapersonal conflicts are based on irrational or 'crooked' thinking, in which all sorts of external and internal pressures distort the decision-making process. The resource guide includes a number of works in this area.

Interpersonal conflict

We are all involved, throughout our lives, in a series of interpersonal relationships—that is, relationships with other people. The most intense conflicts are often those in interpersonal relationships. The more intense the relationship, the more important it is to the individual, and the more threatened the individual is by the prospect of the relationship being damaged or ending, the stronger any conflict within the relationship will be. Interpersonal conflict ranges from that between people in long-term domestic and sexual relationships (including marriage) to that between close friends, and from that between colleagues at work and between acquaintances to that between people who, up to the time of the conflict, were unknown to each other.

Interpersonal conflict is often concerned with the 'rules' of the relationship—that is, how each party believes he or she should behave in relation to the other, and how the other, in turn, should behave. Although social relationships always have rules attached to them, the rules are rarely made explicit. Even in a relationship such as marriage, which is legally and socially defined, the rules applying to each partner in a specific marriage are unlikely to be clearly specified. Both partners are likely to have personal understandings of what marriage means and how each partner should behave, but it may be that these assumptions are never mutually discussed or negotiated. There are some exceptions; in recent years, particularly in the USA, there have been couples who, before marriage, have drawn up contracts specifying the most important rules in their relationship. However, even such a contract will not be able to specify every rule about every situation.

Conflict can arise when one person in a relationship, whether close or distant, feels the other has broken the rules. In some cases, the other person will have known the rules, because they were accepted by both parties; but in many cases, the other person will either not have known, or not have accepted, the rules as prescribed by the person with whom they have a relationship. Some individuals may face a conflict because they have unknowingly broken unspoken rules. To use an example identified in an earlier chapter, if one partner in a personal relationship believes that there is a rule requiring a telephone call if the return home is to be delayed by more than twenty minutes, and the other partner in the relationship believes that there is a rule requiring a telephone call if the return home is to be delayed by more than one hour, conflict is likely to arise over a late home-coming and the lack of a telephone call. The conflict is not essentially about the behaviour (that is, being late in returning home) but about the breach of the rule (which was probably never discussed and made explicit).

All manner of assumptions can be made as a result of believing the rule was broken (for example, 'He or she doesn't really care about me'). In such a case, it needs to be clarified as to whether the issue is the behaviour (returning home late) or failure to comply with the rule (that is, the expectation of the other partner).

Intensity, importance, and investment

Just as all conflict can be thought of as a series of concentric circles, so interpersonal conflict can be conceptualised in the same way. These interpersonal relationships vary in terms of intensity, importance, and investment. Intensity refers to the emotional strength of the relationship; this can range from neutral (for example, people who are dealt with casually at work) to strong (for example, the person with whom a long-term romantic relationship exists). The importance of the relationship derives from the value of the relationship to the participants; this can be, for example, value measured in terms of emotional support or even of money. Investment in the relationship includes financial cost, commitment of time, emotional commitment, or amount of public affirmation and commitment.

Relationships fall within a hierarchy of importance, intensity, and investment. Some are more important, more intense, and more invested than others, and the more investment, importance, and intensity in a relationship, the more the pressure, stress, projection, and risk is involved in any conflict. If one partner in a relationship views it as less intense, less important, and less invested than the other partner does, conflict is certain to arise, and will be dealt with differently by that partner than by the partner for whom the relationship is of greater value. People in relationships rarely discuss their perceptions of intensity, importance, and investment, or the ways in which these perceptions change with time and circumstances.

These general principles apply to all relationships, personal and professional, but they are of special importance in considering conflict in interpersonal relationships.

Conflicts related to stages of relationships

Conflicts are especially common at key stages in relationships. These stages include initiating, maintaining, changing, and concluding. *Initiating* involves the establishment of the relationship, the setting of the rules, and the taking up of roles. *Maintaining* refers to the process of keeping the relationship going, and of coping with external and internal pressures. *Changing*, in response either to internal or external pressures, is highly likely to cause conflict, particularly where the changes are not mutually discussed and accepted. Although relationships often conclude as a result of conflict, the process of *concluding* itself often causes conflict as the relationship, in its present form, is ended. The conflict itself, effectively resolved, can strengthen and stabilise the relationship, even when that relationship, as it previously existed, concludes and a new (potentially) positive relationship develops. The ending of a marriage often leads, unnecessarily, to the conclusion of the old relationship and the emergence not of a state of individual freedom or a new and positive form of relationship between the parties, but of a strong and powerful relationship of hostility based on unresolved conflict.

The conflict at each of these stages will be different for the person who *initiates* and the person who *responds*; for example, the person who starts a discussion about changing the relationship and the person who is confronted by that discussion are likely to view what is happening differently. The manner, style, and timing of initiating a new stage will, largely, determine the response.

Conflict related to change

Particular causes of stress and conflict in relationships include life crises, the changing roles of the parties, the changing interdependence of the parties, and third-party involvement. *Life crises* include the death of people close to either partner, loss of employment, financial problems, retirement, serious illness and injury, and geographic relocation. *Changing roles* can include roles that are changed as a result of life crises (for example, a woman becoming the sole financial supporter of the family when her partner suffers long-term unemployment), or changing needs and expectations (for instance, taking on a new interest or career), or a personal decision to adopt a different style or role in the relationship. *Changing interdependence* usually occurs when one partner in a relationship, having in the past been dependent (financially or emotionally) on the other, now seeks or acquires more independence (for example, a child growing up); it can also include a partner becoming increasingly dependent. *Third-party involvement* can range from the birth of a child for a couple, to a sexual relationship or deep friendship with someone outside the relationship, to criticisms from outsiders.

Categories of interpersonal relationships

Interpersonal relationships fall into a range of categories, depending on the nature of the relationship. Most people will be able to prepare a list of people with whom they consider themselves to be in a relationship, and to define the nature of that relationship. Terms such as 'friends', 'partners', 'lovers', 'husband and wife', 'brothers', 'sisters', 'fellow employees', 'neighbours', and 'mates' may be used. However, not all interpersonal relationships are positive. For a condition of hostility to exist, a relationship of some sort must also exist. Therefore, 'enemy' and 'rival' are categories of interpersonal relationship. Similarly, people may fall into the category of those who previously bore a positive label—for example, 'ex-lover' and 'former friend'.

Friendship

Friendships can be of short or long duration, can be intense and important, or superficial and unimportant, and can regularly involve large amounts of time or occasionally involve short amounts of time. Friendships are characterised by regular minor conflicts that are usually resolved because the friendship is seen by both parties to be more important than the issues over which conflict has occurred.

Co-residents

Sometimes people will live together without having any particular personal relationship other than that of co-residents or co-tenants. This is particularly the case where their reason for co-habiting is convenience or cheaper rents. They may not have met each other before sharing accommodation, may have little in common, and may not see sharing accommodation as any reason to establish any deeper sort of relationship. Sharing accommodation is a frequent cause of a range of interpersonal conflicts, particularly since those involved may have very different views on house management, and different values and expectations, and may not have any overriding commitment to resolving their problems to enable a more positive relationship to continue.

Romantic relationships

When relationships acquire a deeper emotional commitment, they also include a deeper intensity, importance, and investment; they are often thought of as romantic relationships. Each individual may come to depend very much on emotional response and support from the other for identity, self-esteem, and assurance. The intensity of emotion involved in such relationships can increase both the positive and the negative aspects of the relationship. Different expectations about relationships generally, and the present relationship particularly, can lead to conflict.

Sexual relationships

Most people find conflict in sexual relationships, or about sexual matters in relationships that are not primarily sexual, among the most difficult with which to deal. It is often seen, particularly for men, to involve very sensitive and personally threatening issues that have a great effect on self-image and self-esteem. Conflict in sexual relationships often arises in initiating sexual encounters, setting rules for sexual relationships, changes to or in a sexual relationship, rules about monogamy or sexual fidelity, dealing with sexual problems, and responding to the dissatisfaction of one partner. In recent years, concerns about AIDS have led to increasing conflicts and difficulties, including conflicts related to safe sexual practices and the use of condoms.

There are differences in the nature of relationships that are long-term and those that are short-term, between those that are seen to be only or primarily sexual and those that are primarily something else (for example, romantic) but include a sexual relationship as well. Such relationships can be characterised by uncertainty and lack of clarity of the rules, particularly since the rules are rarely discussed. It may be that one partner assumes that a sexual relationship also indicates a romantic relationship, whereas the other makes no such assumption. Many people assume that sexual monogamy can be expected in romantic relationships, especially in marriage, and therefore it is never discussed; severe conflict will arise if one party, not having made that assumption, has sexual relations with a third person.

Marital relationships

Generally speaking, marital relationships refer to relationships between two people who usually have an emotional or romantic relationship, who have a sexual relationship, who co-reside, who share property in common, and who are publicly identified and identify as a couple. This, therefore, includes those couples who are legally married and those who are not, who live in what is often called a 'de facto marriage' (that is, a marriage 'in fact' but not in law). It should be noted that, although in most countries they do not receive legal recognition, permanent relationships that fulfil these criteria for marriage can occur between partners of the same sex, and the issues that can underlie conflict in those relationships are often similar to those in opposite-sex relationships. Same-sex relationships, however, are not only likely to face a lack of positive social support or legal protection, but may also in fact be under pressure to break down.

Marital conflict

The central importance of something called 'the family', the nature of which has been changing over the years, remains constant. When surveyed over the past ten years about their most important goals in life, people in many different countries have given the same answers: they rank family life as the most important, then security (all basic needs and necessities provided for). Prosperity, an important life (achievement, respect, recognition), and an exciting life rank considerably lower. Given the priority placed on marriage, the family, and security, it is understandable that this is an area not only of great importance, intensity, and investment, but also of great potential and actual conflict.

A number of areas commonly lead to conflict in marriage; these include changing models and expectations of what marriage is or should be, sexual differences and dissatisfaction, financial problems, and differences over parenting. Expectations of marriage change, not only individually but also socially. These include changes in what marriage actually is and how easily it can be dissolved, changes to models of how women and men should behave in marriage, changes to models of how a family should function, and changing expectations of married people about what they expect from the relationship. Each partner may have a different perception of what her or his role should be, and how the relationship should operate.

Sexual dysfunction can produce relationship conflict, but it is usually secondary to, and far more often caused by, relationship conflict. Most often sexual conflict arises in relation to frequency, technique, desire for experimentation, contraception, and extramarital sexual relations. Financial conflict includes budgeting, and perceptions of necessary and extravagant expenditure. Conflict can arise over child-rearing, particularly discipline and the exercise of authority, and can include conflict about moral and religious values.

One area of marital conflict that has attracted a great deal of attention and concern is that of domestic violence, which includes physical, emotional, and psychological violence against one partner in a marriage by the other (and most often by men against women), and violence against children. There seems to have been an escalating amount of violence within marriage and de facto relationships; there are questions about whether this is an actual increase, or only increased reporting of such violence, which has in the past remained unreported (and to a large degree still does). Factors involved in domestic violence include alcohol, unemployment, periods of confinement to home (for example, holidays, wet weather, unemployment, school holidays), lack of money, and lack of interests and activities.

There are many excellent studies of domestic violence and the issues raised by it, particularly concerning the role of male and female stereotyping and power balance. It remains a matter of controversy as to whether any non-judicial conflict resolution techniques are appropriate in attempting to deal with domestic violence; for example, could an agreement about it ever be mediated?

A number of specific issues arise in relation to conflict resolution in personal relationships and marriage. The intensity, importance, and investment of the relationship are key factors, particularly where each partner has a different perception. The role of the relationship in building personal identity and self-esteem—and the effect on identity and self-esteem when the relationship is or seems to be threatened—also influences conflict and conflict resolution. The intrusion of an outsider (for example, a mediator or counsellor) into what is essentially an intimate relationship between two people can be difficult, in part because of the importance of confidences, secrets, and hidden issues that the partners may be prepared to share with each other, but not with a stranger. The intensity of emotion that can arise in close relationships is also a factor in heightening the level of conflict.

In marital conflict resolution, additional issues arise: they include those regarding marriage and property, and those that relate to children and to relatives of both partners, who may be direct or indirect participants in any conflict.

In some cases, there will be an overlap between marital therapy and conflict resolution, or between the role of a lawyer representing either of the parties in a separation or divorce and conflict resolution.

Family conflict

Different models of the family exist, not only across different cultures and societies, but also within a single society. Different people in different families may have quite different expectations of how a family will operate. It is therefore difficult to define the 'normal family'. Norms within the family will vary cross-culturally, across economic and social divisions, and geographically (for example, rural as contrasted with urban perceptions). Roles, values, and behaviour in a family in one context may be quite different from those of a family in a different context. What constitutes 'normal' family behaviour can therefore be very difficult to define.

But most people grow up with models of the family that are derived from their own families (for example, men learn how fathers or husbands are supposed to behave from their own fathers), those of friends, and from the media. The media's role is very important; the effect of the 'happy family' model of many television soap operas can be very powerful, and can create expectations that, in reality, will not be met. Significantly, this has changed over the last ten years, with the emergence of dramas in which families survive with virtually no happiness and only conflict. It is instructive to view a range of television dramas portraying family life and family conflict, and to consider how conflict and its resolution (or lack of resolution) are presented.

Role conflict is common in families, particularly as roles within the family change (for example, as a child grows into an adolescent and into an adult, or as a woman goes out to work, or as a husband retires). The focus of authority and power may change, also often leading to conflict. Members of a family may develop different values (for example, on sexual matters), different lifestyles (for instance, wearing clothing considered strange by other family members), or different philosophies (such as converting to a new religious or political movement). Changes and conflicts occur within the family; members often leave (for example, when reaching adulthood), or they may spend more or less time with the family.

Increasing numbers of people within families are now having to play roles that have no real historical base—for example, the relationship between a child and her or his father's second ex-wife's new husband's child of his previous marriage. Role conflict becomes increasingly likely as roles are less familiar and less clearly defined (for example, the amount of authority that an older child of a previous marriage has over a child of the current marriage), and particularly where unclear roles occur within situations of tension (as many, if not most, ex-marriage-partner combinations will be).

The resolution of conflict within families—that is, when it involves all members of the family—raises particular problems, whether for the participant in the conflict who seeks to facilitate resolution or for the mediator. These include the fact that there are likely to be competing interests among members, different perceptions of the role of the family, different perceptions of the role of family members, different (and sometimes conflicting) needs, and changing roles and needs over time. Family conflict resolution can be difficult because the participants spend so much time together; there is rarely an opportunity for anyone physically to separate or to take 'time out' because they live together. There are pressures that arise because of the need for some cooperation in living together, and that arise from the different degrees of dependence of some members on others (including financial dependence).

Sometimes, in situations of extreme conflict, family therapy may be more appropriate than family conflict resolution.

For the mediator or counsellor seeking to assist in family conflict resolution, there are additional problems, particularly that of being the 'stranger'—'the outsider'—in the midst of the family. The mediator may be seen variously as 'saviour', 'intruder', 'scapegoat', 'judge', 'parent substitute', 'confidante', or 'analyst' by different members of the family at different times. As an outsider, the third party does not have access to the family's past, which may, in fact, be the most important dimension in understanding a present problem. This can include not only the past of the family as a whole, but also the past of each parent, and the individual pasts of each of the children, together with those of a range of other family members (for example, parents-in-law).

It is not uncommon in family conflict for participants, particularly parents, to make continual reference to the past, and to talk at length about how people have behaved in the past. While examining some aspects of the past can be helpful, it needs to be used creatively (to help understand and resolve the present problems) rather than accusingly (to punish or make people feel guilty).

Conflict involving children

Virtually all families with children face conflict involving and centring on the children. Conflict is a part of the experience of growing up—testing limits, trying out authority, being rebellious, pushing adults to extremes, and learning what happens when the rules are broken. This is often especially the case in adolescence, when young people begin to develop and test out their adult independence.

Conflict involving children can include generational value conflict—that is, conflicting values between parents (and sometimes grandparents) and children on issues such as morals (including sexual behaviour), appearance (clothing, hairstyles, and washing), work (such as contributions around the home), and behaviour. In some cases, the child may simply be testing parental values; in others, the child may have consciously, or under peer pressure, rejected those values, and may have developed new, personal values.

Children generally respond very positively to non-authoritarian conflict resolution methods, although they are often suspicious and hesitant when such approaches are initially introduced. A considerable amount of material has been written specifically on conflict resolution and children, including material on conflict resolution in schools. Encouraging children to participate in collaborative problem solving, in identifying options, and in recognising that both they and parents, or teachers, have needs that could be met often results in imaginative and effective resolutions of conflict.

The ending of relationships

One area within an interpersonal relationship that is often the focus of conflict is the ending of the relationship, particularly, as in the case of marriage, where there may be many complicated issues to be resolved (for example, the division of property, arrangements about children, and public statements regarding the ending of a publicly recognised relationship).

Among the issues that can arise and cause conflict in separation and divorce are the process of making the decision to separate or divorce, questions of who made the decision and who is responsible or 'to blame', how the non-deciding partner is told, how children and other members of the family are informed, and how the decision is 'published' to the community. The actual process of physical separation, followed by legal separation or divorce, has the potential for powerful conflict, which often finds its focus in the attribution of blame or responsibility. This takes on a particular quality if any third party is involved (particularly one who is identified as having broken up the relationship).

Property division, decisions about custody of and access to the children, and decisions about maintenance and expenses relating to the separation or divorce often become the focus for renewed conflict; they provide disputes over which the participants can fight, usually as a symptom of the underlying, and unresolved, relationship conflict. This will affect future contact and future relationships between the ex-partners. Many of these issues will vary in importance depending on whether or not the parties wish for some ongoing relationship, on how amicable the separation or divorce was, and how much blame each attributes to the other. People other than the ex-partners are also involved in the separation and divorce proceedings: children, any new partners, other family members, and friends.

Emotions are often very strong in the ending of a relationship such as marriage; feelings of loss, grief, anger, accusation, guilt, and blame are common, and have to be worked through. Such emotions can actively hinder the process of conflict resolution, and in many cases, it may be more effective to defer attempts to resolve matters that are not urgent until the parties are no longer 'actively bleeding'. Therapy, whether for an individual, a couple, or a family, can be highly beneficial if the stress of the situation prevents them from participating in its resolution, or if some or all of them find the level of discomfort unbearable.

In many cases, the legal process of separation and divorce will do nothing to resolve, and much to intensify, the conflict between the parties. The fact that a relationship has been legally terminated does not mean that it may not continue indefinitely as the most important, even if most destructive, relationship for either or both people. The resolution of the relationship is essentially unrelated to any legal process. It may require counselling, marital therapy, or mediation to assist the parties, even if they have decided that their relationship is irretrievably broken down, in order to resolve it to the extent of being able to end it, not just legally and physically, but also psychologically and personally.

Men, women, and conflict

Do men and women behave differently in situations of conflict, and in trying to bring about conflict resolution? Some research is beginning to be undertaken in the area of gender and conflict and conflict resolution (for example, Taylor & Beinstein-Muller 1994). While some general conclusions can be drawn from this research, it does not suggest that all men and all women behave in gender stereo-typical ways in all circumstances. It is equally important to recognise that gender differences seem much more likely to derive from culture and socialisation than from biological determinants. Many of the apparent differences between men and women in situations of conflict seem to relate to styles of communication and perception—that is, differences in the ways in which men and women perceive and talk about conflicts and the factors that provoke conflict.

Men	Women
tend to talk the language of facts ('What happened was . . . ')	tend to talk the language of feelings ('When . . . I felt . . . ')
tend to talk the language of 'reality' ('What happened was . . . ')	tend to talk the language of perception ('I felt it was . . . ')
tend not to disclose feelings (and tend to denigrate the expression of feelings)	tend to disclose feelings (and tend to criticise a lack of expression of feelings)
tend to focus on problem solving (the conflict as a single problem, or sequence of problems)	tend to talk about changing a relationship (the conflict as a condition within a relationship)
tend to talk the language of the present (and tend to denigrate reference to the past and the future)	tend to talk the language of the past and the future
focus on content	focus on relationship
tend to be competitive and feel a need to be competitive (that is, to be aggressive) even to their disadvantage	tend to compromise and often appear willing to yield (that is, be submissive)
tend to be very concerned about saving or losing face	tend not to be concerned about saving or losing face

---

Case study 11

Jeff and David have been in a gay relationship for three years. Jeff told his parents he was homosexual shortly after meeting David, and they have hardly spoken with him since then. Jeff's two brothers are very hostile regarding Jeff's sexuality and, on the rare occasions he has spoken with them, always claim that Jeff was 'turned into a homosexual' by David and would be 'normal' if he got away from David.

Jeff hears from a family friend that his father is seriously ill in hospital and may not live more than a few weeks. He contacts his mother, who confirms this, but tells Jeff that neither she nor his father wish him to visit the hospital unless and until he breaks off his relationship with David.

Analyse this conflict carefully, and consider how the pressure of time may affect any attempt at resolution. Explore short-term options for Jeff if he wishes to visit his father, and long-term options if he wishes to resolve the conflict with the family.

Obviously, these are broad generalisations. But if they have any basis in reality, they may be of great significance in approaching conflict between men and women. It may even be the case that, if these two different styles of communicating about conflict are put into effect, the very process of communication may increase the level of conflict. For example, the man may perceive the woman as imprecise, unwilling to focus on the 'real problem', digressing about the relationship when there is a problem to be solved, too emotional and insufficiently rational. She, on the other hand, may perceive him as cold and unfeeling, unconcerned about the relationship, and preoccupied with winning some sort of victory (even if there is harm done to the relationship).

Perceptions of acceptable style in conflict also differ between men and women. What may be regarded as firmness, assertiveness, and strength in a man (for example, raising the voice, being somewhat aggressive, or even thumping a table) is likely to be perceived as unacceptable in a woman's behaviour. He may be seen to be shouting 'because he is tough'; she is shouting 'because she is hysterical'. The expression of emotions within conflict is also subject to gender differences: a man cries 'because he is weak', while a woman cries 'because that is what women do'.

Where conflict involves men and women, and particularly when the conflict is between a man and a woman, differences of perceptions, expectations, and communication styles may need to be taken into account.

Interpersonal and relationship conflict raises a number of particular problems for conflict resolution, mostly relating to the intensity, importance, and investment that either or both parties are likely to place in the relationship, and the often very strong connection between the relationship and personal identity and self-esteem. The degree of emotion in such conflicts can be particularly high, and requires a very sensitive approach. Any distinction between conflict resolution or mediation and therapy is likely to blur when dealing with conflict in close interpersonal relationships, particularly marriage.

12 Neighbourhood and Intergroup Conflict

People not only live in personal relationships such as marriages and families; they also live in geographical and social units, including neighbourhoods, communities, towns, and cities. Some of these units are defined geographically (for example, a neighbourhood) and others by characteristics of their members (such as an ethnic community). The kind of conflict that often occurs within geographical units and community groups raises some issues that tend to be universal to all conflict, but it also raises issues that are specific to this type of conflict.

Territoriality

Territoriality is an important concept in neighbourhood and community conflict. It can also be significant in workplace conflict and, of course, is a central issue in international conflict. Theorists have offered their different explanations for the human tendency to want to possess territory. Robert Ardrey, in *The Territorial Imperative* (1967), popularised the theory that human beings are animals whose behaviour towards ownership, protection, and expansion of territory is analogous to the behaviour of animals; Ardrey suggests that it is similarly genetically inherited. He claims that mutual antagonism increases as natural hazards decrease; as external dangers diminish, internal conflict is likely to increase. Ardrey argues that territoriality is an innate characteristic of all animals, including humans. He defines the territorial imperative as 'the inward compulsion in animate beings to possess and defend' an area of space 'as an exclusive preserve' (Ardrey 1967, p. 3).

When considering the territorial dimension of conflict, it is important to recognise that cultural and individual perceptions of territory may differ, and that territory can be both actual and symbolic. All people have concepts of personal space; this varies between individuals and cross-culturally, and refers to the area around the individual within which intrusions become sensitive and/or threatening. Some people may find close physical proximity reassuring and friendly; others may find it threatening and discomfiting. Territory does not only refer to geographical territory; it can also include symbolic territory (for example, areas of responsibility and authority, work responsibilities, and household tasks).

Neighbourhood conflict

Conflict is very common between neighbours—that is, between people living next to each other or in close proximity. Neighbourhood conflict can be inter-personal conflict but often contains issues and dimensions that are different from that kind of conflict.

Disputes between neighbours tend to fall into clear categories. There are disputes over common or adjoining property, boundaries, and the limits of territory Often related to this, there are disputes over fences, including whether to have a fence and, if so, what sort and how high. Questions of responsibility for meeting the costs of the fence, and repair or replacement of the fence, are also common.

Disputes about intrusion are also frequent. They include intrusion by noise, trees, animals, smoke, smells, water leaking or flooding, children, and buildings. They may be related to disputes about privacy, and to concerns about being over-looked, overheard, or 'spied on'. Noise—including music, arguments, parties, house and vehicle burglar alarms, lawn-mowers, tools, appliances, and backyard workshops—also causes intrusion disputes. Many people argue that they do not mind what the neighbours do, so long as it does not intrude into their territory.

The obstruction of light (for example, building projects), and excessive light (such as a garden floodlight shining into a bedroom) can cause problems, as can trees with branches that overhang, or that drop leaves or fruit, or whose roots damage property (for instance, drains and fences). Animals can intrude by making noise, attacking people, and damaging gardens. Sometimes the dispute relates to claims of excessive numbers or inappropriate types of animals.

Some neighbourhood conflict is centred on children: children who wander, make noise, are aggressive, or engage in verbal abuse. Sometimes conflict arises because of claims of parental maltreatment or neglect.

Disputes can arise over issues of alleged health hazards (including smoke and smells, pollution, and the use of pesticides and other chemicals), over rubbish being dumped over the property boundary or on to common areas, or over the accumulation of garbage. Parking may be a focus of conflict, even when it occurs outside property boundaries; territoriality can attach to spaces in the common roadway or to access ways.

A sort of moral territoriality can lead to conflicts relating to allegedly offen-sive or obscene language, or behaviour that is visible or audible across property boundaries. Such conflict can relate not only to the behaviour, but also to the act of one party in reporting it to the local municipality, to property owners, or to the police.

Conflict also often arises between businesses and local residents in a commu-nity (for example, between a hotel and residents who object to the behaviour of patrons). Such conflicts usually relate to differences over the primary purpose of the neighbourhood, the relative rights (and responsibilities) of the parties, and the source of local power and decision-making.

Some neighbourhood conflicts, although presented as disputes arising from specific behaviour, may have their origins in other conflicts. Interpersonal conflict may lead to neighbourhood conflict; for example, two neighbours who were friends but whose friendship has ended may direct considerable hostility towards each other and use neighbourhood disputes as a means of doing so. Value conflict, including that caused by religious and cultural differences, can manifest in neighbourhood disputes. For example, the dispute may appear to be about the behaviour of a particular neighbour, but may, in fact, be an expression of disapproval of the person's religious or cultural identity. This can be a particular problem between neighbours of different ethnic or cultural backgrounds.

The law and neighbourhood conflict

There are both general legal principles and specific laws that apply to disputes between neighbours. These include laws regarding property, dividing fences, public order, nuisance, water and drainage, and related matters. People in neighbourhood disputes can often apply to local courts for an adjudication and the enforcement of a decision. This can temporarily and superficially settle the dispute, but in general, the use of the law, authorities based on law, and litigation to resolve neighbourhood conflict is more likely to increase the conflict, to make it more bitter, to prolong it as the legal process is carried out, and to add to the cost. Any order made on the basis of law, although enforceable in various ways, is unlikely to be satisfactory or acceptable to both parties. One party, even if prepared to abide by the adjudication, may then seek another basis for taking action against the neighbour (for example, through a series of complaints about the neighbour to various authorities). In some cases, the adjudication may create situations of great discomfort and high tension within the neighbourhood (for example, neighbours refusing to speak to or acknowledge one another). Where the neighbours have some need for occasional cooperation (for example, over a dividing fence), a hostile relationship will ensure that every interaction is characterised by conflict.

Relatively simple disputes, however—where the central question is one of fact, rather than feelings or relationships (for example, a dispute over where a property boundary lies, or what constitutes the type of fence required by law)—may sometimes be quickly and efficiently dealt with by a court or legal authority.

Attempts to resolve neighbourhood conflict need to take account of a number of basic issues, including territoriality, different individual and cultural perceptions of personal space and intrusion, past relationships, the probable future of the relationship between the parties, and the view the parties take of potential ongoing tension and discomfort.

Neighbourhood community justice

Among the most successful models for the resolution of neighbourhood conflicts has been the neighbourhood community justice centre model, which originated in the USA and was introduced into Australia by Community Justice Centres in New South Wales. A similar concept has been taken up in other places, and has also developed with local community-based mediation centres now being established throughout Australia and other countries. These make use of volunteers (who may receive some nominal form of payment for the hours they work) from within the community. They receive a basic training and work, usually in co-mediation, on disputes to which they are assigned by the coordinator(s) of the centre. For many low-level neighbourhood disputes, this form of community-based dispute resolution is very successful.

Tenancy conflict

Conflict is common within a tenancy relationship—that is between the owner and/or agent or manager of a property and the tenant. There is also a high incidence of conflict between tenants in different accommodation in the same building (for example, different apartments in one block). These types of conflict are also often referred to community mediation centres. Interpersonal conflict between co-residents—that is, people sharing the same accommodation—was discussed in chapter 11.

Conflict involving the owner and/or agent or manager of a property and a tenant frequently relates to non-payment or late payment of rent, noise, pets, children, complaints from other tenants or neighbours, and the care and maintenance of the property by the tenant and the owner. It often arises out of disagreements over the rules applying to the occupancy of the property, and to the relative responsibilities, rights, and liabilities of tenants and owners. The issues and problems arising in neighbourhood conflict generally also arise in tenancy conflict, including disputes over common areas, garbage, motor vehicles, the use and maintenance of common facilities (for example, gardens), and allegations of offensive or disruptive behaviour.

Tenancy conflict can be particularly intense and prolonged where one or both of the parties spend most of their time in the building (for example, retired or unemployed people at home all day), and the lack of other interests sometimes means that the monitoring of grievances about accommodation becomes an ongoing pastime or, in some cases, obsession.

Resolution of tenancy conflict must take account of the relative power balance of the parties, the importance of the accommodation for each, and the history of the relationship between them (particularly of all previous problems or disputes), as well as relationships with previous tenants or owners. There are also legal issues, especially where there is a lease, or where the parties may have particular rights or obligations under law. Each party's perception of the appropriate role and behaviour of the other will also be important—for example, the owner's perceptions of the roles of tenant, agent, and owner, as compared with the tenant's perceptions of the same roles. Complications can arise as a result of the participation of other tenants and/or neighbours, in relation both to the owner or agent and to the tenant involved in the conflict. The values held by the owner, the agent, the tenant, and the neighbours are also certain to have an impact on the conflict. For example, an owner's perception of what constitutes 'reasonable tidiness' may differ widely from the perception of the tenant; one tenant's perception of 'excessive noise' may differ from that of an adjoining tenant.

At a time when eviction or non-renewal of a tenancy is threatened or actually carried out, the tenant will often seek out mediation or some other third-party intervention in this area. This places severe strains on any resolution process, even if the owner is prepared to participate. In some cases, the owner may believe it is to her or his advantage to remove a tenant if he or she is able to obtain a more desirable tenant at a higher rent. When there are more tenants seeking accommodation than there are places available, the owners and agents have the advantage, which clearly places the balance of power firmly on their side. This can be particularly the case when the tenant is a single mother or a family with young children; the problems facing such tenants in obtaining accommodation are often such that they have little option but to try to conform to any demands placed on them, however unreasonable or unrealistic (for example, to ensure that 'the children do not make any noise').

Community conflict

As well as existing within a geographical neighbourhood, all individuals belong to communities, and some belong to many different communities. There can be geographical communities (for example, a neighbourhood or town), ethnic communities (for example, people of Vietnamese descent), behavioural communities (for example, Jehovah's Witnesses), and interest group communities (for example, supporters of a particular football team). Some communities live together; some come together frequently; while others rarely meet together. Some people have a strong sense of their community affiliation, and others think of it only on special occasions. Yet other people are only reminded of their community affiliation when others draw their attention to it (for example, a young person, who thinks of herself as Australian, being referred to by her peers as 'Greeks like you').

All communities have implicit criteria, if not explicit rules, for determining membership, and for identifying those who are insiders and who belong, and those who are outsiders and who do not belong. For example, people may say, 'This is how we behave . . . That is not how we behave'.

In some cases, people are born into a community (for example, an Italian Australian); in others, they choose to become a member of it (for instance, by converting to Islam), or community membership is something that they acquire as a result of something else (such as purchasing a house in a particular area).

Intracommunity conflict

Being part of a community provides a further dimension for the occurrence of conflict. It can eventuate within a community, both between an individual or individuals and the community as a whole, or between factions within the community. Intracommunity conflict often relates to the definition of what constitutes the community, and the definition of how the community differs from other communities. It may also involve questions of who is or is not a member, and of what standards and behaviour are appropriate for a member. The definition of community values, particularly when values are challenged or appear to change, and of appropriate responses for those who break the rules of the community are also areas of conflict. Leadership and claims to authority within the community can also be matters for dispute.

Conflicts within a community, although they may nominally be between intracommunity factions, will usually be acted out by individual members of the community who represent or lead the factions (or claim to do so). Such conflict can, of course, have a range of hidden agendas, including attempts by one leader to replace another by making use of an apparent split within the community. All communities have established mechanisms for the resolution of conflict, even if these are often unwritten and not necessarily explicit. In traditional, close-knit communities (for example, rural Aboriginal communities), these may be very clearly defined, although not necessarily formally, and possess great authority and antiquity. Some communities have clear leaders whose role in the resolution of conflict may be crucial; others work on a less structured and more communal basis.

The ultimate sanction that the community has against its members is that of expulsion, and the ultimate sanction members have is that of withdrawal. However, for members of some communities, withdrawal can lead to serious difficulties if they effectively try to cease being a member of one community, but are not accepted by another. The example of the Greek girl given earlier may apply here: if she chooses to reject her identity as a Greek Australian, but is not accepted by her peers, who think of themselves as Australian and of her as Greek, she will be left in something of a vacuum.

The use of external mediators in intracommunity conflict can pose particular problems; not only is the mediator necessarily an outsider, but he or she will also be unaware of the intricacies of the community's past, traditions, and procedures, both formal and informal. Many communities are concerned that they should present a united appearance to society generally, and all parties to a conflict may be eager to ensure that it is contained within the closed and private confines of the community, even cooperating to conceal the truth from an outside party. However, very often only an outsider can facilitate the resolution of such conflicts, since every insider is likely to be identified, by some people and for some reasons, with one or other of the conflicting groups.

Intercommunity conflict

Conflict can occur between two communities, just as it can occur between two individuals. Intercommunity conflict is usually acted out between individual leaders or representatives of the communities concerned. It often relates to disputes over the jurisdiction or the relative rights of the two communities, or to conflicting values or standards of behaviour. Questions of legitimacy and political power, no less than territory, can also provoke conflict.

The use of third-party mediators in intercommunity conflict can only be beneficial if the mediator is clearly not identified or seen to be identified with either community, is recognised as impartial in the conflict, is acceptable to both, and has a good basic knowledge of both. The choice of participants in such conflict resolution (assuming that all members of both communities cannot participate) and the location of any discussions will have an important effect on the outcome.

Intergroup conflict can sometimes arise over difference or non-conformity, particularly where one group is in the minority or where groups have different values. Different groups may have different standards of behaviour (including standards of dress and physical appearance) and different, and sometimes conflicting, values. In some cases, these differences will be public and visible (for example, the wearing of head coverings by some Muslim women) or they may be only occasionally public (for example, dietary rules).

Stereotypes and community conflict

A strong sense of group affiliation and loyalty can lead to positive stereotypes about group members, and to negative stereotypes about outsiders generally or members of other groups particularly. Some other groups may not just be identified as outsiders, but also as enemies. Prejudice towards other groups, particularly where this leads to the identification of enemies, can provide a powerful motivation to seek out opportunities for conflict. For example, stereotypical perceptions of police officers by motor cyclists, and of motor cyclists by police officers, is likely to establish a sense within each group that the two groups are in natural conflict, and opportunities for the manifestation of this conflict are likely to be found. Perceptions that all members of another group are hostile, dangerous, threatening, unreliable, and untrustworthy establish the basis for a relationship in which conflict is inevitable. Such perceptions are often based on a history of conflict and hostility, and on the perpetuation of myths and images of the enemy among the group's members. If it is assumed that the enemy is the manifestation of all that is bad, little value will be seen in talking to them, as opposed to fighting with them. Thus, any attempt to approach such conflict requires an understanding of past relationships, of images and perceptions by each community of the other, and a recognition that these will be powerful influences in shaping the present and the future.

Enmification

An important area of research in the study of conflict relates to the means whereby people choose or create enemies—that is, enmification. This is particularly important in approaching intergroup or intercommunity conflict and conflict based on prejudice, stereotypes, and discrimination. It is also very important in understanding war and intergroup violence. Some may suggest that human beings need to have enemies and that, if no 'natural' or 'logical' enemy exists, an enemy will nevertheless be found.

Thus, in times of very high unemployment, people may focus on immigrants (particularly those of a visibly different ethnic origin) as the enemy: 'Those people come here and take away our jobs'. However, in times of low unemployment and low migration, there is still a tendency to focus on some groups as 'the enemy', attributing to them other anti-social activities. Although the defined enemy can change over time (and former allies can even come to be defined as enemies), there is a tendency for old enmities to be perpetuated across generations, and even over hundreds of years. One ethnic group may, in the present, define its enemy as another ethnic group on the basis of events in the distant past.

Once a relationship of enmity has been established, it will tend to influence all actual and potential relationships between the two parties. If one group is defined as the enemy, possessing all possible negative attributes, then it is unlikely that an effective working relationship can be established with the group or any of its members. There are, of course, exceptions. In some cases, a few members of the hated group will be identified as 'not typical' and can, for some purposes at least, be treated as other than the enemy.

Although there has been increasing research done on enmification in recent years, virtually no research has been undertaken on what might, in order to define an opposite of enmification, be called *amification*—that is, the process by which allies are chosen or constructed. More importantly, work needs to be undertaken on the process whereby it might be possible to transform human relationships so that enemies may become, if not actually allies, at least people who can live together with minimal hostility.

Ethnic conflict

Traditional ethnic rivalries, with long histories of often bitter and bloody conflict in the original homelands of the members of contemporary ethnic communities, can be significant factors in present conflict. Stereotypical beliefs about members of the other community—based on what they or their ancestors did, or are alleged to have done, in the past, and on generations of stories and legends, and large quantities of propaganda from both sides—establish a perception of the enemy that makes conflict virtually inevitable, and conflict resolution very difficult.

The context and the cause of particular conflicts are less important than the fact of a continuing historical conflict. Deep-value conflict is usually a part of such situations. Interethnic conflicts of this kind can involve complex issues of national identity and history, of language, religion and culture, and of past and present territorial divisions and political systems.

Attempts to work towards resolution involve considerations not only of the issues relevant to intercommunity conflict generally, but also of questions concerning the language of resolution: whether it is to be the language of one of the groups (if they have different languages) or a neutral language—for example, English in Australia.

Symbolic conflict resolution

In many traditional societies, conflict between or within groups was often acted out symbolically in ritual, drama, and contest. This allowed for a temporary release from the formal rules of the society, and for the (relatively friendly) expression of inherent competition and conflict. In contemporary society, there are still remnants of this symbolic approach, and these can have important therapeutic effects in reducing the level of tension and conflict between groups without it erupting into open expression or, particularly, into violence.

In a sense, much sporting competition can be seen as symbolic intergroup conflict; it can allow for conflict and competition between groups (including 'natural rivals' such as between different schools, cities, states, and nations) to be expressed through physical activity but (usually) without physical violence, permanent injury, or death. However, the language of sporting commentators, particularly in reporting international sporting competitions, is much like that used by commentators describing war. Although team sports allow for the participation of both teams and supporters, participating in different forms of symbolic conflict, the fine line between symbolic and actual conflict has been demonstrated in recent years at football matches in Europe in which the conflict between opposing team supporters has led to serious violence.

Within and between different communities, different standards are likely to apply regarding the use of physical violence. In some communities, a physical fight may be the normal means of resolving a heated conflict; in others, it will be regarded as unacceptable and abnormal.

Facilitation

There are particular difficulties involved in using conflict resolution techniques, including mediation, within and between groups. The term 'facilitation' is sometimes used to refer to what is effectively mediation but where there are more than two (or perhaps up to six) participants. There are a number of obvious practical problems in acting as a mediator or facilitator for a large group of people, including that of keeping control, maintaining dialogue (rather than a multiplicity of dialogues), and ensuring participation by all members rather than domination by a few. The mediator or facilitator may have to make a practical decision as to how many people can actually participate in any conflict resolution process and how they will be chosen. However, an attempt to resolve

---

Case study 12

Enrico immigrated to Australia two years ago. He moved into a new house with his wife and two children about a year ago. Since then, he has generally been ignored by the neighbours, although he has made a number of attempts to establish a friendly relationship with them.

One evening, one of his neighbours calls out to Enrico as he is walking into his house after coming home from work. The neighbour, Fred, tells Enrico that the large tree in Enrico's backyard has been dropping berries onto Fred's barbecue area. As a result, Fred has arranged for a large branch to be removed from the tree the following week. Enrico is a little confused by the conversation, since his English is not particularly good, but he thinks that Fred said something about the courts and the law.

Enrico is concerned that, if the branch is cut off the tree, the tree is likely to fall into his backyard and possibly to damage the house.

Identify the important issues involved in this conflict, and consider what conflict resolution processes might be appropriate. Consider also processes that might simply make the conflict worse.

---

community conflict by mediation only between the leaders of communities or groups is unlikely to be successful.

In any attempt to resolve such conflict, careful attention must be given to particular issues that arise in dealing with conflict within neighbourhoods and communities. Although some of the general principles and practices of conflict resolution can be applied, specialist methods need to be developed to deal with the special needs of each situation.

13 Industrial and Commercial Conflict

Conflict involving money, especially when the money is of considerable importance to the people concerned, often has particular characteristics. Although sometimes it is suggested that financial or commercial conflict can be managed without emotional or 'deep' issues arising, this is rarely the case. For example, observing two professional commercial negotiators working out a financial deal will disclose a high level of personal emotional involvement, even when the money concerned is not theirs. The two major areas in which such conflict occurs are employment and commerce.

Employment conflict

Employment is very important for many people. Apart from being a means of survival, it is the area in which most people spend about a third of their time and in which they seek a great deal of purpose, fulfilment, and opportunity for self-enhancement and development. Employment usually involves an ongoing relationship like marriage, but, unlike marriage, it is a relationship in which people are brought together without freedom of choice, being forced to relate to and cooperate with one another regardless of personal likes or dislikes. The workplace is the site of much conflict; some of it makes national and international headlines and has significant effects on people outside the workplace (for example, industrial action in the form of strikes). Most of it, however, causes problems only for those directly involved.

The employer–employee relationship

Employment involves a relationship between an individual employee and an employer, who may also be an individual, or a group of individuals, a private company, a community organisation, or a government authority. Power balance is important in employment conflict: if the employee needs the employment more than the employer needs the employee, the power balance in any conflict is with the employer. Consider the situation of an unskilled process worker in an area of high unemployment and low employee demand: what power does that person have in a conflict with an employer who may be able to fill any vacancy many times over without difficulty? On the other hand, an employee with highly specialised skills may hold the power balance working in an area with a high level of vacancies and high competition between employers for the available employees.

In many cases, employees who would be relatively powerless as individuals may be in a powerful position when represented by their unions or professional associations. There are, of course, arguments relating to the relative benefits of an employee negotiating directly with an employer without representation.

The employee–employer relationship covers a broad range of stages and issues, at each of which conflict can occur. The stages and issues include: recruitment, selection, terms and conditions of employment (including salary, status, fringe benefits, insurance, superannuation, leave), promotion, transfer, benefits of employment (including training, fringe benefits), supervision, discipline, discrimination, harassment, termination (whether resignation, dismissal, redundancy), claims of incapacity or incompetence, sick leave, workers compensation, and occupational health and safety.

The employment relationship not only includes the employee and the actual, legal employer (which may be a company or government department), but also runs through a chain of authority from the employee, up through any immediate supervisors (for example, a foreman or section head), through middle management to senior management, and up to the head of the organisation. Different people in this chain of authority will have different levels of power and authority (for example, the level at which a decision can be taken to dismiss an employee will vary from one organisation to another).

Workplace conflict often arises as a result of interpersonal conflict between individuals either *vertically* or *horizontally*. An individual could have conflict with a supervisor (vertical) or with a fellow employee (horizontal).

A range of legal issues important to workplace conflict arises out of the employment relationship, and includes those relating to employer and employee rights, responsibilities and liabilities, and specific statutory provisions (for example, relating to leave, discrimination, occupational health and safety, and the regulation of specific industries and occupations). In looking at workplace conflict, it is important to be aware of any relevant legal issues. As with other forms of conflict, where legal rights or obligations may be involved, it is important to ensure that all parties are aware of their rights and their obligations, and that any resolution is not in contravention of any legal requirement.

Trade unions and employment conflict

Trade unions have an important role in workplace conflict, both in the sense of participating in attempts to bring about resolution, but also, in some circumstances, provoking and maintaining conflict. It is important to recognise that the role of a trade union is advocacy, not simply or even essentially on behalf of the individual member who may be involved in a workplace dispute, but on behalf of the collective interests of the workers in the work area. Thus, in some situations, the union may face a conflict between advocating on behalf of the rights of one member and doing so on behalf of other members, or on behalf of what the union perceives to be the interests of workers in the area generally. This can be a particular problem when the conflict is between members of the same union (for example, one member accused of harassing another member, or one member complaining of harassment by a number of other members).

A further area of conflict involving unions relates to union membership, and whether it should be compulsory or voluntary, and, if compulsory, what provisions should be made for people who have personal objections to joining (for example, religious beliefs).

The role of unions in workplace conflict is generally, and has been traditionally, that of an advocate in an adversarial approach to the employer. This approach may be effective in some cases but, clearly, is unlikely to assist in a non-adversarial approach to resolution. Some trade unions have begun developing alternative approaches to help their members to participate in non-adversarial conflict resolution (for example, mediation).

Conflict management

Conflict in employment covers a broad range, but basically tends to fall into the following categories of conflict: between employer and employee, supervisor and employee, one employee and another, a group of employees and one other, one group of employees and another group, a group of employees and their employer, an employee and a client or customer, a trade union and employer, or a trade union and employee.

Problems arise when a conflict involves two employees but is dealt with by a manager or an employer without the involvement of the direct participants. In such cases, 'conflict management' is often a more appropriate term, since the aim is likely to be containment or suppression. It may be that an employer views dismissing one or both employees involved in a dispute as the most economically efficient response. Although this will often be represented as resolution, it is, at best, management. Its effect may be to remove the immediate cause of conflict, but in general it is unlikely to deal with any underlying issues, and may have the effect of provoking widespread anxiety and conflict within the workplace, and undermining workplace morale.

If the underlying cause of the conflict is not essentially a negative relationship between the two employees but is rather organisational structure, management policy or procedure, or defective supervision or management, the effect will have been to treat a symptom while ignoring the cause.

A positive approach to resolving workplace conflict (for example, by the establishment of effective grievance processes) not only encourages effective resolution, but also promotes good workplace morale and encourages employees to take a positive view of management. To be effective, workplace conflict resolution processes must be, and more importantly must be seen to be, beneficial, impartial, and fair.

Some managers, however, find the sort of conflict resolution processes outlined in this book very threatening, viewing them as in some way undermining managerial authority, and implying that employees ought to have some direct input into management decisions. Large multinational corporations have clearly established that effective grievance handling and workplace conflict resolution are efficient management practice, and are financially advantageous. Large corporations tend to provide effective conflict resolution processes; smaller businesses often take a strong 'employer's rights' position, inevitably to their detriment.

In general, workplace conflicts are more likely to be symptoms of underlying problems than self-contained, individual problems. Seen in this light, they can be used as important opportunities to diagnose underlying problems and to remedy management or system flaws that, if ignored, will lead to more conflicts.

Discrimination

Some conflict in the workplace is a result of prejudice and discrimination on a range of grounds. The most common are race, sex, marital status, and physical impairment. However, discrimination also occurs on the basis of physical appearance, intellectual impairment, homosexuality, parenthood, mental illness, previous criminal record, religious belief or practice, political belief, trade union membership and non-membership, age, social status, or geographic origin. Discrimination on many of these grounds is, under certain circumstances, unlawful in some jurisdictions.

Conflict based on discrimination is usually the result of stereotypical assumptions about people in particular categories—for example, 'Women cannot exercise authority over men; therefore a woman cannot be effective in a supervisor's position, and so a woman cannot be appointed to the supervisor's position for which she has applied'.

Some workplace conflict is based on the harassment of one or more employees by another employee or employees, or by a supervisor or employer. Harassment involves subjecting a person to particular behaviour when it is known that the person finds such behaviour unacceptable, offensive, or distressing. Harassment is really about the exercise of power; victims are inevitably people who, because of their vulnerable positions or personalities, are unlikely to defend themselves against the harassment. Harassment involves a person in a strong position using power over a person in a weaker position. It can be verbal (such as offensive name-calling) or physical (for example, sexual assault). It can be undertaken by a single person against another (for instance, one person sexually harassing another, but only when no one else is present) or can involve, for example, all the other employees in a workplace harassing one individual.

Harassment is usually undertaken on the same grounds as discrimination. In certain circumstances, and in some jurisdictions, harassment is unlawful.

Some workplace conflict results from disputes over occupational health and safety when there is disagreement between the employer and employees or their union over levels of acceptable risk—for example, a dispute about whether or not particular work practices involve unacceptable levels of risk, or whether a particular workplace poses dangers to the health of employees.

Workplace resolution processes

All workplaces have informal mechanisms for the resolution of conflict; this may simply mean that a supervisor intervenes to mediate or arbitrate. In some workplaces, grievance handling or conflict resolution is incorporated into the mainstream of management, without any special policy or procedures. In others there may be specific internal processes for handling grievances and resolving conflict. They can either be integrated into the mainstream management system, or be focused in specialist areas (for example, with a grievance officer appointed).

In general, conflict in the workplace is most effectively and permanently resolved if it is handled quickly and at the lowest possible level; for example, a resolution between two employees should, wherever possible, be attempted at their level, perhaps by their supervisor, before being referred upwards to middle or senior management as a last resort.

Industrial legislation

Most jurisdictions have mechanisms to allow for the formal resolution of workplace conflict: between an individual employee and an employer, and also between an employer and employees represented by trade unions. Access to these mechanisms sometimes requires the participation of a trade union, and this may disadvantage employees who are not members of unions. Such mechanisms include the federal and state conciliation, arbitration, and industrial relations bodies.

Industrial relations mechanisms usually involve both conciliation (which may be a mixture of non-arbitrational approaches, including mediation) and arbitration (in which a legally binding adjudication is handed down). In some jurisdictions, what is described in the USA as 'med/arb' is used—that is, a commissioner or other authority may try to resolve a dispute by conciliation, but if this does not appear possible, he or she may hand down a binding adjudication.

Conflict resolution in industrial relations includes ongoing negotiations (for example, over awards), cyclical negotiations (such as annual reviews), and crisis negotiations (for example, when a strike is called).

Workplace mediation

Although it may be assumed that the use of a third party, like a mediator, will facilitate workplace conflict resolution, this raises a number of important issues, many of which focus on the status and power of the third party, and her or his location in relation to, or within the power structure of, the organisation. The problem of the power balance of the parties to the conflict (for example, between an employee and an employer) is a critical issue. The role of advocates (for example, unions) may also become an issue, particularly where there is an attempt to redress a power imbalance by providing an advocate for the weaker party (usually the employee).

It is not uncommon for individual workplace disputes to become the focus of larger conflict: for example, a minor employer–employee dispute may be taken up by both employer and union as an appropriate matter on which to fight out a broader industrial relations conflict. Either employer or union may take advantage of a particular dispute to attempt to exercise power over the other; this may take place with or without the knowledge or consent of the individual employee involved in the focal conflict.

Just as in interpersonal relationships, intensity, importance, and investment are important in the employment relationship. For some employees, work has both personal and social significance far beyond being just a job. This may make conflict more intense and difficult to resolve, or may facilitate resolution through a commitment to the maintenance of the employment relationship.

The workplace is a common site for conflict ranging from the relatively minor ('problems') to the major ('deep conflict' in Burton's definition) (Burton 1990b, p. 15). A broad range of issues is raised by workplace conflict, including important legal issues, and a wide variety of approaches are necessary if the conflict is to be dealt with effectively.

Commercial conflict

Many disputes occur in relation to commercial and professional matters, particularly between consumers and suppliers (including the suppliers of professional services, such as medical practitioners or lawyers) and, more recently, in regard to environmental matters. Environmental conflict will be considered in chapter 14. Commercial and professional disputes can raise specific problems, and usually differ significantly from interpersonal or neighbourhood disputes. An overview is provided here of those issues that apply particularly in commercial and professional conflict, and that need to be taken into account in analysis of the conflict and preparation for resolution in these areas.

In matters relating solely to money or compliance with the specifications of a contract, resolution may be easily brought about; adjudication or arbitration may be the most efficient means, although negotiation is commonly effective. Resolution may be very difficult in matters involving underlying value conflict.

These include conflicts where perceptions of dishonesty or unfairness are important, and where, although the focus is on tangible matters (such as quality and cost), the underlying conflict relates to intangible issues, often described as 'matters of principle'.

Unlike conflict in the environmental area, commercial conflict can more often be accurately described in terms of disputes, since it is usually resolved by negotiation and other forms of bargaining directed at a settlement of a specific presenting dispute, or by arbitration, and is based essentially on questions of fact and law. A number of basic legal issues can be involved, including specific statutory rights and obligations (for example, any applicable consumer-protection legislation) and a range of common law principles such as negligence, contract interpretation, and compliance, as well as descriptions and promises.

The most common areas of commercial dispute relate to the quality of goods or services, alleged discrepancies between descriptions or advertisements and the product or service provided, price or payment, delay, consumers' rights to repair or replacement, and compliance with contracts and guarantees. These disputes often focus on the rights of suppliers or providers and the rights of customers. It is not uncommon to find two disputes: one arising from the customer regarding the goods or services provided (or supposed to have been provided), and the other from the supplier regarding failure to pay. Disputes regarding contracts often also have that double aspect: each side alleges that the other has failed in some way to meet its obligations.

Commercial conflict can occur between two (or more) individuals, between an individual and a corporation, between two (or more) corporations, between a corporation and a community, and between a corporation and a state authority. Some commercial conflicts occur within one legal jurisdiction (for example, within New South Wales); some occur within different jurisdictions within one nation (for instance, between a company in Victoria and one in Queensland), and some occur internationally. Particular legal and practical problems often arise when conflict occurs across legal jurisdictions.

Consumer conflict

A common, and growing, area of commercial dispute is that of consumer conflict—that is, where the consumer alleges that the goods or services were not provided, were not of advertised or appropriate quality, or were damaged or otherwise inadequate, that the consumer was overcharged, or that supply was delayed. In many cases, the consumer will seek to resolve the conflict directly with the supplier of the goods or the provider of the services, but increasingly governments are providing legislative support for, and agencies to investigate and attempt to resolve, consumer complaints.

Some companies or industries also provide consumer complaint processes in an attempt to resolve disputes quickly, and to circumvent the need for recourse to state agencies or litigation. Effective dispute settlement procedures within commercial organisations can be highly effective, not only in reducing the likelihood of complaints being made to external agencies or developing into litigation, but also in positively promoting good public relations and identifying areas that require improvement.

There are a number of basic problems in the resolution of consumer disputes, generally disadvantaging the consumer. These include consumer ignorance, particularly in highly technical areas. The customer may simply not have sufficient information to respond to claims by the supplier (for example, knowing how long a particular appliance ought to operate without breaking down). Relative consumer powerlessness is a further disadvantage: the limited financial resources of the consumer may not allow legal action, or legal action of the extent that may be taken by the company. The consumer may not know her or his rights, and may have those rights misrepresented by the provider (for example, the supplier may claim that goods cannot be returned, and an uninformed customer may simply accept that to be the case, even where legally it is not).

The consumer may be confused by highly technical information, and the provider may explain the situation in a highly technical way, whether honestly or with the aim of confusing the consumer. For example, a supplier may claim that a motor vehicle needs certain technically described repairs, and the average consumer will have no means of assessing such a claim.

Goods or services can be of relatively low monetary value for the provider, but of relatively high value for the consumer; a large supplier may regard a $5000 transaction as a minor sale, but the customer may see it as an extremely large purchase. The importance of the amount, and the attention it deserves, will therefore differ. Similarly, a matter may have a very great impact on the consumer but be of little importance to the supplier. For example, a faulty water heater may have virtually no significance for a large corporation manufacturing thousands of them a year, but be of critical importance to a family relying on it for hot water.

The consumer and the provider are often affected by a dramatic power imbalance—for example, the provider may be a wealthy, multinational corporation, and the consumer a single individual with limited resources. Power imbalance can result not only from differences in knowledge, money, or resources, but also from differences in the amount of time available to deal with the matter. Resolution of a dispute may be very time-consuming over a long period. This is likely to have minimal impact on the provider or the staff working on the matter, for whom it is usually not an issue of personal concern or inconvenience, but it may have a substantial impact on, and cause significant inconvenience for, the consumer. The consumer may, for example, need a refrigerator that works immediately rather than the possibility of one that will work in six months.

Commercial dispute resolution

A variety of dispute resolution processes exist for commercial conflict. Traditionally, litigation has been the most usual approach. This, of course, advantages the wealthy and disadvantages the poor. It also advantages those who can wait: litigation is rarely quick. It can include taking action for breach of contract or for negligence, and usually looks to the award of damages to compensate for loss or harm. Trade and commerce protection legislation in some jurisdictions has provided a legal declaration of the rights of those involved in trade and commerce, and of the remedies if such rights are infringed.

Many jurisdictions now also have consumer-protection legislation providing processes to protect the rights of consumers, and establishing an alternative dispute resolution process for the settlement of consumer complaints, particularly those of a low monetary value. Such processes are substantially cheaper, quicker, and less formal than litigation generally or the use of trade practices legislation.

A range of dispute resolution processes have also been established by state trade and professional regulatory bodies, which often have the power to penalise or even to deregister companies or individuals who breach prescribed standards. They also encourage low-level, fairly informal dispute resolution through various grievance procedures. In New South Wales, for example, there is the Motor Vehicle Repairs Disputes Committee, which deals with consumer complaints about motor vehicle repairs and uses a conciliation process. But a dispute with a company that is a member of the Motor Traders' Association can also be referred to that association for resolution.

Some voluntary trade and professional associations, which have as their ultimate sanction the power to suspend or cancel the membership of companies or individuals that breach prescribed standards, have also established dispute resolution processes. For example, the Motor Traders' Association has an internal dispute resolution system that can be used by consumers. Many organisations that provide goods and services, particularly the larger ones, have their own internal dispute resolution procedures, either as specialist mechanisms to handle grievances or as part of normal management responsibilities. These procedures attempt to keep complaints within the organisations, thereby avoiding both unnecessary cost and damage to their image.

A range of independent professional specialist services are now available to the parties to a commercial dispute—for example, the Australian Commercial Disputes Centre based in Sydney. This provides a variety of conflict resolution processes for clients who pay for their services. There are also independent professionals who are sometimes used as mediators, arbitrators, or expert assessors.

Increasingly, industry groups are establishing formal mechanisms to deal with consumer complaints. Sometimes this is done through industry associations, but it is now common to find industry groups establishing autonomous (although industry-funded) agencies to deal with conflicts between suppliers and consumers. Examples of these in Australia include the Banking Ombudsman, the Insurance Ombudsman, the Telecommunications Industry Ombudsman, and the Electricity Industry Ombudsman. The obvious advantage of independent agencies is that they are likely to have greater credibility with consumers.

Internal and external processes

There are potential advantages and disadvantages in using either internal or external dispute resolution systems. An internal process may offer greater knowledge of and access to those involved in providing the goods or services, while the external process may offer greater independence and impartiality. A similar situation exists in the matter of regulation by the State as opposed to regulation by an industry, profession, or company. For the consumer, independence and impartiality may be the most important criteria in dispute resolution, and there may be a degree of suspicion of processes operated or paid for by the supplier with whom the consumer is in conflict.

Sometimes the use of a neutral mediator will be effective in resolving a commercial dispute. Commercial mediation is most often concerned with facilitating negotiations, frequently in strictly financial terms, with the aim of settling a specific dispute. It is most often concerned with facts and with law, rarely with any deeper issues. This is not to say that commercial conflict does not involve deeper issues; it frequently does, and these are most often ignored or denied, mostly because those taking part in the conflict believe that emotional and personal issues are irrelevant or unacceptable in the area in which they work. Observing commercial dispute resolution or negotiation, however, discloses a considerable emotional element, and there are often clear indications of unresolved deeper conflict. At its simplest, this is often a strong personal desire to defeat the opponent; this can be such a powerful drive that rational resolution becomes very difficult, and both participants may pay a considerable price for allowing themselves to become locked into unproductive or even counterproductive struggle.

Specialist technical conflict

Where specialist technical issues arise in a commercial or professional dispute, difficult questions are likely to be raised, and these themselves often lead to additional disputes. These disputes are usually related to facts (or alleged facts), their interpretation, and their implications. Conflicting claims about fact may continue even when, to an outside observer, the matter appears to have been objectively determined. This is particularly the case where the debate over facts masks an underlying conflict, and it often leads into conflict over who is or is not an expert.

If the participants to a conflict cannot agree on the facts, it can be useful to have them appoint a mutually acceptable expert whose opinion they have agreed in advance to accept as binding. The expert may have no role other than to determine a question of fact or interpretation, and need not be involved in mediating or arbitrating the overall conflict. Great difficulty arises when a process for determining the facts cannot be found; adjudication is then probably the only option, and should be sought as soon as possible. It remains a possibility, however, for either or both parties to reject the adjudication, even where this has the force of law.

There are arguments in support of both the use of specialists and of non-specialists in the area concerned. Generally, the use of specialists is most effective when confined to those acceptable to both parties in arbitration or fact-finding. There can be problems with using specialists as mediators since they will often find themselves moving, if only unconsciously, into the role of arbitrators. A mediator working in a specialist scientific or technical area does, however, require a basic grasp of the terminology involved to enable him or her to understand the proceedings. For example, a third party attempting to resolve a dispute regarding a complex contract relating to technical specifications for military aircraft computer systems would find the task all but impossible if he or she did not, at the very least, have a basic knowledge of both contract law and computer technology. It is virtually impossible to assess the effectiveness of a resolution process if the very language in which much of it is being conducted is incomprehensible.

Professions and conflict

An area that combines scientific or technical conflict, interpersonal conflict, and commercial conflict—often with some value conflict as well—is that relating to the provision of professional services, as, for example, with medical or legal practitioners. Conflict resolution in such areas will often include issues relating to professions and professional standards, and definitions of professional misconduct, duty of care, and negligence (see pp. 196 and 204 for discussion of these latter two). The regulation of professions—both by their own members and by the State through professional registration Acts and through authorities' professional disciplinary processes—usually provides consumers with some forms of complaint process, although these vary widely in their effectiveness. In most cases they involve some statutory complaint procedure. The issues of relative power imbalance, lack of knowledge and technical language, and differential importance and impact are significant problems in this area.

Conflict in health care

One professional area in which considerable conflict arises is that of medical practice and, more generally, the health professions. Because health care often involves matters of great importance to the individual, and may even involve life-and-death issues, it is often an area of highly emotional conflict, and an area in which value conflict is common.

Conflict involving medical practice can be related to claims of misconduct or negligence (for example, failing to diagnose accurately) and to allegations of fraud (such as overcharging). Some conflict is covered by legislation that deals with the registration of medical practitioners, and establishes procedures for the investigation of complaints; other sorts of conflict are dealt with by internal grievance procedures within hospitals, or within professional associations (such as the Australian Medical Association).

Difficult ethical and professional issues often arise, including questions regarding accuracy of diagnosis, appropriateness of treatment, informed consent and adequate information, and professional manner. Specific areas of conflict may involve problems in communication, breaches of confidentiality, and access to medical records. In some cases, only an expert in the particular medical area in dispute will be able to arbitrate on the appropriateness of a diagnosis or treatment. It may be particularly difficult for the patient, even though the conflict relates to her or his health, to understand the complex issues involved, or to find an independent medical opinion.

Value conflict is often associated with medical and bio-ethical conflict. This may include values relating to: the practitioner's right to decide what a patient should know; the nature of treatment; whether to withdraw treatment, or whether or not to perform certain procedures; and the patient's right to decide whether to have certain procedures performed, to be told certain facts, or even to decide when to die. Additionally, questions about confidentiality often arise. There are numerous works on the ethical and legal issues that can develop in the course of medical practice, and some of these deal with the complex questions that arise in value conflict in health care.

Conflict in legal services

Similar conflict can occur in relation to legal practitioners, including allegations of misconduct and negligence, claims of delays or failure to take action, and fraud (for example, involving trust accounts). Like medical practitioners, lawyers are covered by both legislative regulation and regulation by professional bodies (such as the Law Society). As with medical practitioners, the resolution of conflict with lawyers may involve complex questions of law or legal interpretation, which may be very difficult for the client to understand and which may require expert arbitration.

Conflict arising out of the provision of goods or services ranges from conflict that is often relatively easy to resolve to that involving highly complex technical data and deep-value conflicts. Formal, legal mechanisms, as well as internal mechanisms of organisations and professions, exist for dispute resolution in these areas. Particular problems often eventuate in dealing with conflicts involving scientific and/or technical issues, and with conflict of values, particularly where the matter is of considerable complexity and there is an imbalance of power between the parties.

Complex issues can and do arise in conflict relating to employment, financial transactions, and the provision of services. In many cases, specialist information (including knowledge of the relevant laws) may be an essential part of the resolution process.

Case study 13

Andrew is a senior manager with a large company that runs a number of factories. The position of manager of one of the factories is vacant and has been advertised. The applicants include Stan, the assistant manager who has been at the factory for fifteen years, and Helen.

Helen is of Asian descent, and came to Australia two years ago. She has had extensive experience in management in this type of industry, and has very good formal qualifications. Before being interviewed, Helen visits the factory. The following day, one of the foremen goes to see Andrew and tells him that the staff at the factory, most of whom are men, expect that Stan will get the manager's position, and will certainly not work for any Asian woman. The factory has previously had a record of costly industrial disputes.

Andrew's managing director has seen Helen's application and has met with her. He makes it clear to Andrew that he considers her to be the best applicant for the position, and wants Andrew to inject some new talent into the organisation.

Consider the particular problems Andrew faces, regardless of what he decides to do. Identify the various levels of conflict involved. Attempt to identify any action that Andrew might take, or organise, if he decides to appoint Helen to the position in spite of hostility from the factory staff.

14 Environmental and Technical Conflict

Environmental conflict refers to competing claims to rights to, control over, and use of the environment, or conflict relating to the consequences of use of the environment, including land, water, and other natural resources. More and more disputes have occurred in this area, and with an increasing recognition of the problems inherent in attempting to settle them by court processes, there has developed a considerable interest in the use of conflict resolution processes, including mediation. In the USA there are companies specialising in environmental mediation and dispute settlement. Although environmental conflict involves all the issues inherent in conflict generally, there are some particular issues that need to be taken into account. Some of these also apply in other forms of conflict in which highly specialised technical matters are involved.

Special features of environmental conflict

There are a number of reasons why environmental conflict may differ significantly from more traditional disputes. First, it often involves the possibility of irreversible environmental effects; once an option is implemented, it may simply not be possible to remedy the situation, even if it is recognised to have been wrong. For example, a decision to cut down an area of rainforest, once carried out, is irreversible, even if unforeseen adverse ecological effects are discovered. The use of experimental options, which can be tried out and, if found to be unsatisfactory, abandoned in favour of an alternative, is rarely possible. Testing the toxicity of a factory outflow by releasing it into a lake will have permanent, or at least extremely long-term, effects on the water. If the lake is polluted and all the fish die, it is then impossible to rectify the matter by simply abandoning the release of the pollutant into the lake and finding an alternative means of disposal.

This is probably the major concern of environmentalists and community groups when they consider proposals for environmental change: if something goes wrong, or if an unforeseen (and, perhaps, unforeseeable) adverse consequence occurs, it may simply be impossible to restore the situation. Whenever high risks of irreversible consequences exist in a conflict, the process of resolution becomes very difficult.

It is very important to recognise that risk-assessment is not simply a question of scientific fact. What appears to be a 'relatively low' risk to a company or its scientific advisers (for example, a risk of 1 in 100 000) may appear to be a very high, and therefore unacceptable, risk to those who will be directly effected by the risk if it arises. This relates also to the relative impact of the risk: if it relates to a temporary reduction in the number of fish in a lake, it may be acceptable to local residents (although less so to local people involved in the fishing industry). If it relates to permanent birth defects in children, what a company or its scientific advisers may see as 'an acceptable level of risk' may be entirely unacceptable to the local community. Risk is defined not simply by scientific data and statistical information; it is socially and culturally defined.

The second special feature of environmental conflict is that the effects, boundaries, participants, and costs often cannot be estimated accurately in advance. The full extent of the effect of an environmental decision may not be known until it is carried out and the results monitored; this may be years or, in some cases, decades (or even generations) into the future. A much wider range of people may be directly and indirectly affected than was anticipated; for example, the long-term effects of a chemical agent may be far more widespread than presently known, and may not become apparent until a second or third generation of children is born. It is unlikely that the costs (financial and social) of dealing with unexpected problems can be calculated accurately in advance.

The third special feature is that at least one, if not more, of the parties in most environmental disputes usually claims to represent broader, but imprecisely defined, interests, including 'the public interest', the interests of inanimate objects, wildlife, unborn generations, or 'the future of planet Earth'. Attempts to introduce these issues, or to bring in such indeterminate participants, add a dimension of difficulty, which is increased because these value components are likely to be of intense personal importance to those raising them, but of relative irrelevance to other participants. It is common for governments and developers to refer less than seriously to the sort of moral issues (such as the rights of animals or the future of the planet) that many environmentalists consider to be of fundamental importance in the making of environmental decisions.

The rights of the parties raising such issues are likely to be questioned: two or more participants may each claim to represent public interest, community interest, national interests, or nature itself. Within a community, several groups or individuals (including elected officials and community groups) may each argue that they represent the interests, and the opinions, of the community. Such claims are virtually impossible to test objectively, and are therefore often the subject of considerable, usually diversionary, conflict.

The implementation of agreements for resolution may pose special problems if previously unidentified, or unidentifiable, problems arise after the project is completed on the terms agreed by the participants. For example, the building of a factory may be completed and the factory may be fully operational before it is shown to be an environmental risk as a result of previously unknown factors. The costs of closing down (or even substantially modifying) a recently completed project and beginning again are likely to be considerable.

The range of environmental conflict

Environmental conflict can cover a very broad range of areas: land use; natural resource management (including water, flora, and fauna); air or water quality; the release or disposal of toxins (including pesticides and other hazardous substances); other forms of pollution of air, water, and land; and occupational health and safety. It will often include conflict over the interpretation of scientific or technical information, diverse claims and opinions, and disagreements over the identification of an authoritative expert in the relevant field. Environmental conflict usually includes concern about implications for the future (for example, the effect on future generations or the future status of forests, land, or ocean). Predicting probable and possible outcomes can be difficult, but where there is any suggestion of future problems, particularly if there is a risk to health or life, it will usually assume a critical importance.

In environmental and technical conflict, the use of experts (often described as 'independent experts') can be particularly helpful, particularly if the parties to the conflict agree to accept the determination of the expert or experts. However, given that there can be divergent opinions among experts, such determinations can also lead to another layer of conflict: who is the expert whose opinion is authoritative?

In the process of attempting to resolve environmental conflict, disputes often occur over appropriate and effective means of monitoring and controlling any project, and over appropriate standards of environmental protection. The levels of risk or damage that may be acceptable to a company or a government may be much higher than those that will be accepted by a local community. This often leads to disputes about which interests should prevail in a particular dispute, and to further disputes about who represents particular interests. Terms such as 'community interest' and 'national interest' are often used to lay claim to priority of importance. For a local group, community interest may be far more important than national interest; to a federal government, national interest is likely to take priority. This also often leads to conflict between short- and long-term goals. A local community may demand a much higher standard and guarantee of safety than an industrial corporation is accustomed, or even scientifically able, to give.

Participants

Environmental conflict usually involves a large number of actual and potential participants and interested parties. These can include community and intracommunity groups, residents (often differentiating between long- and short-term residents), local government, local business, property investors, conservation groups (local and external), developers (local, national, and international), and government (local, state, and federal). Groups within these divisions may enter into alliances and oppositions over different aspects of the conflict, and at different times.

Participants are not always constant: individuals or groups may take up and lay down interests and involvement in particular issues, or may have highly specialised interests in only particular aspects of a conflict. In some cases, such specialist participants may be involved in what amount to sub-conflicts with the major participants or among themselves, usually over what constitutes the most important issues in the conflict.

Value conflict

Underlying most environmental conflict, whether or not the parties to the conflict recognise or accept the fact, is value conflict. For example, a conflict will often occur on the basis of values about the relative rights of human beings and other species, or the merits of exploiting natural resources or conserving them, or what constitutes an acceptable quality of life for people in a particular community. These conflicts will usually be expressed in terms of specific disputes (for example, whether to develop a particular mining site), and the underlying values will not necessarily be raised at all. In some cases, the parties themselves may not be aware of the underlying value conflict. It should, however, be brought into open discussion to facilitate resolution.

Although it may not be possible to resolve the value conflict, a recognition of an irresolvable difference in values does not necessarily preclude the possibility that a particular dispute will be settled. In fact, it is more likely that the dispute will be settled if the value conflict has been clearly identified than if it remains undisclosed.

Although a specific conflict may be defined in terms of a proposal to build a particular type of factory in a particular location, a number of value issues are likely to arise, and often make the resolution of the conflict difficult. Different parties to the conflict may have different needs and values: consider, for example, what values and needs can be identified for each of the following parties to an environmental conflict based on a proposal to build a factory in a small country town:

- local business owners
- local unemployed people
- the local member of parliament
- local conservation groups
- residents who retired to the town
- residents who have always lived in the town
- the local council
- the state government

- the federal government
- a national conservation group
- the company proposing the development
- residents whose land will be purchased for the site
- residents living near the site whose land will not be purchased.

The values that often come into conflict include human rights versus the rights of the natural environment, long-term versus short-term goals, and the relationship between human beings and nature. Additionally, different definitions of the quality of life usually reflect value conflicts. The roles of 'experts' and 'ordinary people' in environmental decision-making also become important, as does the location of the decision-making. This is usually seen to be something of a struggle between the local community and the state or national governments, or 'big business', or a combination of these 'outside' powers. The assessment of risks, and the relative acceptability of different levels of risk, will also often mask value conflicts.

The value component may make mediated resolution difficult: if one group believes that no development is acceptable under any circumstances, and the other group seeks to determine the limits of the development, the process may be frustrating and unsuccessful. Likewise, the process becomes fraught if one group believes that the interests of the local community are of the highest importance, and the other that national interests should prevail.

Scientific and technical questions

A further potential problem in environmental conflict is that many people, including many decision-makers, view environmental disputes as essentially scientific disputes that ought to be decided 'on the facts' by experts who can weigh up the evidence, deal with the technical issues, and make informed decisions on behalf of the uninformed public, who would not understand the complexities of the issue even if it were fully explained to them. Environmental conflict, however, is more about conflict of values than about disagreement between scientific experts. The facts are rarely as important as the feelings.

Much environmental conflict has been unnecessarily increased either by the withholding of scientific and technical data or by the provision of the data only in a form virtually unintelligible to all but specialists.

Environmental mediation

The use of third parties to assist in the resolution of environmental conflict has become more common. It is sometimes more appropriately described as facilitation, particularly where a large number of participants are involved.

Environmental mediation is complicated by a number of factors, including the value conflict component, and the complex and often controversial nature of the scientific and technical data on which decisions are usually made (for example, whether a particular chemical will or will not cause health problems). The number, range, and diverse needs and values of the potential participants also add a whole range of complications. Disputes about who is and who is not a 'legitimate' participant (for example, what is the status of environmental activists from outside a town in a conflict over development within a town) often arise and can be difficult to resolve unless the mediator wishes to play the role of arbitrator, at least temporarily.

The political agendas, at local, state, and federal levels, on which final decisions are likely to be based are usually outside the control of almost all the participants to any mediation process, and this can lead to feelings of disempowerment. People may feel, quite legitimately, that no matter what they decide, a final decision will be made by people far away, and for reasons of their own.

Public and publicised conflict

Environmental conflict is usually public, in some cases involving widespread media coverage. This may be the result of publicity-seeking activities by one or more of the participants, or simply because the subject of the conflict, or the conflict itself, provides a good story. All the problems of trying to deal with conflict resolution when the participants also feel the need to play to an audience materialise in this case. The participants' need to take strong public positions and to be seen to be strong and inflexible in media interviews may make the process particularly difficult. This can be especially problematic if participants move out of any mediation session straight into press interviews.

In general, it is much more effective to try to carry out any mediation away from press coverage, and to try to reach a final agreement that can be presented to the media jointly by the participants through a final statement. For political reasons, this is often impossible.

Perceptions

The perceptions of the parties to an environmental conflict are very important. The community or environmental groups may perceive all developers as immoral and dishonest, and assume that they will seek to conceal the facts of any proposal for as long as possible, attempting to use hard-sell public relations techniques to impose their initially undisclosed agenda on the community. A similar view may be held of government. Given the past performance of both developers and governments in using pseudo-consultative processes in which the real intention was to placate and manipulate community groups, this is to some extent understandable.

On the other side, the developers and, in many cases, the government will view local communities and conservation groups as radicals committed to obstructing progress and economic growth. They will be regarded as having some sinister but undisclosed political agenda and as being fundamentally ignorant of the scientific, technical, and economic aspects of the matter in question.

The participants, like those in all conflicts, are likely to approach each other on the basis of their perceptions or projections. Problems of hostile perceptions, distrust, and a poor past relationship hinder effective conflict resolution. To some extent, mediation or facilitation can assist in overcoming these problems, and various forms of mediation have been successfully used in the resolution of some environmental conflicts.

A number of key general issues, some of them related to values, may need to be resolved in mediation before dealing with specific issues. These are likely to include the rights of people outside the local community who may be directly or indirectly affected to participate in the process. Until agreement can be reached on who is entitled to take part in the process, and who is to be accepted as representing which groups, the process cannot proceed. .

Participants in mediation

The number of the potential parties can cause particular problems for mediation or facilitation; the question of who is appropriate and qualified to mediate or facilitate is also difficult to resolve. Questions that often arise relate to whether the third party should come from within the local community or outside it, be an expert on the scientific or technical issues involved, be legally qualified, and/or be paid by the company proposing the development.

Decisions have to be made about who will be involved in any conflict resolution process. The process may include only recognised representatives of the leading groups, or it may involve all people who wish to participate. Both options have potential associated problems. People who feel unjustly denied access to the process are likely to initiate a separate conflict-manifestation process, and can provide a powerful distraction from the main process. Setting an upper limit on the number of participants is a practical consideration, but may alienate some of the participants and (in some opinions) invalidate the process. Large numbers of participants are unlikely to be able to take part in effective collaborative problem solving.

Arbitration

Arbitration has been conspicuously unsuccessful in many environmental disputes because it fails to allow for the active participation of all affected parties, or for dealing with the feelings and values that, rather than the facts or the law, are likely to underlie the conflict. Mediation—or, given the large number of parties, what is more appropriately called 'facilitation'—is more likely to be effective. Problems can arise, however, regarding the perceived partiality of a mediator who is likely to have been recruited and to be paid by one of the parties, most probably the developer or the government. The mediator working with a large number of people on what may be a highly technical and an extremely emotive issue requires considerable skill, and an appropriate amount of technical knowledge. Too much technical knowledge, however, may encourage the mediator to drift into playing the role of either an expert or an arbitrator.

Provention

The concept of *provention* has been developed by John Burton and has particular relevance in environmental conflict. It does not mean *prevention*, but rather the development and implementation of processes that will encourage a conflict to emerge and be approached creatively. This means that the conflict is anticipated and the majority of the participants and issues identified in advance.

For example, a company considering the development of a particular mining project should be able to anticipate any potential conflicts, and to identify those likely to be involved and the matters that will concern them.

Provention is not a variety of public relations in which the predictable arguments of the opposition are met in anticipation. It involves providing all likely participants in the future conflict with an opportunity to learn as much as possible about the matter on which the conflict is likely to focus, and facilitating and encouraging their participation in analysing and evaluating the matter. It poses a major challenge to traditional approaches to environmental conflict, in which developers usually carefully conceal all information until a public decision is made to initiate a project. Being open and honest with those who are traditionally identified as critics and enemies is difficult, but it also poses a challenge for community and environmentalist groups that have traditionally opposed and criticised without necessarily participating positively in the evaluation of proposals.

Complexity of the data

Environmental conflict resolution raises issues that also materialise in other disputes related to scientific and technical matters, in which highly complex and specialist discussions and debates may be involved. These conflicts can be related to facts (or alleged facts), interpretation of the facts, and their implications. Uncertainty of facts, interpretations, or implications is usually a key issue, since most environmental conflict includes some degree of uncertainty, and demands for an 'absolute guarantee' (of safety, for example) are common, and almost always impossible. The question of who is an expert or is not an expert often arises in this connection.

Case study 14

Industrial Developments Pty Ltd has purchased a large site on a lake outside a small town; it proposes to build a factory, and to use the lake water for cooling the plant. Although this much is known, the company has been generally secretive about its proposal, and has stated that full details will only be released when it makes a formal application to the local council to develop the site.

Local opinion is divided. The area has very high unemployment, and some residents believe that the factory development will revitalise the town and provide jobs for young people. The area has a small but developing tourist industry centred on the lake, and those involved in tourism fear that the factory will ruin their plans for future development of tourist sites. Some residents who have moved to the town to escape industrial development in large towns oppose anything that will distract from the quiet, rural nature of the area. A city-based environmental group has already taken a public stand against any development by Industrial Developments Pty Ltd, claiming that it has a bad record in environmental matters.

Analyse this situation with the intention of developing a process to minimise the destructive effects of the emerging conflict. Consider appropriate ways of bringing the participants together to promote collaboration and cooperation rather than antagonism and hostility.

Specialists and non-specialists

The same arguments regarding the use of specialists and non-specialists apply here as in industrial and commercial conflict (considered in chapter 13).

The specialist may be placed in a difficult position if, as is usually the case, he or she is being paid by one party in the conflict. Specialists who regularly work as consultants to large corporations may face personal conflict in particular instances if their findings are adverse to the corporation, or if they support conclusions contrary to the corporation's interests. This is, however, equally a problem for specialists employed by community or environmentalist groups: if specialists' conclusions support the positions of the other parties, they may have difficulties with their clients.

Specialists, whether acting as mediators or as independent experts, also face the general perception of untrustworthiness that is attached to experts by members of community organisations. A community concerned about the quality of life in its area may find little relevance in discussions about scientific or technical issues, and may seek a simple answer (for example, to a question such as 'Will a particular process pollute a waterway?') to what the expert views as an extremely complex and technical question.

If all parties to an environmental conflict have their own specialists, the process of resolution becomes very much a battle of the experts, with each specialist tending to argue for, and vigorously defend, her or his findings. This reinforces the opposing positions of the participants in the conflict, and may make resolution very difficult.

Conflict resolution in both environmental and other areas of scientific or technical specialisation poses particular problems. These problems are principally related to the complexity of the subject matter and the fact that those likely to be most affected by the outcome may be least able to understand or deal with this specialist content. The serious, and often irreversible, results of environmental and technical decisions, and the fact that they often relate directly to value conflicts, add a further dimension of difficulty. Although mediation can be an effective means of seeking to resolve such conflicts, it has limitations in these areas, and poses the particular danger of becoming a process in which those who are already relatively disempowered may become more so. As with all conflict resolution, it therefore needs to be approached with caution, careful analysis, and thorough preparation, and with the option of choosing another process such as adjudication.

15 Conflict Resolution, the Law, and Ethics

This chapter provides an overview of a number of legal and ethical issues raised in conflict resolution. While it is important for the participants in any conflict resolution process to be aware of these issues, it is essential for any third party involved in the process to take account of them.

There are important legal principles that are relevant to anyone engaged in the practice of conflict resolution, particularly where professional practice is involved. The legal system has been the traditional means of resolving disputes and conflicts, especially those that moved from being strictly interpersonal to those having social implications. Different societies have different systems of law, but all societies have legal systems and means of enforcing law and protecting the public order.

In chapter 1 the difference between *disputes* (which can be settled) and *conflicts* (which need to be resolved) was noted. Virtually all of the conflict resolution undertaken in legal or quasi-legal settings can properly be described as *dispute settlement*, since the law is most often concerned with the negotiation or arbitration of a settlement for a presenting dispute, but does not seek to identify or deal with underlying issues or conflicts of which the presenting dispute may be but one manifestation.

Legal processes

Legal processes in modern Western society are characterised by having the power to compel participation and to make decisions without the participation of the disputants. Legal processes do not require, and often discourage, the active involvement of the participants in the process, usually by working through representatives, advocates, or lawyers.

Legal processes have the power to impose a solution by force of the State. They are not required to take the needs, interests, or values of the participants into account when reaching a decision, and indeed, part of being seen to be impartial may involve dealing only with the facts or the law and avoiding any consideration of the people.

The legal process is based on tradition, precedent, and law rather than on equity, justice, and fairness, and is largely inflexible because of its reliance on precedent and law. Much of the legal system is a 'closed shop' within which participation is strictly limited to a defined group of professionals. The legal system generally uses arbitration, or more correctly adjudication, with independent adjudicators (often judges) appointed by the State without consultation with the parties to any dispute on which they may have been appointed to adjudicate.

Alternative dispute resolution

What has come to be called '*alternative dispute resolution*' (ADR) essentially originated in the USA in the 1960s largely as a response to clogged courts, extensive and costly delays in litigation, the cost of litigation, and the fact that by the time the matter was adjudicated both parties had often, in real terms, lost.

To these difficulties was added the problem that, even when an adjudicated determination had been made, parties could often undermine it by unwillingness to comply (in the spirit, if not in the letter) and could continue some form of conflict, whether through repeated use of the courts, or through actions or failures to act that were beyond the power of the courts to resolve.

This led to a search for ways of resolving some of the disputes, which would normally have gone to court, without involving the courts but, usually, still involving lawyers. It was also increasingly recognised that fighting a matter out in court may lead to a victory (of sorts) for one party, but is unlikely to create a feeling of satisfactory resolution for either party, and may irreparably damage the relationship between them. An adversarial system necessarily creates adversaries; if those who have become adversaries have to maintain some form of ongoing relationship, how can this be done?

In Australia, ADR developed at more or less the same pace and in the same areas as it did in the USA. A number of government agencies (for example, the Human Rights Commission and the New South Wales Anti-Discrimination Board) were required by law to use ADR methods. Community mediation centres—sometimes with government funding, but more often without—also developed.

The term 'ADR' includes a wide range of processes such as mediation, adjudication, arbitration, med/arb, mini-trial, 'rent-a-judge', and expert fact finding, some of which are used within the legal system, and some also outside it. These processes vary on matters such as whether they are voluntary or involuntary, binding or non-binding, formal or informal, private or public.

ADR in Australia

ADR occurs in a number of areas within the Australian legal system. It is practised both within the courts—through its use by court officials to try to reduce delays and speed up processes—and by court referrals to outside agencies (for example, the Community Justice Centres) and, in some jurisdictions, by a requirement that an attempt be made at a mediated settlement prior to appearance before the court.

A number of state agencies in Australia are required by legislation to employ ADR processes either as a compulsory prerequisite to adjudication or as the only process available. These include the Industrial Relations Commission, the New South Wales Anti-Discrimination Board, the Human Rights and Equal Opportunity Commission, the Consumer Claims Tribunal, the Residential Tenancies Tribunal, and the Privacy Committee. Additionally, in some states, community mediation services (such as the Community Justice Centres in New South Wales) operate more or less within the legal system, being established by law and having some legal protections.

A number of industry-based dispute resolution organisations, although established by private corporations, have some legal basis for their work (for example, the Telecommunications Industry Ombudsman).

Voluntary and coercive conflict resolution

Although in the best of all possible conflict resolution processes the participants will mutually accept any resolution process and not require any form of enforcement of the outcome, in some cases (for example, where there are legal issues outstanding, where property or legal rights are concerned, and where custody of children is involved) it is often considered appropriate to formalise the resolution to protect the rights of the parties (or any third party) and to try to ensure that the agreed resolution is implemented. This is sometimes done by drafting a contract, agreement, or deed of release to be signed by the parties. If either party fails in her or his obligations to the other, such a document can, in some circumstances, be used as a contract, which can be enforced by action in the courts.

Obviously, there can be some difficulties in conflict resolution in a situation where the parties are moving towards a legally enforceable settlement signified by the formal signing of a legal document. The recording of the settlement can give the proceedings a degree of formality that may make conflict resolution difficult. Parties may be less inclined to accept outcomes that are final in the sense of being legally enforceable, whereas they may be prepared to accept more tentative or provisional settlements. The extent to which such agreements, other than those clearly prepared as contracts, are enforceable largely remains untested in Australian courts.

A number of key legal issues arise in conflict resolution generally, and for mediators, arbitrators, and other third parties particularly. This chapter will outline four of them: confidentiality, duty of care, defamation, and natural justice.

Confidentiality

Although some legislation provides penalties for breaches of privacy or confidentiality under very specific circumstances (for example, the *Sex Discrimination*

Act 1984), there is no general right to either in Australia. *Confidentiality* refers, generally, to the protection of information from access by persons other than those to whom it was given or who have lawful and proper access to it. In giving information to someone, a person may reasonably assume that the information will not be passed on to another person. For example, if an individual tells a mediator that, unknown to his wife, he has had an extramarital relationship, he is not telling his wife, or giving permission for the mediator to tell his wife, or anyone else. Confidentiality becomes more important as an issue when it concerns sensitive or potentially damaging or distressing information.

Privacy

Privacy is a different matter from confidentiality: it refers to the right not to have information gathered. This frequently leads to questions of confidentiality and the two terms are often used interchangeably. However, one might, for example, have no concern about particular information being collected provided it is kept confidential. On the other hand, one might object to information being collected by a particular organisation, even though one has no particular concern about it remaining confidential. Concerns frequently expressed about the collection of data by organisations such as the Credit Reference Association raise both these issues. In general, in Australia, except where the Commonwealth government is concerned, there is no redress against the collection of information by legal means, nor is there any general right of access to information so collected, or any general right to correct errors in the information.

Breaches of confidentiality

Breaches of confidentiality can lead to legal action on one or more of several grounds. It may be claimed that there was a contractual obligation to confidentiality on the part of the defendant, and that a breach of confidence represents a *breach of contract* for which damages may be sought. This, however, presupposes the existence of a contract between the parties—it could, for instance, apply in the case of a mediator who charged a fee for services. A confidentiality provision would not necessarily have to be written into a contract, and nor would there have to be a written contract: it may be held that confidentiality was an implied term of any contract, verbal or written.

Most actions involving alleged breach of confidence are likely to be taken on the ground of negligence—that is, a breach of a *duty of care*. The plaintiff would be arguing that, as a result of a breach of confidentiality by the defendant, the plaintiff has suffered some harm or loss. Negligence will be considered in more detail later in this chapter.

On the general legal issue of confidentiality, mediators can be simply divided into those who have some statutory protection of confidentiality (and usually also have some statutory obligation to maintain confidentiality) and those who do not. For example, mediators for the Community Justice Centres and concil-iators for the Human Rights and Equal Opportunity Commission have some such protections. Most mediators in community mediation centres or private practice have no legal protections for information they acquire in mediation; they can be called to give evidence of it in court, for example, if one party decides to take legal action against the other on the basis of what has been disclosed in mediation.

It is essential that unrealistic and inaccurate claims about confidentiality are not given to those participating in conflict resolution processes. A guarantee of confidentiality would be misleading. Some degrees of legal protection may apply in some circumstances, and both mediators and participants need to be adequately and accurately informed of the situation that applies to them.

Mediators or arbitrators may well face actions for negligence should they breach confidentiality and release information without consent in such a way as to cause harm or damage to the person concerned. In most cases, however, participants in a mediation, other than the mediator, are unlikely to be legally constrained in making use of information obtained. Participants thus need to be aware that, unless there are strict and specific protections for information disclosed in mediation, the other party may make use of it to her or his advan-tage and to the (at least potential) disadvantage of the person providing the information.

Compulsion to give evidence

There are particular legal questions regarding the mediator (or any other third party) being compelled to give evidence or to produce documents in court proceedings. Although some mediators (including conciliation officers with the NSW Anti-Discrimination Board or mediators with the Community Justice Centres) can generally claim immunity from giving evidence or producing documents, most cannot.

If, for example, a mediator took part in a marital mediation session in which various accusations and/or admissions were made, unless he or she had legal protection, the mediator could be called in any subsequent legal proceedings (for example, seeking resolution of disputes regarding division of property). Refusal to do so could render the mediator liable for contempt of court, with consequent penalties (including imprisonment).

In some cases, the parties enter into formal agreements in advance in an attempt to preclude any legal action on the basis of statements made during a mediation session, or to avoid any use of evidence from the session in future legal proceedings. However, whether such agreements would have any effect would depend on the wording of the documents and the decisions of the courts. One obvious area of difficulty relates to the disclosure to, or in the presence of, the mediator of illegal activities, or attempts to negotiate an agreement to undertake or continue illegal activities.

Duty of care

There is a legal concept known as the '*duty of care*': if a person suffers harm as a result of the actions or failure to act of someone who has a duty of care towards that person, then the injured person may have an action for negligence against the person with the duty of care (and generally against persons or organisations employing the individual). The concept of a duty of care is summarised in a judgment in the House of Lords in which Lord Aitken stated that a person must take reasonable care to avoid acts or omissions that can reasonably be foreseen to be likely to injure that person's neighbour. Lord Aitken defined neighbours as 'persons who are so closely and directly affected by my act that I ought reasonably to have them in contemplation as being so affected when I am directing my mind to the acts or omissions which are called into question' (*Donoghue v. Stevenson* [1932] AC 562).

Where a person is engaged in anything that a reasonable person would realise calls for care to prevent damage being caused to others, that person has a duty of care to the people with whom the person deals, and who may rely upon the person's knowledge and skill. It can probably be said that the higher the degree of knowledge and skill relied upon, and the more liable the action to cause harm, the greater is the duty of care.

Where such a duty of care exists, a breach of it may constitute negligence and lead to an action for damages. Although it is generally considered that it is the action or omission of a person with a duty of care that constitutes negligence, it can also be faulty advice that leads to litigation.

To succeed in an action for negligence, the plaintiff must prove that the defendant owed the plaintiff a duty of care, that the defendant failed in that duty, that the plaintiff suffered harm or loss as a consequence, and that there was a direct link between the negligence of the defendant and the loss or harm of the plaintiff.

It seems clear that a person holding him- or herself out as a mediator has a duty of care to anyone who seeks that person's services and, should anyone suffer harm as a result of negligence by the mediator, the injured person may take legal action.

Defamation

Part of any conflict resolution process is likely to involve the parties to a conflict freely and frankly expressing their views of one another and of other people (who may or may not be present). They are very likely, as a result, to defame each other and other people. Defamation, put simply, involves the publication (which includes the saying or writing) of a statement to a person other than the person referred to, where that statement would tend to lower that person in the estimation of right thinking people or, as used to be said, would bring that person into 'hatred, ridicule or contempt'.

For a statement to be defamatory, it must be published, but the motive in publication is not relevant, although it may be relevant in the determination of damages. In some jurisdictions (including New South Wales), the fact that a statement is true does not prevent it from being defamatory: it must be shown to be both true and published in the 'public good'.

To succeed in an action for defamation, the plaintiff must show that the defendant published a statement that caused him or her to suffer a loss in the estimation of right thinking members of society generally. There are situations in which, even if people have been defamed, they cannot take legal action: this is where the person making the statement or the context in which it is made is covered by *absolute privilege*. Courts generally, and some legally based mediation situations (including the Community Justice Centres and the Anti-Discrimination Board), are specifically protected by statute, and action for defamation generally cannot be taken for statements made during proceedings involving them.

In other situations, although a person may have been defamed, the person alleged to have defamed the other person may, if the matter goes to court, offer a defence of what is called *qualified privilege*. That is, even admitting that the statement was defamatory, a person may argue that there was some special reason justifying the defamation. For example, a supervisor making an adverse report on an employee to an employer would generally be covered by qualified privilege; the supervisor would not be so covered if he or she passed on the adverse report to other employees, or to friends.

Parties in mediation should be warned if there is no protection of absolute privilege where they may make statements that are defamatory of each other or—which is probably more likely to lead to litigation—of other parties not involved in the mediation but who may subsequently come to know what was said.

Natural justice

Natural justice is an important legal concept that may well be raised, although it probably has little direct and real relevance in conflict resolution and mediation (it does, however, in arbitration). Case law in Australia is conflicting as to whether those who take part in administering, for example, human rights and equal opportunity legislation, conciliation, and conciliation conferences have to apply the principles of natural justice.

Allowing that whole textbooks have been written on the subject, natural justice, very simply, can be described as a concept of fairness and equity in decision-making. It requires that a person about whom a decision is to be made has the opportunity to know what decision is to be made and on the basis of what information (the accusation and the evidence for the accusation); to be heard before any decision is made; and to be legally represented in any hearing if he or she so wishes.

A person who believes that he or she has been disadvantaged by a decision being made by a public official without these principles being applied can seek a remedy in the court, and if the court finds that the person's concerns are warranted, it can either overturn the decision, order the decision-maker to reconsider, or order a new hearing before a different decision-maker. Obviously, mediation as such does not involve making a decision; a decision may be reached, but if it is, it should be made by the parties to the conflict and not by the mediator. Therefore these principles do not apply. However, mediators may well wish—as an ethical rather than a legal principle—to adopt the principles underlying natural justice. Arbitrators certainly need to be aware of these principles.

Ethics

Ethics include, but are not limited to, law and standards of professional practice. They must also include some of the complex moral, ethical, and political questions with which anyone working in conflict resolution will be faced, including those relating to power imbalance, injustice, inequality, oppression, structural violence, 'learned helplessness', and stereotyping. No practitioner of conflict resolution can realistically claim to operate within a sheltered private world, protected from the often harsh realities of community, nation, and planet. Ethical issues, quite apart from legal issues, are of crucial importance in conflict resolution.

The ethical principles to be discussed in this chapter may seem to apply principally, or indeed only, to mediators. However, ethical principles ought to be considered in all conflict resolution processes and be applied by the parties to conflict resolution as carefully as by any neutral third party.

Ethics is concerned with morality and the rules by which human behaviour is guided, especially regarding how decisions are made about whether particular actions are good or bad, right or wrong. Ethics is thus concerned with the evaluation of human conduct and the ways in which this conduct can be appraised, and this leads to a concern with concepts of right and wrong in actions, motives, and consequences.

Ethical issues in conflict resolution

Conflict resolution raises a broad range of important ethical issues, both for the participants in conflict and for any conflict resolution practitioner, mediator, or facilitator. These ethical issues can be related to the disclosure or non-disclosure of information, including deliberate concealment, honesty and dishonesty, and confidentiality. Often they arise as a result of power imbalance and the personal or positional disadvantage of parties to a conflict, or because of the potential or real manipulation of one party by another (or by a mediator), and unfair or dishonest techniques. For an arbitrator, mediator, or facilitator in particular, ethical issues can relate to overt or covert partiality, fairness and equity, justice and injustice, and to questions of public interest.

As an impartial participant whose primary responsibility is to assist in facilitating the resolution of conflict by the participants, the conflict resolution practitioner or mediator faces specific ethical demands.

Examples of ethical problems

A number of basic examples of situations in which a mediator may be faced with ethical problems will help to identify some of these demands:

- One party discloses information to the mediator in confidence; this information radically affects the position of the other party and, if the other party were aware of it, would lead to a completely different approach being taken. The mediator is faced with a decision as to whether to disclose (and breach confidentiality) or fail to disclose (and breach impartiality and trust, and, possibly, to breach a duty of care).

- Two parties in mediation reach a mutually acceptable resolution that involves their agreeing to breach the provisions of particular legislation and to cooperate in concealing this breach. The mediator has to consider whether he or she has any responsibilities other than to facilitate this mutually acceptable agreement.

- Two parties in mediation appear to reach a mutually acceptable resolution, but it seems to the mediator that this is only happening because one party is intimidated by and frightened of the other, giving in easily to an agreement that seriously jeopardises that party's rights and that is against her or his best interests. The mediator has to decide whether he or she has any responsibility to do anything.

- The mediator acquires some information, from a source other than the two participants in the mediation process, that indicates that the key claim being made by one of the parties is untrue; the other party has accepted the claim, and has agreed to a resolution on the basis of it being true. The mediator is faced with deciding whether he or she has any responsibility to disclose this fact.

- The mediator notices that one participant is less personally skilled, less verbally skilled, less confident, and less assertive than the other and is, accordingly, being dominated and directed by the other. The ethical dilemma here is what, if any, action the mediator should take in this situation.

- The mediator is employed and paid by one party to a conflict, and that party indicates that, if the mediator provides the 'sort of service' the employer expects, a considerable amount of additional (and lucrative) work may be directed to the mediator.

- Immediately before a formal written agreement involving the payment of substantial compensation to one party is signed, that party informs the mediator that the facts as alleged by him or her are false, but that he or she feels entitled to receive the payment for other things. The mediator must determine whether to allow the agreement to be completed, given that it appears to be based on misrepresentation (or even fraud).

Mediators and other third parties involved in conflict resolution need to be able to identify and reflect on ethical problems, and to maintain sound professional (and personal) standards against which any potential breach of ethics can be measured. In some cases, it will be helpful to consult with professional colleagues (without, of course, breaching confidentiality by disclosing identifying details of any case) to seek advice about ethical difficulties.

Expectations of the parties

The expectations of the parties to a conflict resolution process may create ethical dilemmas. It is important for all parties to understand their own and other participants' expectations of the process—that is, their projections of what will, or ought to, or might, happen. Unless these are clarified, there are likely to be incorrect or mistaken expectations, which will lead to increased rather than resolved conflict. Parties need fair and honest descriptions of what is going to be done and not done, what may or may not happen, and what is and is not likely to be achieved. For example, if they imagine that after twenty minutes of mediation the problem will be resolved absolutely and forever, they are being unrealistic and are likely to be disappointed.

In a semi-legal sense, the parties need to give 'informed consent' to participation in the process: they cannot consent to the process unless they have a clear understanding of what it is and what it is not, and how it is to proceed.

Not only do the expectations of both parties need clarification, but the expectation of any third party also needs to be clarified, as does the role of any other person who may be present (for example, friends for moral support, lawyers, or trade union representatives). The expectations of the conflict resolution practitioner or mediator need to be made explicit, particularly where they relate to things that are necessary for all effective resolution processes (for example, preparedness to talk honestly and listen fairly).

The degree of involvement

The mediator may often find that he or she faces an ethical dilemma regarding the degree of active involvement in the conflict resolution process: Should the mediator take any role in directing participants towards resolution? Or should he or she only facilitate? If the parties ask for direction, should it be given? And if the mediator sees an obvious and practical option, should he or she offer it? The choice between facilitating decision-making and directing decision-making (directly or indirectly) is not an easy or clear-cut one; it is possible to offer subtle and implicit direction while appearing and claiming to be non-directive. Indeed, the parties to a conflict-resolution process may want to be directed and may seem to turn a mediator into an arbitrator. This may be particularly the case when the parties know that the mediator has specialist knowledge or skill that they feel they lack, or when their negotiations appear to have reached some form of deadlock.

Neutrality and impartiality

The need to be, and to be seen to be, neutral (that is, not on either side) and impartial (that is, neutral throughout the process, non-judgmental, not reaching conclusions) is central to mediation. Neutrality does not mean a lack of care or interest in the outcome; the mediator's interest is in effective resolution, not in a specific resolution (and certainly not in resolution for its own sake, regardless of quality). Nor does it mean that the mediator has to be value-free or devoid of opinions. Human beings are not capable of such neutrality, even if it were desirable. The only truly neutral mediator is, in fact, a dead mediator. As a living human being, the mediator has values, attitudes, prejudices and beliefs like every other human being, and makes assumptions and reaches judgments (consciously or unconsciously). The mediator must be aware, however, of her or his prejudices, opinions, beliefs, and values, and must ensure that they do not intrude into the process. If this is not possible, the mediator may need to withdraw.

Fairness

Fairness is a concern not only, or even primarily, because of its ethical importance: a process or an outcome that is not fair, while being seen to be fair, will be unlikely to provide an effective and lasting resolution. A sense of justice, equity, and fairness in the process is essential to conflict resolution. Definitions of 'fair' vary, of course, and each participant to a conflict is likely to have a different sense of what would constitute a fair outcome. In general, fairness implies that the rights of the parties are protected, and certainly not violated, and that, as far as is possible, their needs are met. It implies some degree of collaboration in decision-making, and generally precludes coercion or manipulation.

It is important to recognise that both *process* and *outcome* need to be fair. The conflict resolution process itself must be manifestly fair, just, and equitable, even if it does not finally resolve the conflict. However, any resolution that is the outcome of such a process must also be fair. Research on participant satisfaction with conflict resolution processes seems to indicate that participants are more likely to feel satisfied when the process is manifestly fair, regardless of whether or not a permanent resolution is reached. Taking part in a fair process is sometimes sufficient.

It can be argued, however, that the conflict resolution process, as opposed to processes of litigation or arbitration, is less likely to achieve fairness, justice, and equity because it relies so much on the abilities of the individual participants. The more verbally skilled, assertive, confident, and self-controlled a person is, the more likely he or she is to be effective in a conflict resolution process. This may seriously disadvantage participants who are less personally skilled or confident, or who are from minority groups. This raises the critical problem of power balance, which remains probably the most difficult, and the most important, ethical and practical problem facing the mediator.

It is sometimes argued that the adversarial system provides more protection from power imbalance because of its clearly defined rules and methods, and because it involves the presentation of arguments by trained adversaries (for example, lawyers), in a court system within which all parties are—at least in theory—equal. Obviously, however, there is rarely a complete power balance between the advocates. In conflict resolution processes, the individual knowledge and skills of individual participants are crucial to both process and outcome. The mediator must consider what happens if one party is prepared (often on the basis of inadequate information or lack of skills in analysis and evaluation) to accept an inferior or unjust settlement: if the individual chooses it, can or should the mediator intervene?

The rights of participants

The participants in a conflict resolution process must be seen to have a number of basic rights; these rights should also apply to the mediator or other third party. They include the right to know what is going to happen, to know and to understand what is happening, to express their views, to be listened to and to be understood, and to be able to hear and to understand (including questions). The participants have a right to be 'safe' and 'protected', in so far as this is possible; one of the mediator's roles is to provide that safety. The participants must have the right to consider or reflect or take advice, to be treated fairly and with respect, and to take time out when they feel the need for it. They should also have the right to be told the truth and to be actively involved in any decision-making.

Power and power balance

Power can be personal, positional, and situational. *Personal power* relates to the knowledge, skills, and personality of the individual: it includes characteristics such as self-esteem, self-confidence, verbal skills, assertiveness. It also refers to the resources that the individual possesses. For example, someone who has more than enough money to take a matter on to prolonged litigation may have greater power in a mediation than someone for whom the mediation is the only option for resolution.

Positional power relates to the power an individual holds by virtue of her or his position in a structure, which may include a family, an organisation or community, or society generally. For example, a supervisor in a factory holds more positional power than a process worker whom he or she supervises. It may be that the supervisor also has more personal power, but this will not necessarily be the case; personal power is not necessarily equivalent to positional power. In conflict resolution processes, it is personal, rather than positional, power that is predominant, although, of course, positional power can be important (for example, where a conflict involves an employer and an employee).

Situational power is the power individuals have because of the situations in which they find themselves. It often relates to both personal and positional power, but is specifically connected with the context. An employee of very low status in an organisation (who thus possesses low positional power, and may even have low personal power) may acquire very high situational power if he or she possesses essential skills that the company requires in order to complete an urgent project. An individual of both low personal power and low positional power may have very high situational power if he or she knows (or is thought to know) something that the other party is eager should not be disclosed.

Power imbalance between the participants can be a major problem—for example, where one participant is highly assertive, articulate, and confident, and the other is non-assertive, inarticulate, and frightened. This raises the question of whether conflict resolution processes and mediation are intrinsically unfair unless both parties are of roughly equal personal and professional status. Presumably, if this is the case, it would mean that it could rarely work, since most conflict occurs between people of different personal, positional and situational power. It does require that any conflict resolution practitioner or mediator analyses, identifies, and takes account of the power balance, or imbalance, between the participants.

In some cases, this may mean identifying that a non-adjudicatory process is inappropriate because of the extreme disparity in power. In other cases, it may mean that one party requires the presence of an advocate (which, of course, alters the dynamics of the process and may cause difficulties with the other participant), or that the practitioner has to take some action to ensure that, during the process, the disadvantaged participant receives as fair and equal treatment as is possible, given the power imbalance. The question of such imbalance is a crucial and critical one, and requires careful consideration in all conflict resolution processes.

Conflict resolution techniques can be used to manipulate people—particularly by the powerful in order to dominate and control the powerless—and one of the roles of a mediator must be to ensure, as far as possible, that this does not happen.

Rights to privacy and confidentiality

The concept of privacy can create difficult ethical dilemmas in conflict resolution. The right not to have information sought or not to disclose information may seem to be a basic one, but it can often cause difficulties where the resolution may be dependent on disclosure of relevant information. Whether or not a party to a conflict has a right not to reveal this relevant information and, at the same time, to claim to be committed to the resolution of the conflict is doubtful. Self-disclosure is often embarrassing or even personally damaging, but may be essential if the conflict is to be resolved.

The mediator will sometimes face ethical dilemmas, particularly in knowing when to put questions about matters that one party apparently does not wish to disclose or, in some cases, that both parties wish to keep out of discussion. This can become even more complex when one party discloses information to the mediator that is directly relevant to the conflict, but discloses it in confidence and indicates that he or she does not wish it to be disclosed to the other party.

Confidentiality is often an essential quality of an effective conflict resolution process; unless the parties feel comfortable in disclosing information, knowing that it will be kept confidential, the communication process is likely to break down. Things disclosed in the heat of conflict, however, can often be used in the future as weapons in further conflict; this may be something that needs to be directly addressed. It is essential that parties to a conflict resolution process understand what standards of confidentiality apply in the process: it is unethical and dishonest for a mediator to claim, or even to imply, that any form of protection for confidentiality applies when it does not. To say that 'everything said in this process will remain confidential' is, generally, simply untrue, and clearly misleading. Very few conflict resolution processes have any legal basis for total protection of the confidentiality of the proceedings, and where such legal protection exists, it is usually quite narrow and specific, and does not prevent either party, or the mediator, from disclosing information under all circumstances.

The parties should be encouraged to make an agreement to maintain confidentiality; although this only has force of moral persuasion, it will often be effective if the mediator explains carefully the reasons why it is essential. Obviously the mediator or conflict resolution practitioner must maintain as strict a standard of confidentiality as is legally possible. This includes not disclosing anything that may be identifying of the participants or the conflict (and that goes far beyond simply changing their names) to anyone other than, in some circumstances, a professional supervisor.

There are some basic and important exceptions that every conflict resolution practitioner must consider, and on which it is difficult to give clear, simple rules. These relate to situations in which the practitioner receives information disclosing or alleging a crime. Failure to disclose may have serious legal consequences for the individual. For example, in a mediation relating to problems in a marriage, if it were disclosed that one partner had been sexually assaulting a child, and the other partner did not wish to take any action on this, the mediator would face a very serious ethical and legal problem in knowing whether he or she should disclose the claim to the relevant authorities.

Ethical imperatives

Duty of care

The concepts of duty of care and negligence are both legal and ethical issues. It may, however, be possible to maintain appropriate legal requirements of a duty of care while failing to maintain an ethical standard. Any practitioner of conflict resolution, whether professional or voluntary, must recognise the duty that he or she has to all who participate in or who may be affected, directly or indirectly, by the process. This covers not only the practitioner's actions and words, but also what he or she fails to do or say. People who depend upon the skills and knowledge of those who represent themselves, whether explicitly or implicitly, as having special skills and knowledge in the area of conflict resolution have a right to high standards. This must include a right not to be deceived, explicitly or implicitly, about the level of the practitioner's skills. People who describes themselves as 'mediators' may convey to others, who do not know the area, that they have a higher level of skills and knowledge than they in fact possess, and may imply that they have some sort of professional accreditation and recognition that they may not have.

Ethical standards require that the practitioner considers not only the literal and technical meaning of any claims that he or she may make, but also what the ordinary, perhaps poorly informed, member of the public may understand those claims to mean.

Recognising limits

A key ethical skill must be the ability to recognise limits to personal competence, and to know when and how to refer the client to a person who is qualified, or better qualified, to assist. The desire to help anyone who seeks help may be noble, but it may equally be misguided and ultimately harmful. Conflict resolution techniques are not infallible solutions to every human problem; they are sometimes just clearly inappropriate, and should not even be attempted. The skilled practitioner should know when to say 'no'.

Appropriate professional standards

Another key ethical imperative is the maintenance of appropriate professional standards. This involves not only adequate education and training, and ongoing professional development, but also appropriate means of review and evaluation, including peer review. Providing services of an inadequate standard must be recognised as unethical.

Identification of the client

Considerations of duty of care also raise questions about the identity of the conflict resolution practitioner's client: in mediation, for example, it is both parties to a conflict (or, all parties, if there are more than two). This means that both should be involved in organising and (where appropriate) paying for the process equally. Particular problems arise where the practitioner is employed (whether as an employee or as a consultant for a specific situation) by an organisation of which one party is an employee.

Conflict of interests

Sometimes the conflict resolution practitioner will face competing or conflicting interests. This can be especially true when the mediator works for the same organisation as the disputants, and it is one of the particular difficulties of conflict resolution processes within organisations. To whom is the mediator essentially responsible if he or she is employed by an organisation to resolve conflicts within it: the participants to the conflict who are (whether in a voluntary context or under direction) using the mediator, or the organisation that employs the mediator?

Sometimes ethical dilemmas arise in conflict resolution because the participants to a conflict reach an agreement that may meet their needs and satisfy them both, but that is either not in the broader interests of the community or may even be against the law. For example, in an employment conflict, an employee might agree to accept a sum of money by way of compensation for a workplace injury resulting from an illegal work practice, and as part of that agreement the employee may undertake not to disclose that the employer had been, and still was, in contravention of occupational health and safety laws. The employer is essentially paying not only compensation for injury, but also 'hush money'. The responsibility of any mediator in such a case is divided between the clients (employer and employee) and the community (for safety at work and for compliance with the law).

Feelings in conflict resolution

All sorts of professional people claim that their personal feelings are not allowed to 'get in the way of' their professional practice, but since all human beings have feelings, the emotional dimension of the relationship between a conflict resolution practitioner and the participants to the process must be considered. Individual practitioners may automatically, and inexplicably, find one party as personally attractive as they find the other objectionable, or on the basis of learning more about the conflict, they may feel that one party is clearly the victim and the other the villain.

Effective ethical practice requires that such feelings must be recognised, acknowledged, and evaluated to determine whether or not they may interfere with the conflict resolution process. Pretending that they do not exist, or suppressing them, is more likely to lead to their becoming problems, albeit unconsciously.

Professional competence

One of the key ethical responsibilities of any conflict resolution practitioner is professional competence. This is both a general and a particular requirement. It means that the practitioner should not practise *at all* without having attained an adequate standard of knowledge and skill, and it means that the practitioner should not participate *in specific cases* in which he or she does not have the necessary specialist knowledge or skill. Because there are generally no formal standards for conflict resolution or mediation in Australia, it is difficult to offer clear guidelines as to how a conflict resolution practitioner or mediator should be tested for competence. Different organisations offering training and accreditation have different standards, some of them clearly inadequate.

Case study 15

Joe and Mary have been married for seven years and have been experiencing difficulties in their relationship for the past two. They seem to disagree about almost everything and have finally reached a crisis over Joe's wish to accept a position in another city. He wants the family to move, but Mary wants them to remain where they are. She particularly wishes to stay close to her elderly parents and her younger sister. Mary and Joe decide to ask a mediator to help them to resolve the conflict over moving.

The mediator speaks with Joe and Mary separately. Joe tells the mediator, in strict confidence, that he is only taking part in mediation to relieve some of the stress that the conflict has been causing. In fact, unknown to Mary, he has established a relationship with another woman in the other city, and is planning to accept the new position and to leave Mary in three months or so. He wants things to be calm before then and intends to leave without making any prior statement to Mary.

Consider the mediator's position; identify what options are available, and evaluate the implications of each. Assuming the mediator decides to proceed with the mediation, consider the problems that will arise.

Resolving ethical dilemmas

If and when ethical problems arise in the course of conflict resolution practice, they must be clearly identified and effectively dealt with. This will often include a discussion with one or both of the participants to the process, and perhaps with professional colleagues or supervisors, almost always with the case being described in ways to prevent breaches of confidentiality. An ethical dilemma in which one party is not prepared to disclose relevant information to another party, but has told the mediator, is usually best dealt with in discussions with the party who made the disclosure.

Practitioners of conflict resolution need to be able to identify their ethical standards for participants, and to state clearly the limits of their preparedness to take part in processes that seem to be unethical. Provided this is done using a collaborative problem-solving approach, rather than one that is judgmental and accusatory, it will usually be appreciated and understood.

Ethics are an essential and crucial element of any conflict resolution process. It is vital that all those participating in conflict resolution, particularly those who provide services, whether professional or voluntary, have clear concepts of what constitutes ethical conflict resolution practice, and have given adequate time and effort to the development of appropriate ethical standards and ethical decision-making abilities.

The conflict resolution process raises a number of important legal and ethical questions for participants, including mediators. For conflict resolution to work effectively in the long term, it must be based on sound ethical practice, and mediators must have given consideration in advance both to legal and ethical issues in general, and, in each specific case, to those particular legal and ethical questions likely to be raised. Ethical questions cannot be resolved without appropriate thought and reflection. Simple sets of ethical rules can be useful as guides, but do not allow for the complexity and unpredictability of human conflict.

16 Making Conflict Resolution Work

The aim of this book is to provide an outline of the broadest possible range of issues relating to the practice of conflict resolution. Some of the material may seem irrelevant to the particular personal or professional interests of individual readers. Having reached the end of the book, however, the importance of a wide, general understanding of conflict and its resolution should be evident.

There are issues that arise in narrow areas of conflict that have significance in other areas, and for conflict more generally.

Theory and conflict resolution

Underlying every system of conflict resolution is a theory of the nature of conflict and its resolution, and, ultimately, of the nature of human beings and human society. Whether or not the theory is consciously and explicitly identified, it nevertheless underlies and, usually, prescribes the practice.

Conflict resolution practice is *not* value-neutral. For example, if it is believed that human beings are innately and biologically aggressive, the approach to conflict resolution will be radically different from that taken if the belief is that human beings are innately peaceful and cooperative. If conflict is innate, a different approach must be taken than would be used if conflict is learnt: in one case, mechanisms for control are likely to be seen as necessary; in the other, education and training will be appropriate.

This book has not dealt explicitly with the theory of conflict resolution. A number of key references in this area are included in the reading guide and should be consulted.

The majority of those practising conflict resolution seem to operate as if in a theoretical vacuum, where no assumptions, theories, or beliefs get in the way. Indeed sometimes practitioners explicitly declare that the practice of conflict resolution can take place in such a vacuum. All practitioners of conflict resolution, of course, have clear theoretical orientations, from Freud to Marx and beyond, but many seem to prefer to deny these, or to conceal them. The majority of agencies offering conflict resolution processes seem, like individual practitioners, unwilling to disclose their reasons for doing so, the beliefs upon which their practice is based, or the assumptions (tested or more usually not) upon which they base their work.

It is important for all practitioners to spend some time thinking about their own personal approaches to conflict and conflict resolution, and this usually means examining their own views of the nature of human beings biologically, psychologically, and socially, as well as their views of society. Ideally, reading this book will have resulted in some consideration of theoretical assumptions, and the development, even if informal, of theories of conflict and conflict resolution. It is useful to reflect on personal assumptions and theories, and to speculate on how differently conflict would be approached if a different theory were held, or a different model of human nature and behaviour accepted.

It is unlikely that any one theory in isolation can satisfactorily and entirely explain conflict or enable resolution. Approaching all conflicts on the basis of a single theory (for example, that of Marx or Freud), regardless of the people, issues, or context involved is unrealistic. Different aspects of the same conflict may be illuminated by approaches based in different theoretical models. For example, there may be aspects that require some analysis based in psychological theory, others that require a sociological approach, and yet others that have an economic basis.

The development of conflict resolution skills requires exposure to a wide range of theories and practices, and an ability to explore them all critically and creatively. Individuals need to explore, reflect on, and develop their own approaches, and to become increasingly sensitive to human diversity, unpredictability, and complexity. It is for this reason that simplistic approaches to conflict resolution (such as those that offer 'ten steps to resolution' or prescribe quasi-magical formulae 'guaranteed to resolve') are, at best, naive and, at worst, fraudulent. There is, however, a more serious problem: every unsuccessful attempt at the resolution of a particular problem has the potential to undermine any further attempt at resolution, to encourage perceptions of powerlessness and helplessness in the participants, and to complicate the conflict. Just as (one hopes) a medical practitioner would not prescribe the same medication for all patients, regardless of their symptoms or illness, or prescribe medications at random in the hope that, eventually, the appropriate one will be found, so the conflict resolution practitioner must approach her or his work carefully, seriously, and with a sound analytical approach.

A theoretical approach to conflict resolution must also take account of cultural issues, and must address complex and controversial questions of social justice, structural conflict, structural violence, and social inequality. Pretending that conflict is simply something unfortunate that occasionally occurs between two or more otherwise nice people is, at best, naive.

Conflict resolution training

Conflict resolution is fundamentally a set of practical skills, or a complex of skills. Therefore the development of conflict resolution skills must focus on practical skill development. But it is important to recognise that attempts to provide rules or laws or quasi-magical formulae by which all conflict can always and everywhere be resolved is simplistic, misleading, and dangerous.

Conflict resolution training should expose participants to the widest range and variety of conflict resolution strategies, techniques, and practices, and should enable them to select from these those elements that will best meet the needs of the specific situations with which they are dealing. Flexibility, innovation, imagination, and creativity are important personal and professional qualities of the conflict resolution practitioner. Although broad general principles can be established, laying down laws of conflict resolution seems a dangerous, and ultimately fruitless, pastime.

The cultural context

It is important to be aware of the quite specific cultural context within which what is generally known as conflict resolution, alternative (or additional) dispute resolution, negotiation, mediation, or conciliation arose. It is not a culturally neutral process, and cannot simply be imposed upon or integrated into other cultures. It is primarily the product of an educated, verbally skilled, industrialised, middle-class, white (and predominantly male) Western society. This fact creates problems that must be explored, particularly when attempting to apply the skills of conflict resolution to people who may not fit this description. Essentially Western models of conflict resolution cannot appropriately be exported into other cultures. Some of the elements of Western conflict resolution models may be of use in other cultural contexts, but these need to be identified through appropriate and adequate research and consultation.

Some approaches taken in Western conflict resolution directly conflict with rules about conflictual behaviour in other cultures, and it is certainly not the case that the Western approach is better or more effective. For example, the tendency to encourage direct and explicit identification of the conflict and direct dialogue between the participants may not only be unacceptable, but may also be highly counterproductive in cultures in which such direct confrontation is regarded as rude, aggressive, and even a 'declaration of war'.

Basic principles

A number of basic principles can he identified that are applicable in all conflicts, and that positively promote effective conflict resolution. It must be remembered, however, that these are principles for conflict resolution, not laws or 'scientific' formulae or guaranteed techniques that work at all times and in all circumstances. Despite this, there is an overriding key principle: conflict resolution depends on adaptability, flexibility, creativity, motivation, innovation, willingness to experiment, critical and imaginative thinking, and effective communication.

Analysis

The first principle in conflict resolution is that there is a need for analysis—essentially a thinking skill. Analysis was considered in chapter 2 and includes identifying, mapping, and recognising multiple factors and dimensions.

Preparation

The second principle is that there is a need for preparation or planning for resolution, which is also a thinking skill. This was discussed in chapter 4.

Effective communication

The third principle is the need for effective communication. This includes taking account of perceptions, feelings, and needs, as well as developing assertiveness and self-esteem. It involves effective use of language (both verbal and non-verbal) and active listening. Although communication is thought of as a talking skill, it must begin as a thinking skill, and must also include listening skills. Communication was considered in chapter 3.

Collaboration

The fourth principle is the need for collaboration or participation, involving the participants to the conflict as fully and as actively as possible (even if, in some specific cases, this is only minimally) in the whole process of resolution. This involves issues of motivation, projection, perception, and pressure. This was particularly dealt with in chapter 5.

Process

The fifth principle is that conflict resolution must be recognised as a process. It is important to perceive and apply conflict resolution as a process—one that may take time—rather than something that simply happens. Situations rarely move from conflict to resolution instantaneously; there is almost inevitably a process through which the participants, and the conflict, move. When an apparently immediate resolution occurs, it is more often because the process has gone largely unnoticed. The conflict resolution process was explored in chapter 8. 'Quick fixes' or fast settlements are very rarely resolutions, although they may, in the short term, appear to make the conflict go away. In some cases (for example, purely commercial disputes), disputes may be settled quickly, but there is still a process of settlement. Conflict resolution is a process in which the participants to the conflict need to collaborate; it should, and ideally will, continue as part of, and enhance, the relationship between the participants, even when the original conflict has been resolved.

Conflict resolution is essentially a process of changing relationships. If that is what it is in practice, it will not only resolve a specific conflict, but also enable the participants to resolve future conflicts. Any approach to conflict resolution that creates a dependency on external processes (for example, through ongoing use of the courts or mediation) is disempowering.

Problem solving

The sixth principle is that conflict resolution needs to be problem-solving, but this relates to the real problem or conflict, rather than to the resolution of a symptom of an underlying cause. The emphasis needs to be on the identification and resolution of the real problem through a process in which the relationship between the participants changes; the problem can be solved because the relationship is changed.

This principle draws attention to the fact that conflict resolution needs to focus on the problem, not on people or positions that may be taken. It seeks to explore options, often by 'brainstorming' and related techniques, and to encourage collaborative problem solving. This principle was considered in several chapters, including chapters 2, 4, 5, and 8. Conflict resolution is a process of solving problems in the context of changing relationships.

Negotiation

The seventh principle is that conflict resolution usually involves some form of negotiation. Negotiation is not always a part of conflict resolution, but it is common for all conflicts to involve at least some issues that require negotiation between the participants.

It is possible, of course, to negotiate a settlement to a dispute without resolving an underlying conflict. Sometimes this is entirely appropriate and necessary: there may be preliminary matters that must be resolved before central or core matters can be approached. The case of property division and child access and custody arrangements in a marital breakdown is an example. It is rarely possible to leave issues relating to property and children undecided until the couple have worked through the conflict underlying their separation. There are practical questions (for example, 'Where are the former partners and the children going to live?' and 'Who will make the payments on the mortgage?') that need prompt resolution, and this is almost inevitably done through negotiation. It is important, in such cases, to recognise that the negotiation of settlements in preliminary disputes does not resolve the underlying conflict.

Generally participants in a conflict resolution process will be involved in some form of negotiation, and will need to be prepared to offer and to listen to offers—to give and to receive. Effective conflict-resolving negotiation is based on a positive, honest, relationship-building style. Negotiation was considered in the context of collaborative problem solving in chapter 5.

Third-party facilitation

The eighth principle is that, in some conflicts, *third-party facilitation* may assist in or expedite the conflict resolution process. This can include processes ranging from mediation, arbitration, and expert appraisal through to adjudication or even therapy and counselling.

Third-party involvement needs generally to be viewed as a second option; the first option should always be direct collaboration between the participants to the conflict. Where this is either impossible or ineffective, or where it may involve extensive delays and even the real possibility of escalation of the conflict, the involvement of an appropriately trained neutral third party may be beneficial. The range of third-party processes was outlined in chapter 4. Mediation was discussed in chapter 6, and arbitration in chapter 7.

Flexibility

The ninth principle is the need for *flexibility* and *change*, both during the process and with regard to any outcome. Rigid positions that do not allow for movement or change are, effectively, refusals to attempt resolution. Once an option has been selected as a possible resolution, it is likely to be most effectively implemented if it can be seen as a trial solution that will be (at a specified time and on specified criteria) reviewed and, if necessary, revised. The importance of flexibility, innovation, and change has been emphasised throughout the book.

Resolution

The tenth principle is the need for *resolution* itself; that is, there must be a point at which the participants to the conflict agree that it has been resolved. Allowing resolution to appear to be achieved without any explicit recognition of the fact is rarely effective. The participants must both cognitively and emotionally recognise resolution if it is to have been accomplished. Very often this will be signified by some symbolic action (for example, shaking hands, signing an agreement, or making an announcement of the resolution to others). This principle was considered at the conclusion of chapter 8.

Reality

The eleventh principle is the need to recognise and take account of *reality*. Approaches to conflict resolution that operate without a recognition of the limitations, constraints, difficulties, and unpredictability of real people in the real world are of little practical value.

For example, agreements that sound wonderful, and are utopian and idealistic, but which will be highly unlikely to work in practice, do little to resolve conflict. They may promote immediate feelings of euphoria and satisfaction, but they are unlikely to be capable of translation into practice.

Processes that depend upon people being able immediately to change their personalities, behaviour, and lives, not to mention the world in which they live, are equally impractical. It may sometimes be depressing to accept, but in the real world difficulties often arise, people sometimes fail to live up to their undertakings, the unexpected happens, people and situations are rarely entirely consistent and predictable, and occasionally things go wrong. Conflict is rarely resolved by wishful thinking and overly optimistic speculation.

The reality that needs to be recognised includes *power*, power differentials, and power imbalance. There is no magical means of redressing power imbalance, or empowering everyone in every situation. The question of power also relates to the need to recognise that sometimes there are real risks and dangers, and that there may be serious costs if attempts at resolution are not successful. Sometimes there are real dangers in even attempting to bring about resolution. Employees who raise workplace problems with their employers may, for example, find that their employment is placed in jeopardy, or even terminated.

Conflict does not exist in some sort of vacuum, away from the real difficulties of the real world, and effective conflict resolution must, as far as is possible, take account of reality.

Training

The twelfth and final principle is that there is a need for *training* if conflict resolution is to be effective. Participants and practitioners in conflict resolution require training in a range of basic skills. To some extent, this is because most people have been trained out of many of those skills (for example, collaboration) through socialisation and education. Conflict resolution training should include experiential and collaborative learning, and the development of interpersonal skills. The conflict resolution process should be an educational process in itself, assisting the participants to develop new skills for future use. The process through which parties to a conflict work together to develop the skills of resolution can actively create a more cooperative and trusting relationship between them, facilitating resolution.

These twelve principles should be considered when approaching the resolution of conflict. They represent a checklist of considerations, not a formula for resolution.

The physiology of conflict resolution

Conflict has a personal physiological dimension: the fight-or-flight reactions are biological responses that bring about changes in the body. Conflict usually produces physical stress; it can also be argued that physical stress can provoke conflict. Thus there can be a conflict–stress cycle: conflict creates stress, which increases sensitivity and susceptibility to conflict, which in turn increases stress.

The psycho-physical aspects of conflict and conflict resolution are an interesting area and require further research. Certainly, the development of personal stress-reduction techniques and the ability to recognise and to deal with negative physical effects of conflict are important for effective resolution.

Personal development and conflict resolution

Conflict and conflict resolution both have their origins in the mind. In some cases, as was identified in chapter 2, the origin of conflict may be in deep and unconscious elements, and it may be necessary for an individual to look at techniques of personal deep-conflict resolution or therapy as a basis for the resolution of conflict with others. A number of theorists have looked at what might be called the deeper personal and collective aspects of conflict. Obviously, Freud and others in the psychological traditions were among these theorists.

In the cases of interpersonal conflict considered throughout this hook, the assumption has been that resolution will occur as a result of the involvement of both (or all) participants in the conflict. This is the ideal situation, and indeed, conflict resolution is very difficult without that participation. Situations sometimes exist, however, in which such participation is simply not possible (for example, when a party to a conflict has died). A conflict does not simply die because one of the participants has done so. It can, and often does, continue as a powerful and negative force in the mind of the living participant. Therefore individual intrapersonal conflict resolution techniques must be used. In general, such techniques are only effective where the participation of the other party is not possible; they rarely succeed where that participation is simply difficult or undesirable.

Individual counselling or therapy should be considered in any situation in which the level of individual or joint distress effectively prevents the application of the principles that have been outlined.

Conflict should not be seen as inevitably or innately destructive. It is usually painful to some degree, but the pain can be the pain of growth and exploration. Effective conflict resolution can lead to creative conflict, characterised by innovation, collaborative problem solving, and enhanced relationships. Most people already possess the necessary skills; they require only identification and enhancement to make them more effective.

Case study 16

Daniel and Katrina have been partners in a medium-sized retail business for the past four years. Business has been good and has every prospect of getting better, but it requires considerable effort from both of them to keep it that way.

Over the past year, some differences have developed between them, mainly over management style. Daniel has commented that Katrina is too hard on the staff and too interested in making money, even at the expense of good personnel relations. Katrina has responded that Daniel is too easily influenced by staff, and that he undermines her authority in the business. She believes he is too friendly with the staff; he believes she is too formal.

The business has an excellent opportunity to expand in a way that will financially benefit both Daniel and Katrina. But Daniel announces that he wants to look at the option of ending the partnership and dividing the business into two smaller businesses. This would be financially disastrous for both of them.

Review the principles of conflict resolution and identify how each could be applied in this case study. Consider what additional information you would require if you were planning to resolve the conflict.

17 An Example of Analysis and Planning

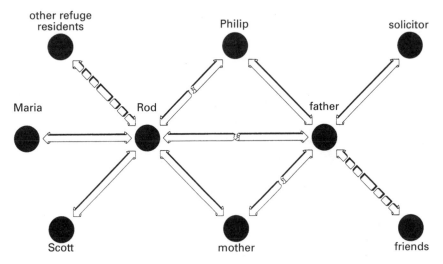

Figure 17.1 The participants in the conflict

Friends of all the identified participants are likely to be influential in various ways—for example, the father's friends may be encouraging him to exercise his authority over his son, while Rod's friends at the refuge may be encouraging him to reject his father.

The focal conflict is that between Rod and his father, and relates to where Rod lives. Underlying that are other conflicts relating to power and author-ity—for example, whether Rod, at fifteen years of age, ought to have the power to make independent decisions against the wishes of his father. Beneath this, and undisclosed, may be issues arising from the father's treat-ment of Rod in the past. There is also an undisclosed conflict between Rod's parents, specifically in relation to Rod, but probably also more generally concerning their relationship.

There are both immediate and long-term conflicts that require resolution, and they have different degrees of urgency. In the short term, the father's inter-vention with the refuge and with his son needs resolution. In the long term, the relationship between father and son needs resolution.

The past would need to be explored, particularly the reasons for the break-down in relations between Rod and his father, and between Rod and his brother.

The pressures or needs of the two major participants are relatively easily identified. Rod needs somewhere to live where he does not feel under attack (and, possibly, where he is not at risk of physical assault), and he probably also needs to exercise some independent power in making decisions about his life. He needs to be treated in an adult way. This need particularly is probably being met in his relationships with the refuge worker and the social worker, but not in his relationship with his father. Rod's father needs to be seen to play the role of father, to be able to control and support his family; he seems also to need to be

where Rod lives

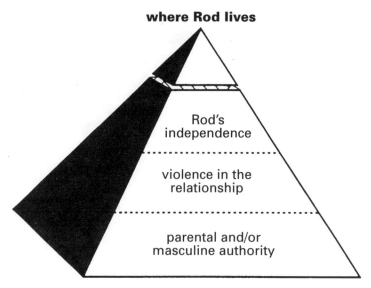

Figure 17.2   The conflict

seen to exercise power over his son. This may relate, at least in part, to his concerns about how his (male) friends see him.

Both father and son have clear projections or fears. Rod fears that, if he returns, the situation will be the same as when he left, and this will be intolerable. He also fears that once he gives in to his father's demands, he will have surrendered the personal power he has taken by leaving home. However, he probably also has fears for the future: he cannot stay in the refuge permanently, and knows that his future will be seriously affected by not living at home. He has fears associated both with living at home and with staying away.

Rod's father fears the loss of his son, possibly more as a visible sign of his failure as a father than anything else. He may also fear the consequences of the process that has been initiated by Rod: if he was involved in beating his son, this may, eventually, become the subject of open discussion.

This is a fairly superficial analysis, but it identifies the key elements. A more detailed analysis, involving discussions with the key participants, would certainly disclose additional information of critical importance in understanding the situation.

In planning for resolution, it is clear that two conflicts need to be addressed: the conflict between Rod and his father, and that between Rod and his brother. For resolution to be effective, it would also be useful to look at the conflict between Rod's mother and father. It seems unlikely that either collaborative problem solving or arbitration has any chance of success in this case. The relationship between Rod and his father seems to be so impaired that collaboration seems impossible, and neither is likely to accept arbitration unless the decision was in his favour. Some form of mediation is likely to be most effective, but it should ideally be combined with therapy. In this case, it might be argued that a number of the participants require some form of therapy before, during, and after any mediation process.

Planning would need to consider both the short-term and long-term conflicts; the former should be dealt with as soon as possible to establish something of a basic working relationship between Rod and his father while the long-term matters are worked through. So long as the immediate crisis conflict exists, the larger issues effectively cannot be approached. Over the next three months, some form of agreement would seem an appropriate aim for immediate mediation. Such an agreement would probably need to be fairly formal and in writing, and would deal with the relationship between father and son, including relations with the refuge. Included in the agreement could be provision for ongoing mediation or therapy. It seems probable that the father would be more willing to participate in something described as *mediation* than in something described as *therapy* if there were any suggestion in the latter that he, rather than Rod, had problems to be worked through.

Appendix

John Burton, Conflict Theory, and Conflict Resolution Practice

The theories of conflict and conflict resolution upon which this book is based derive largely from the work of Professor John Wear Burton. Burton is probably the world's most distinguished theorist of conflict resolution, and one of very few scholars who has attempted to develop a unified theory of conflict and its resolution. He has been prolific not only in his writings but also in inspiring and assisting in the establishment of centres for conflict resolution at universities in the United Kingdom, the USA, and Australia.

Before beginning an academic career, Burton was a distinguished public servant and diplomat. He joined the Australian Department of External Affairs (now the Department of Foreign Affairs) in September 1941, and was appointed departmental Secretary to the Minister the following month, working very closely with the Minister, Dr H.V. Evatt. He represented Australia at the United Nations Charter Conference in 1945, and became the Permanent Secretary of the Department of External Affairs in 1947, the youngest person ever appointed to that position at thirty-two years of age. He resigned after a change of government and was appointed Australian High Commissioner to Ceylon from 1951 to 1955. An excellent introduction to Burton's remarkable and controversial career in the Australian public service is found in Gregory Pemberton's article 'John Burton: The Heretic' (1995).

Burton was Lecturer in International Relations at the Australian National University (1955–63) and Lecturer in International Relations at University College, London (1963–78), where he founded the Centre for the Analysis of Conflict. He was Director of the Centre for the Analysis of Conflict at the University of Kent (1978–82) and Director of the Conflict Resolution Project of the Center for International Development at the University of Maryland (1982–85). Burton was appointed as Distinguished Visiting Professor of Conflict

Resolution at the Center for Conflict Analysis and Resolution at George Mason University, Fairfax, Virginia in 1985, and was named Distinguished Jennings Randolph Fellow at the United States Institute of Peace in 1989.

Burton has facilitated numerous efforts in international conflict resolution, including attempts to resolve conflict in Ceylon (now Sri Lanka), Cyprus, Northern Ireland, the Falklands-Malvinas Islands, and Lebanon.

There are seven essential principles that characterise the ideas that Burton brings to the study of human conflictual behaviour.

1 The a-disciplinary approach

Burton writes:

> Conflict, its resolution and prevention, comprises an a-disciplinary study, that is, a synthesis that goes beyond separate disciplines, beyond interaction between separate disciplines, and beyond any synthesis of approaches from several disciplines. An a-disciplinary approach accepts no boundaries of knowledge. Consequently it has as yet no shelf in any discipline-based library (Burton 1988, p. 2).

In *International Relations: A General Theory* (1965), Burton warned of the dangers of simply transferring concepts from other disciplines or from areas of what was then called 'peace research'. His opposition to an inter-disciplinary approach was thus established.

Burton's approach to conflict and its resolution is revolutionary not only in intellectual terms (where almost all discussion occurs in artificially constructed divisions), but also in institutional terms. Seeking to pursue an a-disciplinary approach, he sets himself clearly outside the traditional intellectual framework, not to mention the traditional institutional structures for academic work or conflict resolution, which seek to compartmentalise people and processes (for example, by making divisions between legal, social, and psychological approaches to the resolution of conflict).

2 The holistic approach

Burton further notes:

> Conflict, its resolution and prevention, is inevitably a study which knows no boundaries of thought. It involves the whole person, the nation or identity group of the person, the political system, and the physical environment. It is a study with universal application. It cuts across cultures. It cannot be broken up into 'aspects' of behaviour. Conflict resolution is a study that transcends separate compartments of knowledge, known as disciplines, and seeks to take a holistic view of human conflictual behaviour, without being politically unrealistic or in any sense superficial (Burton 1990b, p. 20).

In suggesting that conventional approaches to human conflict that examine it from a historical, an economic, a psychological, an anthropological, or a political approach are plainly inadequate, Burton throws down a blatant challenge to those who operate within those specialist areas. Burton does not suggest as an alternative even the usual interdisciplinary approach—in which, for example, a biologist might consider the biology of conflict, and a sociologist the sociology, and a psychologist the psychology.

One of the most radical demands made by Burton's approach to conflict resolution (and one that none of his critics seems to have considered) is that human beings must be considered as total beings in a total environment. It is unhelpful, if reassuringly easier, to work on 'the economic person' or 'the sociological person' or 'the legal person' or 'the biological person', as if human beings consisted of interlocking but independent components. These constructs not only fragment any understanding of human beings, but they also incapacitate any attempt to understand the origins or resolution of conflict. It is difficult to imagine a conflict that is economic, but not social or psychological, or one that is psychological, but not social and economic. It is equally fruitless to talk of the war in the Balkans (for example) as political or historical, as if it were not also social, psychological, and economic, as well as geographical, religious, and cultural. Nor is it a conflict simply between two formalised factions; rather, it involves a multiplicity of interconnected groups (formal and informal), networks, and individuals.

3 The unified theory

Following on from an insistence on a unified approach to human beings, Burton requires a unified theory of conflict and its resolution. Throughout his work there has been a developing recognition that conflict is conflict is conflict: not that all conflicts are the same, but that in all conflicts there are significant common elements.

In one of his earliest writings in the area, *Peace Theory: Preconditions for Disarmament* (1962), Professor Burton sought to develop a unified theory of conflict by identifying the factors common to conflict at all levels, from the interpersonal to the international. He concluded that the common factors were more than analogy. He sought to develop a new theory of conflict, and thus of conflict resolution, and throughout his works—from *Peace Theory* (1962), *International Relations* (1965), *Conflict and Communication* (1969), and *World Society* (1972) to *Deviance, Terrorism and War* (1979) and *Global Conflict* (1984b)—there is a development towards a unified theory.

But it was essentially not until 1990 that he published in full his central and universal theory: that conflict at all levels of society has its origins in the systemic or structural deprivation of non-material human needs. This theory was developed and expanded in the four-part *Conflict* series.

His approach to human needs theory is significantly original in that he gives recognition, and indeed primacy, to innate, non-tangible needs—needs that can very rarely be compromised and that powerfully motivate individuals.

These needs can be too strong to allow the shaping or reshaping of the individual by even much more powerful external forces.

The concept of the almost infinitely malleable human being, so central to traditional political (and indeed social) thought, has rarely in practice been shown to apply. As Burton has noted, street battles and wars are regularly being lost by authorities possessing overwhelming force. Increased punishment rarely decreases crime.

Analytical conflict resolution seeks to identify the needs that drive individuals in a conflict, and to explore options for redirecting the satisfaction of the needs, rather than by seeking to suppress either the needs or their satisfaction. If, for example, group affiliation and identity are more powerful needs for a group of youths on the streets than are physical safety or social and parental approval, then control methods (such as increased policing, enhanced punishments, and the use of guilt) will be unlikely to diminish group activities (such as car racing, vandalism, and crime) that meet those needs. The problem is not to suppress the need (Burton's assumption being that that cannot be done) but to look for innovative and non-destructive ways of allowing it to be met.

4   The analytical approach

A further characteristic of Burton's approach to conflict resolution is that it must be analytical; this distinguishes it from bargaining, negotiation, most forms of mediation, the judicial processes, and most alternative dispute resolution processes, which rarely seek to reveal the underlying issues that are the source of the conflict. In Burton's terms, resolution is only possible if an adequate analysis—or to use a medical model, diagnosis—is made. To be most effective, this process of analysis should involve the participants in the conflict; they need to analyse and understand (which does not necessarily mean accept, approve, or agree with) the needs of each other.

This can be politically difficult. Professor Burton has, for example, carefully identified the role of domestic sources in international conflict, notably in his work *Global Conflict* (1984b). But it will be next to impossible for political leaders to openly acknowledge that domestic political considerations may, for example, drive international military operations.

But, despite the difficulties, analysis is essential. If, for example, an international conflict is driven by a domestic conflict, attempts at an international resolution will inevitably fail.

5   The proventive approach

If analysis is not only possible but also essential for present conflicts, what of future conflicts? Burton has emphasised that much, if not most, conflict is predictable. He requires conflict resolution to seek 'explanations of conflict that make possible prediction and, thereby, not merely prevention but provention also. '"Provention" implies the promotion of an environment conducive to harmonious relationships. The study thus enters the fields of political philosophy and policy making' (1988, p. 2).If indicators of potential conflict can be developed, then proventive action (to use Burton's term) can be taken. This may eliminate the factors that would otherwise lead to the conflict or, if that is not possible, minimise them and establish, in advance, processes that will enable the conflict, when it arises, to be dealt with more effectively. Although a little work has begun in the area of international conflict prediction, it is a field that remains undeveloped.

The concept of provention reflects Burton's impatience with the assumption that each conflict is new and surprising, even when it is more likely to be a recycling of old conflicts, or to have been foreseeable. In interpersonal relations, industrial relations, and international relations, patterns and cycles of conflict are common and predictable. But relatively rarely are underlying causes analysed and processes for resolution established. It is all too common for each conflict to provoke expressions of surprise or alarm, and reactions suggestive of a totally new experience.

6 The paradigm shift

Professor Burton has sought to motivate what he has called a 'paradigm shift': the term itself has provoked criticism of him. He did not seek to reapply old concepts, theories, and methodologies; he began with an assumption (which the evidence seems to support) that these had mostly failed. He wanted to begin again, as it were, by looking anew at the problem of human conflict, and by recognising how little is known about it that can be shown to be pragmatically effective, as opposed to theoretically descriptive or academically respectable. Conventional theories about conflict, while perpetuated in academic institutions and applied in social and political policy, essentially failed to deliver in practice. More research into street crime, for example, has not led to less street crime. Nor has increased policing. In fact in some places, the increase in street crime has become proportional to the increase in police on the streets.

From his place in international relations, Burton recalled being challenged by the manifest failure of traditional theory:

> Thinking in the late 1950s and early 1960s, stimulated by World War II and its consequences, led to a questioning of the underlying thesis of the power elite frame. That deterrence deters was the underlying assumption on which [traditional] processes were based. If deterrence did not deter in certain circumstances, the dominant power politics theories of the time were false, whether applied at the domestic or at the international level (1988, p. 2).

A dramatic increase since the 1950s in the amount of study, research, teaching, and discussion in areas such as peace research, international relations, and military and strategic studies has not been paralleled by a decrease in the amount of war or an increase in the effectiveness of interventions in inter- and intranational conflict. Most scholarship in these fields appears content with describing conflict. The approach that Burton proposes analyses rather than describes, and seeks practical strategies for prediction and provention.

For Burton, the new approach to conflict resolution is necessarily political. That is not to say it is party-political or ideologically aligned, but rather that it involves a radical change in the conceptualisation of human problems, including individual, social, and global problems, and in the approach to the solution of such problems.

7 Analytical problem-solving conflict resolution

The approach that Burton sometimes calls 'analytical problem-solving conflict resolution' can perhaps most readily be understood using a medical model: if the theoretical understanding of the illness is accurate, then, on the basis of sound diagnosis and appropriate prescription, some observable cure should be evident or an explanation should be available to account for the lack of cure. Existing approaches to conflict, as Burton repeatedly notes, fail in this respect. If deterrence works (whether at an international level, or at the level of street crime), why does more force or threat of force not bring about the desired change? An equally interesting question must surely be: why, given the overwhelming evidence of lack of effectiveness, are the same old theories and the same old practices perpetuated? Here Burton moves into the dangerous area of politics: institutions tend to be self-perpetuating, being maintained not because they work effectively, but because they exist.

A new area of study, and one that takes such an unconventional approach, almost inevitably requires a new language. Although Burton has initiated the use of only a few new terms—'provention' being the most notable—he seeks to use terms from other areas of study in new ways. Those who criticise Burton for failing to come up with a definitive 'scientific' method for resolving conflict miss the point. A key feature of his work is the emphasis on the complexity of human relationships. Those scientific or pseudo-scientific approaches (from Marxism to behaviourism) that seek to provide a single magical formula for the cure of all problems have failed, not because they were necessarily theoretically flawed, but because they just did not work. The resolution of conflict is a complex, unpredictable process. Burton provides clear guidelines for the operation of the process but does not presume that every conflict will or can be resolved in the same way.

The ideas and the ideals that underlie Burton's work are summarised in the term 'conflict resolution'. Rather than engage in seemingly endless description, he has sought to understand the forces that create conflict, and thereby to develop principles for its resolution, rather than its management, displacement, suppression, or containment. This presupposes a preparedness to let go of traditional constructs, institutions, intellectual constraints, and all the accumulated baggage of the years, and look anew at the problem of human conflict, which daily increases in extent, intensity, and cost.

Suggested reading

This appendix is based on Gregory Tillett, 'The Ideas and Ideals of John Burton' (1995). For the writings of Burton, see the entries for Burton in the Bibliography. A critical assessment of Burton's theoretical approach is found in K. Avruch and P. Black, 'A Generic Theory of Conflict Resolution: A Critique' (1987); for Burton's response see Burton and Sandole (1997).

Reading Guide

This reading guide is intended to provide some suggestions for initial reading. A more detailed Bibliography follows the reading guide to assist those who wish to undertake further and more detailed study, and suggestions for reading under subject headings are provided at the conclusion of this guide. Most of the books suggested contain bibliographies, which can be used to locate further works.

The best works on the theory and practice of conflict resolution generally are those in the *Conflict* series by John Burton. Each of the volumes includes extensive bibliographies, and some have annotated reading guides. Burton's *Conflict: Resolution and Provention* (1990b) provides a clear overview of the theory and practice of conflict resolution, and develops both Burton's particular theoretical approach, based on human needs theory, and his approach to the practice of what he calls 'conflict *provention*'.

Conflict: Human Needs Theory (1990a), edited by Burton, brings together key papers on human needs theory, all of which provide both sound theoretical supports for practice, and examples of the application of human needs theory in the resolution of conflict.

Conflict: Practices in Management, Settlement and Resolution (Burton & Dukes 1990a) provides a broad and concise overview of the whole range of conflict resolution practices and processes, including material on the application of such processes to specific types and areas of conflict.

Conflict: Readings in Management and Resolution, edited by John Burton and Frank Dukes (1990b), is a collection of basic readings in the study of conflict and conflict resolution, providing a basic library for the practitioner. Further works by Burton are included in the Bibliography.

An excellent introduction to interpersonal conflict is Susan Heitler's *From Conflict to Resolution: Strategies for Diagnosis and Treatment of Distressed Individuals, Couples, and Families* (1990). This book contains very useful guides for the diagnosis of conflict in individuals, relationships, and families, and for both 'symptom relief' and therapy. It provides an invaluable theoretical and practical background for those working with interpersonal conflict.

Two books provide particularly good introductions to mediation. Jay Folberg and Alison Taylor's *Mediation* (1988) provides an excellent introduction to the broad range of issues involved in mediation, including its relationship with counselling, practical psychology in mediation, ethical considerations, and the establishment of mediation services. The book gives a concise overview of a range of theories and practices.

Christopher Moore's *The Mediation Process: Practical Strategies for Resolving Conflict* (1996) is an extremely detailed introduction to conflict and its resolution generally, with a highly detailed outline of the principles and practice of mediation. The material is presented in a style and structure that makes it readily applicable in practice. The book includes a detailed bibliography.

An excellent introduction to alternative dispute resolution (ADR) in Australia is Hilary Astor and Christine Chinkin's *Dispute Resolution in Australia* (1992), although the general outline of ADR presented does not apply only within Australia. It includes helpful material on the relationship between ADR and the traditional system of litigation, and outlines the practice of a range of ADR processes (including negotiation, mediation, arbitration, and expert appraisal), as well as exploring the relationship between ADR and the legal profession, mediator training, and ethics.

Conflict analysis requires clear, analytical, creative thinking. There are many works that include practical suggestions for enhancing the ability to think, to analyse, and to make rational decisions. Robert H. Thouless's *Straight and Crooked Thinking* (1974), although a little dated, is a classic in this area. It includes interesting and entertaining material on a range of crooked thinking styles and how they can be overcome. John Adair's *Effective Decision-Thinking* (1985) and Ben Heirs's *The Professional Decision Thinker* (1986), although directed towards managers in business, contain valuable material on decision-making generally, and on those factors that obstruct effective decision-making and those that facilitate it.

Karl Albrecht's *Brain Power* (1987) and James Adams's *Conceptual Blockbusting* (1987) are excellent introductions to imaginative, innovative and creative thinking, and include challenging exercises to stimulate the thinking processes. A number of Edward de Bono's works are relevant to conflict analysis and resolution; *I am Right. You are Wrong* (1990) is particularly challenging to conventional linear thinking (or 'rock logic', as de Bono calls it in this book), and suggests a variety of ways to work towards more effective, problem-solving thinking. De Bono's *Conflicts: A Better Way to Resolve Them* (1985) applies de Bono's approach specifically to conflict resolution.

Rather than taking one theory or approach to practice and concentrating on it, readers are encouraged to read widely and critically, exploring a range of approaches to conflict resolution. Suggested reading for each of the key subjects considered in this book is provided in the following list. Full references are provided in the Bibliography.

aggression: Storr 1968; Zillmann 1979

alternative dispute resolution (ADR): Abel 1982; Auerbach 1983; Brown & Marriott 1993; Fulton 1989; Goldberg et al. 1985; Goldberg et al. 1992; Mackie 1991; Stein 1984

alternative dispute resolution (ADR) in Australia: Astor & Chinkin 1992; Ingleby 1991; Mugford 1986; Pears 1989

Bibliography

Abdennur, A. 1987, *The Conflict Resolution Syndrome: Volunteerism and Beyond*, University of Ottawa Press, Ottawa.

Abel, R. (ed.) 1982, *The Politics of Informal Justice*, Academic, New York.

Acland, A. 1990, *A Sudden Outbreak of Common Sense: Managing Conflict through Mediation*, Hutchinson, London.

Adair, J. 1985, *Effective Decision-Thinking*, Pan, London.

Adams, J. 1987, *Conceptual Blockbusting*, Penguin Books, Harmondsworth.

Albrecht, K. 1987, *Brain Power*, Prentice Hall, New York.

Amy, D. 1987, *Environmental Mediation*, Columbia University Press, New York.

Ardrey, R. 1967, *The Territorial Imperative: A Personal Inquiry into the Animal Origins of Property and Nations*, Collins, London.

Argyle, M. 1975, *The Psychology of Interpersonal Behaviour*, Penguin Books, Harmondsworth.

—— 1978, *Bodily Communication*, Methuen, London.

Argyris, C. 1970, *Intervention Theory and Method: A Behavioral Sciences View*, Addison-Wesley, Reading, Mass.

Astor, H. & Chinkin, C. 1992, *Dispute Resolution in Australia*, Butterworths, Sydney.

Auerbach, J. 1983, *Justice Without Law: Resolving Disputes without Lawyers*, Oxford University Press, New York.

Augsvurger, D. 1992, *Conflict Mediation across Cultures*, Westminsters, Louisville, Ky.

Avruch, K. & Black, P. 1987, 'A Generic Theory of Conflict Resolution: A Critique', *Negotiation Journal*, vol. 3, no. 1, pp. 87–96.

Avruch, K., Black, P., & Scimecca, J. 1991, *Conflict Resolution: Cross Cultural Perspectives*, Greenwood Press, New York.

Bacow, L. 1984, *Environmental Dispute Resolution*, Plenum Press, New York.

Banks, M. (ed.) 1984, *Conflict in World Society: A New Perspective*, Wheatsheaf Books, Brighton, Sussex.

Baruch Bush, R.A. & Folger, J.P. 1994, *The Promise of Mediation: Responding to Conflict through Empowerment and Recognition*, Jossey-Bass, San Francisco.

Bazerman, M. & Lewicki, R. (eds) 1983, *Negotiating in Organizations*, Sage, Newbury Park, Calif.

Biddle, A. et al. 1982, *Corporate Dispute Resolution*, Bender, New York.

Bingham, G. 1986, *Resolving Environmental Disputes: A Decade of Experience*, Conservation Foundation, Washington DC.

Bisno, H. 1988, *Managing Conflict*, Sage, Newbury Park, Calif.

Blake, R. & Mouton, J.S. 1984, *Solving Costly Organisational Conflicts: Achieving Intergroup Trust, Cooperation and Teamwork*, Jossey-Bass, San Francisco.

Blake, R., Shepard, H., & Mouton, J. 1964, *Managing Intergroup Conflict in Industry*, Gulf, Houston.

Blumberg, A. & Golembiewski, R. 1976, *Learning and Change in Groups*, Penguin Books, Harmondsworth.

Bochner, S. (ed.) 1981, *The Mediating Person: Bridges between Cultures*, G.K. Hall, Boston.

Bolton, R. 1987, *People Skills*, Simon & Schuster, Sydney.

Borisoff, D. & Victor, D.A. 1989, *Conflict Management: A Communication Skills Approach*, Prentice-Hall, Englewood Cliffs, NJ.

Boulding, K. 1962, *Conflict and Defense*, Harper Collins, New York.

Boulle, L. 1996, *Mediation: Principle, Process, Practice*, Butterworths, Sydney.

Brown, D.L. 1983, *Managing Conflict of Organisational Interfaces*, Addison-Wesley, Reading, Mass.

Brown, H. & Marriott, A. 1993, *ADR Principles and Practice*, Sweet & Maxwell, London.

Bunker, B.B., Rubin, J.R., & Associates 1986, *Conflict, Cooperation and Justice*, Jossey-Bass, San Francisco.

Burton, J. 1941, *Restrictive and Constrictive Intervention*, University of London, London.

—— 1962, *Peace Theory: Pre-conditions for Disarmament*, Knopf, New York.

—— 1965, *International Relations: A General Theory*, Cambridge University Press, London.

—— 1968, *Systems, States, Diplomacy and Rules*, Cambridge University Press, Cambridge.

—— 1969, *Conflict and Communication: The Use of Controlled Communication in International Relations*, Macmillan, London.

—— 1972, *World Society*, Cambridge University Press, Cambridge.

—— 1979, *Deviance, Terrorism and War: The Processes of Solving Unsolved Social and Political Problems*, St Martin's Press, New York.

—— 1982, *Dear Survivors*, Francis Pinter, London.

—— 1984a, *Conflict in World Society: A New Perspective on International Relations*, St Martin's Press, New York.

—— 1984b, *Global Conflict*, Wheatsheaf Books, Brighton, Sussex.

—— 1986, 'History of Conflict Resolution', in L. Pauling (ed.), *World Encyclopedia of Peace*, Pergamon, Oxford.

—— 1987, *Resolving Deep-Rooted Conflict: A Handbook*, University Press of America, Lanham, Maryland.

—— 1988, *Conflict Resolution as a Political System*, Working Paper No. 1, Centre for Conflict Analysis and Resolution, George Mason University, Fairfax, Va.

—— (ed.) 1990a, *Conflict: Human Needs Theory*, Macmillan, London.

—— 1990b, *Conflict: Resolution and Provention*, St Martin's Press, New York.

—— 1996, *Conflict Resolution: Its Language and Processes*, The Scarecrow Press, Lanham, Md.

Burton, J. & Azar, E. 1986, *Conflict Resolution: Theory and Practice*, Wheatsheaf, Brighton, Sussex.

Burton, J. & Dukes, F. 1990a, *Conflict: Practices in Management, Settlement and Resolution*, St Martin's Press, New York.

—— (eds) 1990b, *Conflict: Readings in Management and Resolution*, St Martins Press, New York.

Burton, J. & Sandole, D.J.D. 1986, 'Generic Theory: The Basis of Conflict Resolution', *Negotiation Journal*, vol. 2, no. 4, pp. 333–4.

—— 1997, 'Expanding the Debate on Generic Theory of Conflict Resolution: A Response to a Critique', *Negotiation Journal*, vol. 3, no. 1, pp. 97–9

Cahn, D.D. (ed.) 1990, *Intimates in Conflict: A Communication Perspective*, Lawrence Erlbaum Associates, Hillsdale, NJ.

—— (ed.) 1994, *Conflict in Personal Relationships*, Lawrence Erlbaum Associates, Hillsdale, NJ.

Campbell, D. & Summerfield, P. (eds) 1989, *Effective Dispute Resolution for the International Commercial Lawyer*, Kluwer, Boston.

Carpenter, S.L. & Kennedy, W.J.D. 1988, *Managing Public Disputes: A Practical Guide to Handling Conflict and Reaching Agreements*, Jossey-Bass, San Francisco.

Condliffe, P. 1991, *Conflict Management—A Practical Guide*, TAFE Publications, Melbourne.

Constantino, C. & Merchant, C.S. 1995, *Designing Conflict Management Systems: A Guide to Creating Productive and Healthy Organisations*, Jossey-Bass, San Francisco.

Coogler, O.J. 1978, *Structured Mediation in Divorce Settlement*, Lexington Books, Lexington, Mass.

Coombs, C.H. & Avrunin, G.S. 1988, *The Structure of Conflict*, Lawrence Erlbaum Associates, Hillsdale, NJ.

Cornelius, H. & Faire, S. 1989, *Everyone Can Win*, Simon & Schuster, Sydney.

Coser, L. 1956, *The Functions of Social Conflict*, Free Press, New York.

—— 1967, *Continuities in the Study of Social Conflict*, Free Press, New York.

Crum, T.F. 1987, *The Magic of Conflict*, Simon & Schuster, New York.

Davis, G. 1988, *Partisans and Mediators*, Clarendon Press, Oxford.

de Bono, E. 1985, *Conflicts: A Better Way to Resolve Them*, Penguin Books, Sydney.

—— 1990, *I am Right. You are Wrong*, Viking, London.

Deetz, S.A. & Stevenson, S.L. 1986, *Managing Interpersonal Communication*, Harper & Row, New York.

de Mare, P., Piper, R., & Thompson, S. 1991, *Koinonia: From Hate, through Dialogue, to Culture in the Large Group*, Karnac Books, London.

Deutsch, M. 1973, *The Resolution of Conflict*, Yale University Press, New Haven.

De Vito, J.A. 1995, *The Interpersonal Communication Book*, Harper & Row, New York.

Dewdney, M. & Charlton, R. 1995, *The Mediator's Handbook: Skills and Strategies for Practitioners*, LBC Information Services, Sydney.

Dingwall, R. & Eekelaar, J. (eds) 1988, *Divorce Mediation and the Legal Process*, The Clarendon Press, Oxford.

Donohue, W.A. 1992, *Managing Interpersonal Conflict*, Sage, Newbury Park, Calif.

Druckman, D. (ed.) 1977, *Negotiations: Social Psychological Perspectives*, Sage, Newbury Park, Calif.

Duffy, K.G., Grosch, J.W., & Olczak, P.V. (eds) 1991, *Community Mediation: A Handbook for Practitioners and Researchers*, Guilford Press, New York.

Dukes, F. 1996, *Resolving Public Conflict: Transforming Community and Governance*, Manchester University Press, Manchester.

Egan, G. 1994, *The Skilled Helper—A Problem-Management Approach to Helping*, Brooks/Cole Publishing, Pacific Grove, Calif.

Ellis, A. 1989, *Rational-Emotive Couples Therapy*, Pergamon Press, New York.

Filley, A. 1975, *Interpersonal Conflict Resolution*, Scott, Foresman, Glenview, Ill.

Fischer, R.J. 1997, *Interactive Conflict Resolution*, Syracuse University Press, Syracuse, NY.

Fisher, R. 1969, *International Conflict for Beginners*, HarperCollins, New York.

—— 1978, *International Mediation: A Working Guide*, International Peace Academy, New York.

Fisher, R. & Brown, S. 1988, *Getting Together: Building Relationships that Get to Yes*, Houghton Mifflin, Boston.

Fisher, R. & Ury, W. 1981, *Getting to Yes: Negotiating Agreement without Giving in*, Houghton Mifflin, Boston.

Folberg, J. & Milne, A. 1988, *Divorce Mediation: Theory and Practice*, Guilford Press, New York.

Folberg, J. & Taylor A. 1988, *Mediation: A Comprehensive Guide to Resolving Conflicts Without Litigation*, Jossey-Bass, San Francisco.

Folger, J.P., Poole, M.A., & Stutman, R.K. 1997, *Working through Conflict: Strategies for Relationships, Groups and Organizations*, HarperCollins, New York.

Frankl, V. 1969, *The Will to Meaning: Foundations and Applications of Logotherapy*, World Publishing Co., New York.

Frost, J. & Wilmot, W. 1978, *Interpersonal Conflict*, Brown, Dubuque, Ia.

Fulton, M. 1989, *Commercial Alternative Dispute Resolution*, Law Book Co., Sydney.

Geldard, D. 1989, *Basic Personal Counselling*, Prentice-Hall, Sydney.

Glasser, W. 1965, *Reality Therapy: A New Approach to Psychiatry*, Harper & Row, New York.

—— 1985, *Control Theory: A New Explanation of How We Control Our Lives*, Perennial Library, New York.

Goldberg, S., Green, E., & Sander, F. (eds) 1985, *Dispute Resolution: Negotiation, Mediation and Other Processes*, Little, Brown & Company, Boston.

Goldberg, S., Sander, F., & Rogers, N. (eds) 1992, *Dispute Resolution: Negotiation, Mediation and Other Processes*, 2nd edn, Little, Brown & Company, Boston.

Gray, B. 1989, *Collaborating: Finding Common Ground for Multiparty Problems*, Jossey-Bass, San Francisco.

Grieger, R. & Boyd, J. 1980, *Rational-Emotive Therapy: A Skills Based Approach*, Van Nostrand Reinhold Co., New York.

Grimshaw, A.D. (ed.) 1990, *Conflict Talk: Sociolinguistic Investigations of Arguments in Conversations*, Cambridge University Press, Cambridge.

Gulliver, P.H. 1979, *Disputes and Negotiations: A Cross-Cultural Perspective*, Academic Press, New York.

Hare, A.P. 1985, *Social Interaction as Drama: Applications from Conflict Resolution*, Sage, Newbury Park, Calif.

Hawkins, D., Hudson, M., & Cornell, R. 1991, *The Legal Negotiator: A Handbook for Managing Legal Negotiations More Effectively*, Longman Professional, Melbourne.

Haynes, J. 1981, *Divorce Mediation: A Practical Guide for Therapists and Counsellors*, Springer Publishing, New York.

Haynes, J. 1994, *The Fundamentals of Family Mediation*, State University of New York Press, Albany, NY.

Haynes, J. & Haynes, G. 1989, *Mediating Divorce: Casebook of Strategies for Successful Family Negotiations*, Jossey-Bass, San Francisco.

Heirs, B. 1986, *The Professional Decision Thinker*, Sidgwick & Jackson, London.

Heitler, S. 1990, *From Conflict to Resolution: Strategies for Diagnosis and Treatment of Distressed Individuals, Couples, and Families*, W.W. Norton, New York.

Hocker, J.L. & Wilmot, W.W. 1985, *Interpersonal Conflict*, Wm C. Brown, Dubuque, Ia.

Ikle, F. 1981, *How Nations Negotiate*, Praeger, New York.

Ingleby, R. 1991, *In the Ballpark: Alternative Dispute Resolution and the Courts*, Australian Institute of Judicial Administration, Melbourne.

Irving, H. & Benjamin, M. 1987, *Family Mediation: Theory and Practice of Dispute Resolution*, Carswell, Toronto.

Jandt, F.E. 1975, *Conflict Resolution through Communication*, Harper & Row, New York.

Janke, P. (ed.) 1994, *Ethnic and Religious Conflicts*, Dartmouth Publishing, London.

Johnson, D. & Johnson, F. 1991, *Joining Together: Group Theory and Group Skills*, Prentice-Hall, New York.

Katz, N.H. & Lawyer, J.W. 1985, Communication and Conflict Resolution Skills, Kendall/Hunt, Dubuque, Ia.

Keen, S. 1986, *Faces of the Enemy: Reflections of the Hostile Imagination*, Harper & Row, San Francisco.

Kennedy, G., Benson J., & McMillan, K. 1984, *Managing Negotiations*, Hutchinson, Melbourne.

Kolb, D. 1983, *The Mediators*, MIT Press, Cambridge, Mass.

Kolb, D. & Associates 1994, *When Talk Works: Profiles of Mediators*, Jossey-Bass, San Francisco.

Kressell, D., Pruitt, D., & Associates (eds) 1989, *Mediation Research: The Process and Effectiveness of Third Party Intervention*, Jossey-Bass, San Francisco.

Kressel, K. 1985, *The Process of Divorce: How Professionals and Couples Negotiate Settlements*, Basic Books, New York.

Kritek, P.B. 1994, *Negotiating at an Uneven Table: Developing Moral Courage in Resolving our Conflicts*, Jossey-Bass, San Francisco.

Lake, L. 1980, *Environmental Mediation: The Search for Consensus*, Westview Press, Boulder, Coll.

Lall, A. 1966, *Modern International Negotiation: Principles and Practice*, Columbia University Press, New York.

—— (ed.) 1985, *Multilateral Negotiation and Mediation: Instruments and Methods*, Pergamon Press, New York.

Landau, B., Bartoletti, M., & Mesbur, R. 1987, *Family Mediation Handbook*, Butterworths, Toronto.

Lawson, M. 1991, *Facing Conflict*, Hodder & Stoughton, London.

Lax, D. & Sebenius, J. 1986, *The Manager as Negotiator: Bargaining for Cooperation and Competitive Gain*, Free Press, New York.

Lederach, J.P. 1995, *Preparing for Peace: Conflict Transformation across Cultures*, Syracuse University Press, Syracuse, N.Y.

Lemmon, J. 1985, *Family Mediation Practice*, Macmillan, New York.

Lewicki, R.J. & Litterer, J.A. (eds) 1985, *Negotiation: Readings, Exercises and Cases*, Irwin, Homewood, Ill.

Likert, J. 1976, *New Ways of Managing Conflict*, McGraw Hill, New York.

McCarthy, J. (ed.) 1980, *Resolving Conflict in Higher Education: New Directions for Higher Education*, No. 32, Jossey-Bass, San Francisco.

McCarthy, P. 1989, *Developing Negotiating Skills and Behaviour*, CCH, Sydney.

Mach, Z. 1993, *Symbols, Conflict and Identity: Essays in Political Anthropology*, State University of New York Press, Albany, NY.

Mackie, K. (ed.) 1991, *A Handbook on Dispute Resolution: ADR in Action*, Routledge, New York.

Maggiolo, W. 1972, *Techniques of Mediation in Labor Disputes*, Oceana, Dobbs Ferry, NY.

—— 1985, *Techniques of Mediation*, Oceana Publications, New York.

Marlow, L. & Sauber, S. 1990, *The Handbook of Divorce Mediation*, Plenum Press, New York.

Maslow, A. 1959, *New Knowledge in Human Values*, Harper, New York.

—— 1987, *Motivation and Personality*, Harper & Row, New York.

Mernitz, S. 1980, *Mediation of Environmental Disputes: A Sourcebook*, Praeger, New York.

Messmer, H. & Ottoc, H.-U. 1992, *Restorative Justice on Trial—Pitfalls and Potentials of Victim–Offender Mediation: International Research Perspectives*, Kiuwer Academic Publishers, Boston.

Mille, G. & Simons, H. (eds) 1974, *Perspectives in Communication in Social Conflict*, Prentice-Hall, Englewood Cliffs, NJ.

Moore, C. 1996, *The Mediation Process: Practical Strategies for Resolving Conflict*, 2nd edn, Jossey-Bass, San Francisco.

Moscovici, S. & Doise, W. 1994, *Conflict and Consensus: A General Theory of Collective Decisions*, Sage, London.

Mugford, J. (ed.) 1986, *Alternative Dispute Resolution*, Australian Institute of Criminology, Canberra.

Mulholland, J. 1991, *The Language of Negotiation*, Routledge, London.

Murray, J., Rau, A., & Sherman, F. 1989, *Process of Dispute Resolution: The Role of Lawyers*, Foundation Press, New York.

Mustill, M. & Boyd, S. 1989, *Commercial Arbitration*, Butterworths, London.

NADRAC. See National Alternative Dispute Resolution Advisory Council.

National Alternative Dispute Resolution Advisory Council (NADRAC) 1997a, *Alternative Dispute Resolution Definitions*, NADRAC, Canberra.

—— 1997b, *Issues of Fairness and Justice in Dispute Resolution*, NADRAC, Canberra.

—— 1997c, *Training and Qualifications Standards for Mediators*, NADRAC, Canberra.

New South Wales Law Reform Commission 1989a, *Alternative Dispute Resolution: Training and Accreditation of Mediators*, Discussion Paper 21, New South Wales Law Reform Commission, Sydney.

—— 1989b, *Training and Accreditation of Mediators Report*, New South Wales Law Reform Commission, Sydney.

Pe, C., Sosmefia, G., & Tadiar, A. (eds) 1988, *Transcultural Mediation in the Asia Pacific*, Asia-Pacific Organization for Mediators, Manila, Philippines.

Pears, G. 1989, *Beyond Dispute: ADR in Australia*, Corporate Impacts Publications, Australia, Sydney.

Pemberton, G. 1995, 'John Burton: The Heretic', *Evatt Papers*, vol. 3, no. 2, pp. 93–105.

Pillar, P. 1983, *Negotiating Peace: War Termination as a Bargaining Process*, Princeton University Press, Princeton.

Pneuman, R.W. & Bruehl, M.E. 1982, *Managing Conflict: A Complete Process Centred Handbook*, Prentice-Hall, Englewood Cliffs, NJ.

Porter, J.N. & Taplin, R. 1987, *Conflict and Conflict Resolution: A Sociological Introduction with Updated Bibliography and Theory Section*, University Press of America, Lanham, Md.

Pretorius, P. (ed.) 1993, *Dispute Resolution*, Kenwyn, Juta & Co, South Africa.

Princen, T. 1992, *Intermediaries in International Conflict*, Princeton University Press, Princeton, NJ.

Pruitt, D.G. 1981, *Negotiation Behaviour*, Academic Press, New York.

Pruitt, D.G. & Carnevale, P.J. 1993, *Negotiation in Social Conflict*, Open University Press, Buckingham.

Pruitt, D. & Rubin, J. 1986, *Social Conflict: Escalation, Stalemate and Settlement*, Random House, New York.

Rahim M.A. 1985, *Managing Conflict in Organizations*, Praeger, New York.

—— 1989, *Managing Conflict: An Interdisciplinary Approach*, Praeger, New York.

Raiffa, H. 1982, *The Art and Science of Negotiation*, Belkap Press of Harvard University Press, Cambridge, Mass.

Rausch, H., Barry, W., Hertel, R., & Swain, M. 1974, *Communication, Conflict and Marriage*, Jossey-Bass, San Francisco.

Reiber, R. (ed.) 1991, *The Psychology of War and Peace: The Image of the Enemy*, Plenum, New York.

Robert, M. 1982, *Managing Conflict from the Inside Out*, Learning Concepts, Austin, Texas.

—— 1988, *Mediation in Family Disputes: A Guide to Practice*, Wildwood House, Aldershot, Northampton.

Rogers, C. 1961, *On Becoming a Person: A Therapist's View of Psychotherapy*, Houghton Mifflin, Boston.

—— 1980, *A Way of Being*, Houghton Mifflin, Boston.

Roberts, S. 1979, *Order and Dispute: An Introduction to Legal Anthropology*, Penguin Books, Sydney.

Rogers, N. & McEwan, C. 1989, *Mediation—Law, Policy, Practice*, Lawyers Cooperative, New York.

Rogers, N. & Salem, R. 1987, *A Student's Guide to Mediation and the Law*, Matthew Bender, New York.

Rothman, J. 1992, *From Confrontation to Cooperation: Resolving Ethnic and Regional Conflict*, Sage, Newbury Park, Calif.

—— 1997, *Resolving Identity-Based Conflict*, Jossey-Bass, San Francisco.

Rubin, J. & Brown, B. 1975, *Social Psychology of Bargaining and Negotiation*, Academic Press, New York.

Rubin, Z., Pruitt, D., & Kim, S. 1984, *Social Conflict: Escalation, Stalemate and Settlement*, McGraw-Hill Inc., New York.

Sandole, D.J.D. & Sandole-Staroste, I. 1987, *Conflict Management and Problem Solving: Interpersonal to International Applications*, Frances Pinter, London.

Sandole, D.J.D. & van der Merwe, H. 1993, *Conflict Resolution Theory: Integration and Application*, Manchester University Press, Manchester.

Saposnek, D. 1983, *Mediating Child Custody Disputes: A Systematic Guide for Family Therapists, Court Counselors, Attorneys and Judges*, Jossey-Bass, San Fransisco.

Schelling, T. 1960, *The Strategy of Conflict*, Harvard University Press, Cambridge, Mass.

Scott, B. 1981, *The Skills of Negotiating*, Gower Publishing, Aldershot.

Seward, G. 1972, *Psychotherapy and Culture Conflict*, Ronald Press, New York.

Simmel, G. 1955, *Conflict and the Web of Intergroup Affiliations*, Free Press, New York.

Smith, C.G. (ed.) 1972, *Conflict Resolution: Contributions of the Behavioral Sciences*, University of Notre Dame Press, Notre Dame, Indiana.

Stein, P. 1984, *Legal Institutions: The Development of Dispute Settlement*, Butterworths, London.

Storr, A. 1968, *Human Aggression*, Allen Lane, London.

Stulberg, J.B. 1987, *Taking Charge/Managing Conflict*, Lexington Books, Lexington, Mass.

Sullivan, T. 1984, *Resolving Development Disputes through Negotiations*, Plenum, New York.

Suskind, L. & Cruikshank, J. 1987, *Breaking the Impasse: Consensual Approaches to Resolving Public Disputes*, Basic Books, New York.

Tavuchis, N. 1991, *Mea Culpa: A Sociology of Apology and Reconciliation*, Stanford University Press, Stanford Calif.

Taylor, A. & Beinstein-Muller, J. (eds) 1994, *Conflict and Gender*, Gamer Press, Hampton, NJ.

Tedeschi, J.T., Schlenker, B., & Bonoma, T.F. 1973, *Conflict, Power, and Games*, Aldine, Chicago.

Thouless, R. 1974, *Straight and Crooked Thinking*, London, Pan.

Tillett, G. 1995, 'The Ideas and Ideals of John Burton', *Evatt Papers*, vol. 3, no. 2, pp. 106–14.

Turner, S. and Weed, F. 1983, *Conflict in Organizations: Practical Solutions Any Manager Can Use*, Prentice-Hall, Englewood Cliffs, NJ.

Ury, W. 1991, *Getting Past No: Negotiating with Difficult People*, Business Books, London.

Ury, W., Brett, J., & Goldberg, S. 1986, *Getting Disputes Resolved: Designing Systems to Cut the Costs of Conflict*, Jossey-Bass, San Francisco.

Volkan, V. 1988, *The Need to Have Enemies and Allies: From Clinical Practice to International Relationships*, Jason Aronson, Northvale NJ.

Walton, R.E. 1969, *Interpersonal Peacemaking: Confrontations and Third-Party Consultation*, Addison-Wesley, Reading, Mass.

Wehr, I. 1979, *Conflict Regulation*, Westview Press, Boulder, Col.

Williams, A. 1991, *Forbidden Agendas: Strategic Action in Groups*, Routledge, London.

Wright, M. & Galway, B. (eds) 1989, *Mediation and Criminal Justice: Victims, Offenders and Community*, Sage, Newbury Park, Calif.

Zartman, I.W. (ed.) 1978, *The Negotiation Process*, Sage, Beverley Hills, Calif.

Zartman, I.W. & Berman, M. 1982, *The Practical Negotiator*, Yale University Press, New Haven, Conn.

Ziegenfuss, J. 1988, *Organisational Troubleshooters: Resolving Problems with Customers and Employees*, Jossey-Bass, San Francisco.

Zillmann, D. 1979, *Hostility and Aggression*, Lawrence Erlbaum Associates, Hillsdale, NJ.

Index

Page numbers in **bold** type refer to main entries